Jeff Smith, star of the popular Public Television cooking series, believes that frugal cooking is an attitude toward food, that *frugal* doesn't necessarily mean sparing. It means getting the most for your money by buying the best meats, grains, fruits, and vegetables you can afford and putting them to the best possible use.

Gourmet cooking doesn't require complicated recipes with dozens of ingredients. Jeff Smith can show you how to turn two salmon steaks, soy sauce, ginger, and a few spices into a tasty meal—one of many that illustrate his principles of simple elegance and economy.

Best of all, you don't need a lot of know-how in the kitchen to cook sumptuous dishes that make the most of your time and money.

Also by Jeff Smith:

THE FRUGAL GOURMET COOKS WITH WINE

THE FRUGAL GOURMET COOKS AMERICAN

THE FRUGAL GOURMET

Jeff Smith

Illustrations by Gary Jacobsen

BALLANTINE BOOKS • NEW YORK

Library of Congress Catalog Card Number: 84-60208

ISBN 0-345-33523-6

This edition published by arrangement with William Morrow and Company, Inc.

Recipe for Bean Curd in Hot Meat Sauce reprinted from *Henry Chung Hunan Style Chinese Cookbook* by Henry Chung, copyright © 1978 by Henry W. S. Chung. Used by permission of Harmony Books, a division of Crown Publishers, Inc.

Recipe for Melitzanosalata courtesy of St. Demetrios Greek Orthodox Church, Seattle, Washington.

Manufactured in the United States of America

First Ballantine Books Edition: February 1987

40 39 38 37 36 35 34 33 32

For my sons,

Channing and Jason

*Joyful dinner partners and serious food
critics since their births*

Acknowledgments

*T*here is no banquet table in the world large enough to seat all the persons whom I must thank for their help in connection with the television shows and this book.

The great cooks who have taught me include my mother, Emely Smith, my uncle Victor, dear Mary Young, the Bill Campbells, and the William Ches. And a thousand chefs whose names I do not even know, especially the old chef at Tai Tung in Seattle when I was a boy, and the chef at old Maison Blanc.

My philosophy of the table has been shaped by great thinkers who are also great eaters. Sara Little, the Lester Baskins, Father R. F. Capon, and all of the university students in that very first class I taught on food and theology.

And the television people! Roger Allen, who first produced *The Frugal Gourmet* at KTPS in Tacoma, and Tim Ward and Friends at WTTW, Chicago, KING television in Seattle, Hearst/ABC in New York. Many of these recipes were first offered on one of the above stations. Still other recipes were developed for the Bob Hope International Heart Research Center in Seattle. Headed by Dr. Lester Sauvage, they were able to bring me to the table with a whole new hymn of thanksgiving.

The encouragement of my editor, Maria Guarnaschelli, and my friend Bill Adler has been at once a blessing and a kick. I had no idea that I would have an editor who knew food much better than I, and an agent who has not been seen eating in three years. My cousin David Smith, of San Francisco, already knows how important he was to the whole project of *The Frugal Gourmet*. Phil Donahue and his great staff have been more help to me than they will ever know.

Finally, my family has always been inspiring in terms of their hunger and patience. My wife, Patty, who still wonders about all of this, has quietly washed a thousand dishes while I was testing in the kitchen. She thought up the name "The Frugal Gourmet," but after testing all of these recipes she has other names for me. I am sure you understand. My sons, to whom this book is dedicated, kept me honest in the quest with their remark, "Oh Lord, he's still on the Tomato Show."

Would that all of us could feast together at once.

Contents

Introduction

*I*t is the journey that seems to provoke the question, and the question is always the same: "How did you get from the university chaplaincy to the television kitchen?" The answer is not complicated because I think each location is consistent with the other.

I am primarily a people lover, then a food lover. The events of the meal, the friends gathered, the family excited over the coming dishes are much more important to me than what is on the plate. While teaching religion at a Methodist school, the University of Puget Sound, I became very interested in the meaning of the event of the table and the concept of food as history. Out of this study came a class that investigated the meaning of food as celebration and, of course, that studied cooking techniques. And we ate. We ate the cuisines of many cultures, and we finally realized that a cuisine is a way of thinking as much as it is a way of cooking. I was already very comfortable with such thinking, and with cooking, for I had been brought as a child to the stove by my Norwegian mother. She instilled in me the love of cooking and of food that I now more than enjoy. I was further trained in the kitchen by my Lebanese uncle. It was he who first taught me that cooking is neither a feminine nor a masculine category but is always a joyful and noisy event. He removed from me, even as a child, all fear of the kitchen. And he talked. He talked about how a dish had been prepared in the old country and how food had functioned in the land of his ancestors. His parents had given him a great gift: They had taught him how to cook with his memories.

My attempts at teaching my students to "eat history" rather than to analyze it gave rise to more cooking classes. My students helped me open a cooking school called the Chaplain's Pantry, and soon I was invited by KTPS, educational television for Tacoma, Washington, to do some cooking shows. That was 200 television shows ago, and I have loved the whole event, the entire journey.

Eating as a way of understanding and celebrating other cultures and histories sounds strange to the fast-food crowd, but the popularity of the television shows, which explain this very concept, means that we are dealing with more than one kind of hunger when we cook. The hunger for affection, for community, for feasting in order to remember cannot be satisfied by a fast-food french fry. It can be met with a good meal shared with the whole family, a meal that will ensure memories for many years to come. And we can learn to do this from other cultures. Our own culture seems to have gotten so involved with TV trays and privacy that we have forgotten how to eat together, a sure sign of the collapse of communication ... maybe even the whole culture.

Our current economic bind also pushes us to think carefully about what it is we are cooking, and why. I dislike most instant food products not just because they lack flavor and fascination but because they are too expensive. Cooking from scratch is much less costly and is certainly much more fun for everyone in the household. But you must organize yourself and learn to cook seriously one day a week.

The growing interest in health has also contributed to the reason for this book. We are much more aware of the dangers of living on food additives and chemicals, and we seem to be taking a much more serious view of our own responsibility for what we put into our bodies.

To complicate matters, we are dealing with an era in which most of us are burdened by stress. As an attack on this contemporary problem, I advocate a good glass of wine, your friends or children gathered about the table, and at least five courses. Relax and enjoy. The idea of eating on the run or eating without my wife and children causes me to become nervous even now.

The concept behind *The Frugal Gourmet* is a simple one. The term *frugal* does not necessarily mean "cheap." It means that you use everything and are careful with your time as well as with your food products. Fresh foods, prepared with a bit of care and concern, will result in terrific meals with lower costs. And the term *gourmet* does not mean "food snob." It means lover of good food and wine and, as far as I am concerned, of people. So we all can qualify by preparing meals for one another. We know deep in our hearts that the table is the proper place for understanding.

I offer you these recipes so that you will have a good time in the kitchen, and since few of the recipes are complicated, both adults, men and women, and children should enjoy creative cooking. Read each recipe through before you shop or start to cook. You might also consult the glossary for information on kitchen equipment and ingredients and to acquaint yourself with some definitions. Finally, I hope you can find the time to read a bit in each section about the history of the culture or the food products, so that when you come to the table serving your treasures, you will have gained insight that will help draw the peoples of the world closer together. Eat well!

I bid you peace.

Jeffrey Smith

Tacoma, Washington
December 14, 1983

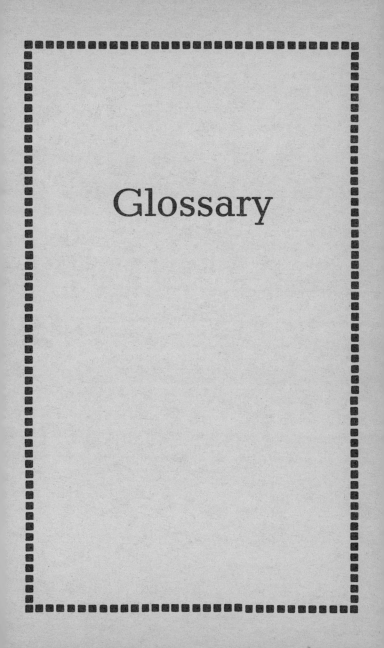

Glossary

Practical Hints

Kitchen Equipment

Good cooking equipment is an absolute must for me. I see no point in investing good money in cheap equipment, only to have to replace it again within a very short time. *Frugal* means that you are not wasting your time or your money...and we can certainly waste a fortune on cheap equipment.

Nothing in your house is more important to your good health, and to the health of your family, than good cooking equipment.

■ HINT: On Kitchen Design

When designing your kitchen, consider the galley concept. When the kitchen is long and narrow, you need not run about all the corners of the room. With little effort you can plan a kitchen that will keep things close about you and thus eliminate the problem of people sitting about the kitchen when you are trying to work. Let them sit and talk on the other side of a counter. Don't forget to include space for those who may be helping you in food preparation, such as your mate or children. Set up additional work areas so that you will not get in one another's way. It will be worth the effort and cost, and it will help keep your family together.

Knives

There are more phony items on the market in the knife department than in any other field, I am sure. Choose knives that feel good to your hand and that will not tire you while you work. How do you tell? Does the handle feel good in your hand? Do your fingers bang on the counter when you are trying to cut with the knife? Is the knife made of stainless steel, so that it can go into the dishwasher but is so hard that it can never be sharpened properly or hold an edge? I never buy stainless steel knives. Never! Choose good high carbon steel so that you can sharpen them . . . and never put them in your dishwasher.

I use the following constantly:

10-inch chef's knife
Boning knife
Paring knives
Long slicing knife (thin)
Sharpening steel

Keep your knives very sharp. A dull knife will force you to work too hard, and it will slip and cut you. Better to have a very sharp knife that will work for you with little effort. Use your sharpening steel often, and carefully.

I am very fond of Henckels knives, and Sabatier's are good, too.

Chinese Cleaver: Finally, I love my Chinese cleaver. This is not an expensive item, running about $10. Once you learn to use yours, you will begin giving Chinese cleavers to your dearest friends. That is how helpful this item will be! Find one in a Chinese or Oriental market. Do not buy a stainless steel cleaver.

■ HINT: Hold Your Knife Properly When Cutting

I find that the easiest and most efficient way to handle a knife is also the safest. Hold the knife as shown in the illustration, and hold the food with the opposite hand, *with your fingers bent under.* Let your knuckles be your guide to where your knife is cutting. If you stick your fingers out, you will cut yourself. Keep them bent under.

Pots and Pans

Second only to the knife, your pans are most important. Through the years I have found many charming and intelligent persons who felt they were poor cooks because they kept burning things, or had lumpy sauces, or could not make a good omelet or crepe. The problem was with the pan, not with the person.

Choose good equipment. I like to deal with a restaurant supply house for many things. The following hints will help you with your necessary purchases:

1. Don't buy pans with plastic or wooden handles. They mean that you cannot ever put the pan in the oven or under a broiler.
2. Buy pans that will be functional for you. Just because a pan looks stylish or up-to-date doesn't mean that it will help you in your cooking. I am conservative when it comes to good cooking gear. If it has worked for many decades, why change it?
3. Aluminum is fine for cooking, but you must keep it clean, and you can never store food in it. Copperware is a joy, but the original investment is considerable. Just remember that your copper pans will always be worth more than what you paid, with decent care, of course. Stainless steel is fine for small pans and pots, but you must have a heat diffuser under them. In our time stainless steel is so thin that you will burn everything. And never buy a stainless steel frying pan. The steel is so hard that you cannot cure it; thus everything will stick or burn. I am very fond of cast-iron ware, coated with porcelain enamel—heavy, yes, but it works great.

The items that I use the most:

20-quart aluminum stockpot, with lid
12-quart aluminum stockpot, with lid
4-quart aluminum sauteuse, with lid
10-inch aluminum omelet and crepe pan, lined with Silver-
    Stone, with lid
12-inch aluminum frying pan, lined with SilverStone, with
    lid
Several cast-iron casseroles, with lids; varying sizes (I like
    Le Creuset)
Several cast-iron saucepans, with lids; varying sizes
Copper baking pans and saucepans; varying sizes

■ HINT: To Cure or Season Your Pans

Remember the rule: *Hot pans, cold oil, foods won't
stick.* That means that you never put the oil in the pan
and then heat the pan. You heat the pan first; add the
oil and then, immediately, the food. You will have much
less sticking that way.

An aluminum frying pan is cured, or seasoned, by
this simple method. First, wash the pan with soap and
water, using a cloth or sponge, never a steel soap pad
or steel wool pad. Rinse the pan, and dry it. Never put
soap in your frying pan again! Heat the pan on a burner
until quite hot, and then add 2 or 3 tablespoons of peanut oil. Gently swirl the oil about the pan, and allow the
pan to cool. Heat the pan again, add more oil, cool, and
repeat once more. Your pan is now ready for use. If
foods should stick or if you have trouble getting the pan
clean, do not resort to soap. Instead rub the pan with a
green scouring cloth, or try a bit of peanut oil and salt;
rub with a paper towel to clean.

Stainless steel frying pans cannot be cured. Everything will stick. For this reason I urge you never to buy
stainless steel frying pans.

Chinese woks are cured according to the directions
on page 354.

SilverStone frying pan: This excellent product from
Du Pont is easy to care for. Wash once with soapy water,
and cure just as you cure aluminum frying pans (see
above). Care for the pan in precisely the same way.

Black iron pans are cured as you would a wok (see page 354).

Casseroles and Baking Pans

I have a good selection of porcelain casseroles with lids. They make any dish look great. I also enjoy the Le Creuset cast-iron–enameled casseroles. Finally, Corning Glass is bringing in a great selection of baking pieces made in France. They are clear glass, easy to clean, and very attractive.

Machines

I have very few machines in my kitchen. The reasons are simple. You can get carried away with buying appliances that you do not need, and if you have children in the kitchen, those machines are dangerous.

I do regularly use:

KitchenAid Food Machine and Mixer: It will make bread, grind meat, slice, and mix anything. And it is made by a restaurant equipment company.

KitchenAid Food Processor: I use this one less than my food mixer, but it is a great help and a fine product. I prefer it to those machines that are made in Japan, such as the Cuisinart.

Food Blender: There are many on the market, and they all seem to work well.

Electric Coffee Grinder: This small German gadget is great for grinding spices and herbs. I rarely use mine for coffee.

Microwave Oven: Yes, I do have one. I love it for heating up leftovers or for assisting when I am in the midst of a big meal. It is a very frugal gadget since it helps you eat up your leftovers.

Special Items

Wok: I use my Chinese wok constantly. It is an ingenious device that is actually much larger than it appears because of its shape. Buy a plain steel wok. Aluminum woks heat too evenly, and the advantage of a Chinese wok is a "hot spot" in the center of the pan where juices and liquids can evaporate; an aluminum wok does not have the necessary hot spot. A copper wok will have the same problem. A stainless steel wok cannot be seasoned properly, and food will always stick. Finally, an electric wok generally heats too slowly and cools too slowly, so the advantage of the wok—quick heat and rapid cooking—is lost.

Bamboo Steamers from China: These stackable steamers, usually three or four in a set, allow you to steam several dishes at once. The advantage that these have over metal steamers stems from the fact that bamboo will not cause moisture to condense and drip on your food. Metal steamers drip, always. I use bamboo steamers for Chinese cooking and for warming up leftover dishes. Find them in Oriental markets or in any good gourmet shop.

Special Gadgets

Garlic Press: I cannot abide garlic in any form except the form which the Creator intended. Buy a SUSI garlic press. Looks expensive to start with, but it remains the best on the market.

Lemon Reamer, Wooden: Any good gourmet shop should have one of these for you. Works better than any other lemon juicer I have ever seen.

Heat Diffuser or Tamer: This is an inexpensive gadget that you place on your burners to even out and reduce the heat. It will save you from a lot of burned sauces. Any gourmet shop or hardware store should have this item.

Wooden Spoons and Spatulas: I never put metal spoons or gadgets into my frying pans or saucepans. Metal will scratch the surface, causing food to stick. Buy wooden gadgets, and avoid that problem. Yes, they will be clean if you wash them in soap and water and allow them to dry before putting them away. Never soak your wooden cooking gear.

Pepper Mill: I love fresh-cracked black pepper. You cannot get that kind of flavor in something preground. I have three good mills: one for the dining-room table, one for the kitchen stove, and one for my traveling cooking kit. Buy pepper mills made in France. They last much longer than the Japanese versions.

Flour Dredger: Looks like a big salt shaker. Fill it with flour, and have it ready to help you flour things with much less waste and time.

Meat Pounder: A heavy disk of metal with a handle that will help you prepare thin slices of meat. You can also use a short length of two-by-four wood.

Fire Extinguisher: A must for your kitchen. Buy one that will work on electrical fires as well as stove fires. Talk to the salesperson. You will sleep better at night.

Marble Pastry Board: These can be purchased in many sizes. I could not make bread or pastry without one.

Plastic Sheeting: Very helpful when you are pounding meat thin or when you need another piping bag. Inexpensive and available at most large lumberyards. Ask for clear vinyl sheeting, 8 mil. thick. See Hint, page 412.

Wine Bottles: Save old ones for oils, soy sauce, vinegars, and, of course, wine.

Oil Can: I keep near the stove a tiny spouted little can filled with peanut oil. The little spout means that I use less oil in my cooking. Found at any gourmet shop.

Kitchen Scale: Buy something that is fairly accurate. It will be helpful in baking perfect French bread and in judging the size of meats. You will be able to buy things in bulk and save some money.

Stainless Steel Steamer Basket: This is a great help. It will fit any size pan and is readily available and very cheap.

Cheese Thermometer: This is an absolute necessity if you are going to make your own cheese and yogurt. Buy a thermometer that goes from 100° to 250° Fahrenheit. If it covers that range, it will work well for you.

Things I Love But Could Probably Do Without

When I buy a new piece of cooking equipment, I must always ask myself, "Do you really need this to be creative?" Often the answer is no, but I buy it anyway. I have few electric gadgets like hot dog cookers or electric egg poachers or upside-down chicken cookers or upside-down electric crepe makers. These I can do without. But the following items are in my kitchen because I love them:

Glass Plates, Dessert Size: These are cheap, and I use them for salads, pastas, and desserts. They make the food look attractive.

Big Dinner Plates: I hate eating a nice dinner that has been squeezed onto a regular plate. Buy big ones, 12 inches in diameter. You may have to go to a restaurant supply house.

Good Wineglasses: I do not enjoy drinking wine from a glass with a lip or heavy rim. Shop carefully, and you will find good wineglasses without lips, and they are not expensive. I own several dozen big ones, glasses big enough to make even a medium-class wine look and taste fine. You can get carried away with wineglasses because there are many different kinds for several different wines. Start with a 10-ounce clear tulip glass; it will do fine for any wine. Your collection can grow as your wine cellar grows.

Big Serving Platters: I find these in antique and junk shops—serving platters from a time gone by. It is great fun to put an entire main course on a gigantic platter and bring it to your friends and family.

Big Wooden Salad Bowls: I don't really believe that you can make a good salad in glass or metal. Metal is harsh in its appearance, and glass is too fragile for a proper mixing or tossing of the salad. A wooden bowl can be seasoned with a clove of fresh garlic and thus impart a most delicate flavor to your greens.

Pitchers and Serving Jugs: My sons never put a container of milk on the table, and every liquid is served in a pitcher of some sort. It makes the event of the meal seem a little more important to all of us.

Potato Bird-Nest Fryer: A pair of small baskets that allow you to prepare little nests made of fried potato. More fun, and any gourmet shop will have one for you.

Piping Bags and Tips: These will help you add some class to your efforts in the kitchen. I use three sizes the most—10, 12, and 14 inches. Choose several tips that will be helpful in cake icing, in piping cheese, in piping mayonnaise or potatoes.

Cooking Terms

Blanching

Plunging a food product into boiling water for a very few minutes (the time varies and will be explained in each recipe). The food is then removed and generally placed in cold water to stop the cooking process. The purpose is to loosen the skin of a vegetable or fruit, to set the color of a vegetable, or to cook a food partially in preparation for later completion of the dish.

Browning Meat

When preparing stews and cassoulets, do not flour the meat. You then end up with browned flour instead of browning the natural sugars that are in the meat itself. Use a hot pan, and do not crowd the meat or cook it slowly. The meat should be seared or browned very rapidly, thus giving color to the stew and sealing the meat cubes.

Chow (stir-fry)

A basic cooking method in the Chinese kitchen. Generally a wok is used, but you can also do this in a frying pan. The food is tossed about in a hot pan with very little oil, in a process not unlike sautéing.

Dash

Generally means "to taste." Start with less than 1/16 teaspoon.

Deglazing a Pan

After meats or vegetables have been browned, wine or stock is added to the pan over high heat, and the rich coloring that remains in the pan is gently scraped with a wooden spoon and combined with the wine or stock.

Dredging in Flour

Meats or fish, generally sliced thin, are rolled about in flour in preparation for frying or sautéing. The flour is usually seasoned.

Marinating

Meats or vegetables are soaked for a time in a flavoring liquid, such as soy sauce, wine, oil, or vinegar. The time of the marinating varies with the recipe.

Matchstick or Julienne Cut

Cut vegetable into thin slices, stack the slices, and then cut the slices into thin sticks, like matchsticks.

Mirepoix

A blend of vegetables and herbs sautéed and used to flavor other dishes (see page 278).

Pinch of Herbs or Spices

Usually means "to taste." Start with less than $\frac{1}{16}$ teaspoon, and then increase if you wish.

Poaching

Gently cooking fish, meat, or eggs in stock or water at just below a simmer. The liquid should just barely move during the poaching process. When fish or eggs are poached, a little vinegar or lemon juice is added to the liquid to help keep the food product firm.

Reducing

Boiling a sauce or liquid over high heat until it is reduced in volume, generally by half. The result is a very rich concentration of flavors.

Roux

A blend of oil or butter and flour used to thicken sauces and gravies. The fat and flour are mixed together in equal amounts over heat. If a white roux is desired, the melting and blending are done over low heat for a few minutes. If a brown roux is desired, the flour is cooked in the fat until it is lightly browned.

Sauté

This term comes from a French word which means to jump. In cooking *sauté* means to place food in a very hot pan with a bit of butter or oil and to shake the pan during the cooking process so that the food jumps about. Thus one can cook very quickly over high heat without burning the food. Not unlike Chinese chowing or stir-frying.

Shot

A liquid measurement which amounts to very little or to taste. A shot of wine is about an ounce, but a shot of Tabasco is less than 1/16 teaspoon.

Steaming

Cooking with steam as the heat source. See page 301 for a full discussion. This method is not to be confused with pressure cooking.

Stir-fry

See Chow.

Terrine

A dish used for the cooking and molding of coarse-ground meat loaves or pâtés. Also the meat itself. The dishes can be found in many styles and materials.

Ingredients and Food Definitions

Anchovies (flat, canned)

Used for salads and Italian and French cooking. Buy in cans from Portugal or Spain. Very salty.

Bean Curd

Cheeselike product made from soybean milk. Buy fresh in cakes at Oriental markets or in produce sections of most supermarkets. This can also be purchased in cans, but the flavor is far inferior. Fresh bean curd looks very much like a 5-inch rectangular block of soft white cheese.

Bean Sprouts

You will find these fresh in most produce sections. The canned variety is so tasteless that you should omit them unless you can find them fresh.

Béchamel Sauce

Basic white sauce made of milk or stock and thickened with a roux of flour and butter. See page 259 for recipe.

Beef Stock

Please make your own. Canned consommé or bouillon is little more than salt. Real beef stock is rich in flavor and inexpensive to make from fresh bones. See page 47 for recipe.

Bok Choy

A vegetable resembling Swiss Chard in shape, but much lighter in color and flavor. A member of the mustard family, it can be found fresh in most supermarket produce sections and in Oriental markets.

Bulgur Wheat

Processed wheat for Middle Eastern dishes. Three grinds: fine, medium, and coarse. Find in Middle Eastern stores or in fancy supermarkets or gourmet stores.

Capers

Pickled buds used in salads and dressing. Found in any good supermarket.

Cellophane Noodles

Noodles from China made from the mung bean, the same bean from which bean sprouts grow. Find in Oriental stores and in some supermarkets. Also called glass noodles, Sai Fun, or bean threads.

Cheese

This list is offered simply because I use all these in my recipes, though I rarely have them all on hand at once. Buy fresh cheeses, and grind or grate your own. Find a good delicatessen or cheese store, and you should find each of the following:

    Parmesan (imported, aged Italian, if you can afford it)
    Romano
    Swiss (Wisconsin fine for baking; imported for snacking)
    Monterey Jack
    Kasseri (Greek)
    Asiago (my favorite Italian pasta cheese for grating)
    Bleu (imported Danish excellent for cooking)
    Feta (Greek)
    Mizithra (dried ricotta in hard ball)
    Ricotta

Chili Sauce

Bottled product found in the catsup section of market.

Chinese Ingredients

Please look under individual headings for each of the following items:

> Bean Curd
> Bean Sprouts
> Bok Choy
> Cellophane Noodles
> Dow See
> Fermented Black Beans
> Five Spice Powder
> Glass Noodles
> Hoisin Sauce
> Hot Bean Sauce
> Hot Pepper Oil
> Mein See
> Mushrooms, Chinese
> Napa
> Oyster Sauce
> Red Chili and Garlic Paste
> Rice Wine Vinegar
> Sai Fun Noodles
> Sesame Oil
> Soybean Condiment or Jam
> Soy Sauce
>   Light, Dark
> Turnip Ball

Coconut Milk

Canned or frozen in Oriental markets or fancy supermarkets.

Cream

When the term is used in this book, I mean Half-and-Half or whipping cream. Either may be used, or you may dilute whipping cream with milk.

Cream Sauce

See Béchamel Sauce. Same item, only made with cream instead of milk; very rich.

Dijon Mustard

A style of mustard from France. A good American brand is Grey Poupon.

Dow See

See Fermented Black Beans.

Fermented Black Beans

These fermented black beans from China are a classic condiment in Chinese cuisine. Buy in Oriental markets, and then keep in tightly sealed glass jars. No need to refrigerate.

Five Spice Powder

A Chinese blend of spices. Find in any Oriental market, or blend equal amounts of powdered cinnamon, ginger, anise, fennel, and clove. Some blends contain a bit of black pepper.

Fillo Dough (Phyllo)

Thin sheets of dough for Middle Eastern baking. Can be found in most delicatessens. Also called phyllo dough.

Glass Noodles

See Cellophane Noodles.

Grape Leaves

Treasures from Greece; can be found in Middle Eastern markets in glass jars, packed in brine. Drain, and use.

Herbs and Spices

See page 26.

Hoisin Sauce

A soybean and pepper sauce common to Chinese recipes. Find in any Oriental market.

Hot Bean Sauce

Found canned or in jars in Oriental markets. It is mein see with hot pepper oil. That blend would be a good substitute.

Hot Pepper Oil

May be purchased in Oriental markets, or see page 353 for a recipe that is easy.

Hot Sauce

Tabasco or Trappey's Red Devil will do well. Found in any supermarket.

Imitation Mayonnaise

Low-fat mayonnaise and called imitation simply because it does not have all the fat of ordinary mayo. Good for low-fat diets.

Leeks

These look like very large green onions in the produce section. Wash carefully because they are usually full of mud.

Liquid Smoke

For use in barbecue sauce. Find in the condiment section of the supermarket. I like Wright's.

Low-Fat Mayonnaise

See Imitation Mayonnaise.

Mein See

The remains of the process of making soy sauce. Very rich soybean jam used in many Chinese dishes. Can be found in Oriental markets under this name or soybean jam or condiment. Refrigerate after opening.

Mock Sour Cream

Made from cottage cheese in order to eliminate fat. Easy to prepare. See footnote on page 276.

Mushrooms, Chinese

Find in any Oriental market. Soak for 1 hour in water before cooking. Trim the stems, and save for Chinese Chicken Soup (page 365).

Mushrooms, Dried

Dried mushrooms called cepes or boletus. See page 231 for discussion of less expensive sources.

Napa

Sometimes called Chinese Celery Cabbage, it can be found in many supermarket produce sections and in Oriental markets.

Oils

  Butter
  Olive Oil
  Peanut Oil
  Sesame Oil

These are the common oils that I use in my kitchen. I use little butter, but I enjoy the flavor and dislike margarine. For fuller discussion of cooking oils, see page 58.

Orzo Pasta

Pasta shaped like rice. Great for pilaf. Find in Middle Eastern or Italian shops or in a good delicatessen.

Oyster Sauce

Classic cooking sauce from China. While actually made from oysters, it has no fishy taste. Found in Oriental markets. Refrigerate after opening.

Pesto

A sauce of northern Italian origin, made from fresh basil, olive oil, garlic, cheese, and pine nuts. Great for pasta or in soups and sauces. You can purchase this frozen or in glass jars at Italian markets. For a recipe, see page 147.

Pine Nuts

Expensive little treasures that actually do come from the large pinecone of Italy. Find in Italian markets, or substitute slivered almonds.

Red Chili and Garlic Paste

Very hot Chinese sauce made of red peppers and garlic. Find in Oriental market, or substitute garlic and Tabasco. It is worth the effort to find this delicious sauce.

Red Chili Paste with Garlic

See above. Same product.

Rice Wine Vinegar

Delicious vinegar used in Oriental cooking. Find it in Oriental markets.

Saltpeter

A common kitchen chemical used in preserving meat or preparing corned beef or pork. May be purchased at a drugstore.

Sai Fun Noodles

See Cellophane Noodles.

Sesame Oil

Used as a flavoring in Oriental cooking but not a cooking oil. Find this at an Oriental market. Used for flavoring a dish at the last minute. The health food store version is not made from toasted sesame seeds, so the flavor will be very bland.

Sesame Seeds

Buy in the bulk, and then toast them by stirring them in a hot frying pan until lightly browned.

Shallots

A cross between garlic and onion. Classic part of French cuisine. Find in the produce section or substitute a blend of onion and garlic.

Soybean Condiment or Jam

See Mein See.

Soy Sauce

Light: To be used when you do not wish to color a dish with caramel coloring, which is what dark soy contains. Find in Oriental market by this name.

Dark: Used in dishes in which you wish to color the meat and sweeten the flavor with caramel sugar. Most common soy sauce.

Tahini

A light paste made of toasted sesame seeds and sesame oil—almost like a peanut butter. Used in many Middle Eastern dishes, it is to be found in Middle Eastern delicatessens or fancy supermarkets.

Turnip Ball

A preserved vegetable from China used in the making of a good Chinese Chicken Soup (page 365) and other dishes. Found in Oriental markets.

Vinegars

These are the vinegars that I use most in my cooking. They are all readily obtainable in most markets.

   Red Wine Vinegar
   White Wine Vinegar
   Plain White Cider Vinegar
   Tarragon Wine Vinegar
   Rice Wine Vinegar

White Sauce

See Béchamel Sauce.

Wines for Cooking

All these wines are readily obtainable. Please do not buy wines that have salt added; they are labeled "Cooking Wines" but really should not be used at all. My rule is "If you can't drink it, don't cook with it."

Dry Sherry
Dry Red Wine
Dry White Wine
Sweet Vermouth
Marsala

Herbs and Spices

■ HINT: Buying, Storing, and Grinding Herbs and Spices

Herbs and spices are some of the most important ingredients in your kitchen. Try to keep them as fresh as possible, so don't buy them in large amounts. Keep them in tightly sealed jars. Try to buy most herbs and spices whole or in whole leaf form; they have much more flavor that way. Crush the leaf forms as you add them to the pot. Or use a wooden or porcelain mortar and pestle. For seeds that are hard to grind, I use a small German electric coffee grinder. I have one that I use just for spices; it works very well.

Try to buy your herbs and spices in bulk, and then put them in your own spice bottles. The saving realized here is about 70 percent. Hard to believe, but it is true. Find a market that has big jars of spices, and you will also be amazed at the difference in flavor.

Allspice

Not a blend of spices at all, but a single one. Basic to the kitchen. Buy it ground because it is hard to grind.

Basil

Common in French and Italian cooking. Grow it fresh or buy it dried, whole.

Bay Leaves

Basic to the kitchen for good soups, stews, etc. Buy whole, dried, or if your area is not too cold, grow a bay laurel tree. I have one in Tacoma.

Bouquet Garni

A bouquet of fresh herbs, generally tied in a bundle or in a cheesecloth sack. Usual ingredients include parsley, thyme, and bay leaves. You can use all these dried.

Caraway

Whole seed, dried.

Cardamom

Common in Scandinavian and Middle Eastern dishes. Rather sweet flavor. Expensive. Buy whole seed, and grind as you need it.

Cayenne Pepper

Fine-ground red pepper, very hot.

Chervil

Mild French herb that resembles parsley in flavor. Buy dried, whole. Use in soups and sauces.

Chili Powder

Actually a blend of chili peppers. Buy in the can, ground. Usually I use the hot blend.

Cinnamon

Hard to grind your own. Buy it powdered.

Cloves

I use both the powdered and the whole.

Coriander

The dry, whole seed is common in Mediterranean cooking. The fresh plant, which looks like parsley, is common in Chinese, Indian, and Mexican cuisines. You may see the fresh form in your supermarket listed as cilantro or Chinese parsley.

Cumin

Used in Mexican cooking a great deal. Buy powdered in the can, or buy the whole seed and grind it. The flavor is much brighter in the whole seed.

Curry Powder

An English blend of many spices. Many brands are on the market, so choose one that seems to fit your family. I like Sun from India. Or a much brighter blend may be made at home. Find a recipe in any good Indian cookbook.

Dill Weed

Dried, whole. Great for salad dressings and dips. Common in Middle Eastern cuisine.

Fennel

A seed that resembles anise or licorice in flavor. Produces that special flavor in Italian sausage. Buy it whole, and grind it as you need it.

Filé

Ground sassafras leaves, along with a bit of thyme. Essential in New Orleans cooking. Also called gumbo filé.

Fines Herbes

A blend of parsley, chervil, tarragon, and chives. Very mild and very French. Used in everything from salads to soups and stews.

Garlic

The bulb, of course. Use only fresh. See section on garlic (page 317) for purchase and storage. And buy a good garlic press!

Ginger, Fresh

Very common in Chinese dishes. Buy by the "hand" or whole root at the supermarket. Keep in the refrigerator, uncovered and unwrapped. Grate when needed.

Mace

The outer covering of the nutmeg. Not as strong as nutmeg, but rich in flavor. Buy ground. Common in early American cooking.

Marjoram

Common kitchen herb, light in flavor. Buy whole, dried.

Mint, Dried

Common in Middle Eastern dishes. Buy whole. Also makes a great tea.

Mint, Fresh

Grow this in the backyard if you can. Great for salads, mint juleps, Middle Eastern dishes.

Mustard, Dry

Absolute necessity if you love salad dressings. I buy Colman's, from Britain.

Nutmeg

Basic to the kitchen. Buy it whole in bulk, and grate your own with an old-fashioned nutmeg grater.

Orange Peel, Dried

Great for Italian tomato sauces for pasta. Dry your own by saving the peelings and letting them sit on the top of the refrigerator.

Oregano

Basic to the kitchen. Salads, meats, sauces, etc. You can grow your own, but the best comes from Greece. Buy whole, dried.

Paprika

Light, lovely flavor and color. Buy ground, imported from Hungary.

Parsley, Dried

I use this rarely because fresh is better. But in salad dressings or anything that is to be kept for a few days the dried lasts much better. Buy whole.

Parsley, Fresh

Buy in the supermarket produce section, or grow your own. I like the Italian variety, which has flat leaves and a bright flavor.

Peppercorns, Black

Buy whole, and always grind fresh. See page 11.

Red Pepper Flakes, Hot, Crushed

Also labeled "crushed red pepper flakes." Buy in bulk, and use sparingly. The seeds make this a very hot product.

Red Peppers, Hot, Dried

Buy whole. Necessary for many Chinese dishes and in southern cooking.

Rosemary

Basic to the cooking of Italy and southern France. Grow your own, or buy whole, dried.

Saffron

Real saffron is from Spain and is the dried stamens from the saffron crocus . . . and costs $2,000 a pound. Buy it by the pinch or use Mexican saffron, which includes the whole flower and is very cheap. Works well; just remember to use much more.

Sage

Basic kitchen herb. Grow your own, or buy it whole, dried.

Savory

Close to thyme in flavor. Common in French cooking. Buy it whole, dried.

Thyme

Necessary to good French cooking—soups and stews to meat dishes. Buy it whole, dried, or grow your own.

Turmeric

Bitter orange-colored spice that gives the flavor and color to pilafs, curry powders, and Indian braised dishes. Buy it ground. Cheaper in Middle Eastern and Indian stores.

Zaartar

From Lebanon. Find in Middle Eastern delicatessens or mail-order houses. A blend of sumac bark, thyme, and chick-peas or sesame seeds, common in foods from the Middle East.

The Television Shows and Recipes for Each

SHOW 130   Simmer a Turkey

SHOW 131   Addictive Pastas

SHOW 132   The Mushroom

Some Hints on Menu Planning

Every meal should certainly have a purpose, even if it is simply to eat a short but satisfying snack. Rarely, however, is the point of the meal just food. We plan meals for the sake of talking with friends, family, or new acquaintances. We create special celebrations that are best enjoyed around the table. Or we carefully plan menus that will help us understand other people, other cultures, other nations. Finally, the table can be used for feasting, that special celebrative eating in which we attempt to remember something that is important to our past or will be important to our future.

When I plan a menu, I first think about the nature of the event. If it is a simple meal, then a good entrée, a fresh salad, perhaps some fruit and wine will suffice. But if we are to have a feast, an event in order to recall, then menu planning is something else altogether. There always seems to be an excuse for having a grand time at the table, and certainly the menu should not be bound by any rules whatsoever. Half the fun in planning a great meal comes in serving an unusual assortment of food, one that will help us remember who we are in terms of a family or the background of friendship. If you always serve the same style of food to your eaters, how are you going to say something new? I recall a meal in which my wife served grits to the family . . . on the day of Jimmy Carter's inauguration. After all, the boys knew nothing about the South, and the table would be a perfect place in which to begin the discussion. Anything goes at the celebrative table. A feast is defined not by what is eaten but by what is remembered.

I know that you may just have to get dinner on the table. Even under those boring pressures you still have the chance to create an unusual menu if you simply do some planning. Plan out the week, and cook for more than one meal each evening. In that way you will have a couple of nights off, and you will probably be more creative on the nights that you cook like a mad chef. See the discussion on cooking one day a week. It's on page 60.

The index has been designed to help you in your planning. You can choose dishes from a whole nation or even a continent. Or you can go through the lists and put together your own unusual collection of favorites. In any case, enjoy the feast. Sorry about the lack of desserts. I have so much fun with the earlier courses in a meal that I just have never gotten into the sweet trip.

Soups

I know of no single food product that is more useful in the frugal kitchen than a basic brown soup stock. Just the fact that this lovely fluid is in your refrigerator will help you relax in the kitchen since you always know that you can fall back upon the soup stock. It is rich and versatile and inexpensive.

Remember, *frugal* does not necessarily mean cheap. It means that you use everything and waste little or nothing, and that includes both time and food products. You will find yourself saving vegetable skins and scraps for the soup pot. Only green onions and cabbage should be avoided because they will sour the stock. You can use almost everything else. Very French!

Basic Brown Soup Stock

Bare rendering bones, sawed into 2-inch pieces
Carrots, unpeeled and chopped
Yellow onions, unpeeled and chopped
Celery, chopped

Tell your butcher that you need bare rendering bones. They should not have any meat on them at all, so they should be cheap. Have him saw them up into 2-inch pieces.

Roast the bones in an uncovered pan at 400° for 2 hours. Be careful with this, because your oven may be a bit too hot. Watch the bones, which you want to be toasty brown, not black.

Place the roasted bones in a soup pot, and add 1 quart water for each pound of bones. For 5 pounds bones, then add 1 bunch carrots; 1 head celery; and 3 yellow onions, chopped with peel and all. (The peel will give lovely color to the stock.)

Bring to a heavy simmer, uncovered, and cook, for 12 hours. You may need to add water. Do not salt the stock.

Strain the stock, and store in the refrigerator. Allow the fat to stay on the top of the stock when you refrigerate it; the fat will seal the stock and allow you to keep it for several days.

MAKES 5 QUARTS OF STOCK.

■ HINT:

If you do not wish to watch the pot all day long, bring the soup to a heavy simmer, cover the pot, and place it in a 225° oven overnight. This works very well.

Italian Barley Soup

This is a great dish, and talk about frugal. Note that there is no meat in this dish because you are using our rich beef stock. No meat is needed. And the lemon peel will surprise you.

> 1½ quarts Basic Brown Soup Stock (page 47)
> 2 cups water
> ¾ cup barley
> 1 cup celery, chopped
> 1 cup grated carrot
> 1 cup yellow onion, peeled and chopped
> 4 cloves garlic, crushed
> ½ cup red wine
> 1 piece lemon peel, about 1 inch by ½ inch
> Pepper to taste (I like plenty)
> Salt (if you must)

HERBS
- ½ tablespoon basil
- ¼ tablespoon oregano
- ½ cup fresh parsley, chopped
- 2 bay leaves
- ½ tablespoon whole rosemary

- 2 tomatoes, chopped
- 4 tablespoons tomato paste
- Fresh-grated Parmesan or Romano cheese

Bring the stock and water to a boil. Add the barley and turn down to a light simmer. Add the celery, carrot, onion, garlic, red wine, lemon peel, pepper, and salt and simmer for 2 hours. Stir often, or the barley will stick to the bottom of the pot.

At the end of the 2 hours add the herbs, tomatoes, and tomato paste. Continue cooking the soup for 1 more hour, the total cooking time being 3 hours. Leave the lid on during the whole operation, and remember to stir often and check to see if you need to add water. Stir in a handful of grated cheese before serving.

This thick and flavorful soup is a terrific main dish for the whole family, and it tastes better on the second day. Serve with a deep red wine and a crisp green salad. Crunchy Italian rolls would be perfect.

SERVES 8.

Sauerkraut Soup
(Austria)

Even those who dislike sauerkraut will love this rich and warming dish. Yes, it is peasant food, but then the peasants have always known how to eat.

    1 large yellow onion, peeled and chopped
    3 slices bacon
    1 clove garlic, crushed
    ½ lb. lean pork, diced
    2 generous cups fresh or raw sauerkraut (or
           sauerkraut in a glass jar, not a tin)
    1 tablespoon tomato paste
    ½ teaspoon paprika
    ¾ teaspoon caraway seed
    8 cups Basic Brown Soup Stock (page 47)
       Roux of 1½ tablespoons flour and 1½
           tablespoons butter
       Pepper and sugar to taste (optional)
       Sour cream for garnish

Brown the onion in the bacon fat, along with the garlic. Add the pork, and cook for about 20 minutes. Add the sauerkraut, tomato paste, paprika, caraway seed, and soup stock. Simmer for about 45 minutes, until the sauerkraut is soft. Thicken with the roux, and correct seasoning (you may wish to add pepper or a pinch of sugar).

    Serve hot with garnish of sour cream. If you wish a milder flavor, cook the soup a bit longer.

SERVES 8.

Beef Soup with Meatballs

This blend of herbs and spices, coupled with the rich beef stock and the little meatballs, offers a very unusual full-meal soup. My camera crew in Chicago went crazy over this one.

3 small hot green peppers, fresh
½ pound ground beef
½ pound lean ground pork
2 cloves garlic, crushed
1 teaspoon salt
¼ cup tomato sauce
1 teaspoon chili powder
1 teaspoon cumin, ground
1 tablespoon parsley, chopped
½ cup bread crumbs
2 eggs, beaten
3 tablespoons butter for browning
6 cups hot Basic Brown Soup Stock (page 47)
½ cup dry red wine

Remove the seeds and chop the peppers. Mix all ingredients except the butter, soup stock, and the wine. Blend well. Form the meat mixture into 48 meatballs and brown them in the butter. Add the meatballs to the soup stock along with the wine. Simmer 10 minutes before serving. The soup may need additional salt.

For a full meal serve this soup with a large hearty salad, such as Pea Salad with Bacon (page 99). Either a white or a red wine will do well.

SERVES 8.

Lettuce Soup
(Early American)

This is a very nice dish, easy and cheap, that I found in a cookbook published in 1907. You will be surprised by the flavor of cooked lettuce.

This can be served as the first course in almost any type of meal. It is not strong in flavor but supports whatever may follow.

    1 large head iceberg lettuce
    1 tablespoon butter
    1 teaspoon sugar
    2 tablespoons tarragon vinegar
    1 tablespoon flour
       Salt and pepper to taste
    1 egg, beaten
    6 cups Basic Brown Soup Stock (page 47)
    ½ cup cream
       Toasted croutons

Chop the lettuce. Sauté in a frying pan with the butter, sugar, and vinegar, stirring constantly until lettuce is barely wilted. Add the flour, salt, pepper, and egg. Mix well, and then pour in the soup stock. Bring to a boil, remove from the heat, add the cream, and serve with the croutons.

SERVES 8.

French Onion Soup

This soup, made with a proper beef stock, will not have that salty flavor you find in restaurant soups. Why? Because the restaurants usually use instant stock. For shame!

    ½ yellow onion, peeled and sliced for each bowl
    1 tablespoon butter for each bowl
       Dash of dry sherry for each bowl
       Fresh-grated Parmesan or Romano cheese
    1½ cups Basic Brown Soup Stock (page 47), boiling
       Salt to taste
       French bread, toasted
    1 slice Swiss cheese for each bowl

Sauté yellow onions in butter. Place 2 tablespoons onions in a 12-ounce soup bowl, and add dry sherry and Parmesan or Romano cheese. Add soup stock and salt to bowl.

    Serve with a boat of French bread covered with Swiss cheese in the bowl.

Lentil Soup
(Germany)

This dish is terribly rich and wonderful. Plan to serve it on a cold winter evening with lots of bread and wine. I served this very recipe for years in my restaurant in Tacoma. No meat need be added, and the nutritional value is very high.

> 2 **cups dry lentils**
> 1 **quart water**
> 2 **quarts Basic Brown Soup Stock (page 47)**
> 1 **potato, peeled/diced**
> 2 **carrots, grated**
> 3 **tablespoons white vinegar**
>   **Salt to taste**
> ⅛ **teaspoon ground cloves**
>   **Dry sherry**
>   **Parmesan cheese**

Soak the lentils in the water for 2 hours. Place (water included) in soup pot, and add the soup stock, potato carrots, vinegar, salt, and cloves. No pepper! Cook over low heat for 3 hours, and serve with sherry and Parmesan cheese in a bowl.

SERVES 8.

Chicken Soup Stock

If you have a bit of this in your refrigerator, you will think of marvelous soups to make. Jews call this *Gildern yoich,* or golden soup.

   3 pounds chicken necks and backs
   4 stalks celery, chopped into large pieces
   6 carrots, chopped into large pieces
   **2 yellow onions, peeled and chopped into large
      pieces**
   Salt and pepper to taste

Boil the chicken necks and backs in water to cover. Add the
celery, carrots, and yellow onions. Add salt and pepper. Simmer
for 2 hours. Strain and refrigerate.

MAKES ABOUT 2½ QUARTS.

■ HINT:

To remove fat from the top of soup stock, use a plastic
tube. Plastic tubing about ⅓ inch in diameter can be
purchased at hardware stores. Strain the stock, and
then remove the stock from beneath the fat by siphoning with the plastic tube. Tip the kettle holding the
stock so that you can always keep the siphoning tube
beneath the level of the fat. This works very well.

Celery Soup

This is so easy, and it is a most satisfying way to tell your guests
or family that you care about them. Be frugal, and use the leaves
as well as the stalk . . . and make your own chicken stock!

   1½ cups chopped celery stalks and leaves
   ½ cup chopped carefully cleaned leeks
   2 large tomatoes, chopped
   3 tablespoons butter
   6 cups hot Chicken Soup Stock (page 53)
   Fresh-chopped celery leaves for garnish
   Salt and pepper to taste

Sauté 1½ cups celery and leaves, leeks, and tomatoes in the butter. Add the soup stock, and cook for 30 minutes. Strain, and serve with some fresh-chopped celery leaves and salt and pepper.

SERVES 6.

Chicken with Mushroom Soup

What to do with that little bit of leftover chicken? This is a snap, and after all, soups should lengthen the time that you spend at table with your friends or family. Such a good use for a cup of chicken.

> ½ cup sliced fresh mushrooms
> 2 tablespoons butter
> 6 cups Chicken Soup Stock (page 53)
> 1 cup cooked chicken
> ½ cup white rice, uncooked
> 2 tablespoons lemon juice
> Chopped green onions for garnish

Sauté the mushrooms in the butter. Add to the soup stock along with the chicken and rice. Cook until the rice is puffy, and serve with a little lemon juice and chopped green onions in a bowl.

SERVES 6 TO 8.

Cream of Broccoli Soup

At times I have made this just with the hard ends of the broccoli. It is delicious, and already you feel so frugal.

> 2   **pounds broccoli**
> 2   **tablespoons butter**
> ½   **cup yellow onions, chopped**
> ¼   **cup chopped green pepper**
> 2   **tablespoons flour**
> 6   **cups Chicken Soup Stock (page 53)**
> 1   **bay leaf**
>   **Parsley**
> 1   **teaspoon ground thyme**
> 6   **black peppercorns**
>   **Pinch of nutmeg**
> 3   **egg yolks, whipped and blended with 1 cup milk**
>   **or cream**

Chop up the broccoli, saving some of the small buds and flowers for later use. Sauté in the butter along with the onions and green pepper. Sprinkle with the flour, and stir. Add to the soup stock, along with the bay leaf, parsley, thyme, and peppercorns. Cook for 30 minutes, and purée the mixture in a blender or sieve. Add the nutmeg, strain the soup from the pulp, and return to pan. Add a bit of the purée to the egg yolk and milk or cream mixture, then pour into hot soup. This will prevent curdling.

Serve with some of the reserved broccoli buds floating in the bowl.

SERVES 6 TO 8.

Spinach and Dandelion Soup

The first time I made this for my sons they thought I was crazy, marching through the city park, picking dandelion greens. Now I shall let them do it.

6   cups Chicken Soup Stock (page 53)
3   cups fresh dandelion greens,* chopped
3   cups fresh spinach, chopped
3   green onions, chopped
1   clove garlic, crushed
    Salt and pepper to taste
    Pinch of nutmeg
2   eggs, hard-boiled and chopped

To the soup stock, add the dandelion greens, spinach, green onions, garlic, salt, and pepper. Cook until the greens are tender, and offer in bowls with the nutmeg and eggs.

SERVES 6.

Beer and Cheese Soup

This recipe is for the law students at the University of Puget Sound. When I put this on the menu, they shouted, "Relevance at last!" It is delicious. You see, I don't even waste stale beer.

My wife, Patty, loves to serve this soup along with bagels and beer for a party. That's the whole menu, and it is always a hit.

1   cup carrots, chopped
1   cup celery, chopped
1   cup yellow onions, peeled and chopped
2   teaspoons peanut oil
6   cups Chicken Soup Stock (page 53)
1   cup cheddar cheese, grated
2   teaspoons flour
    Salt and pepper to taste
½   teaspoon dry mustard
⅛   teaspoon Tabasco or more to taste
⅛   teaspoon Worcestershire sauce
1   12-ounce bottle beer
    Parsley for garnish
    Polish sausage or knackwurst (optional)

Sauté the carrots, celery, and onions in the oil until lightly browned. Bring the soup stock to a boil, add the vegetables, and simmer for 45 minutes.

(continued)

*Find nice leafy dandelion greens that have no fuzz on them.

Dredge the cheese in the flour, and mix into the soup, *stirring constantly* until the mixture thickens. Keep stirring often until you serve.

Add the salt, pepper, mustard, Tabasco, and Worcestershire. Finally, add the beer, and stir until all is hot. Garnish with parsley, and serve.

You may add sliced cooked sausage to this soup; add just before serving.

SERVES 6 TO 8.

■ HINT: Cooking Oils

I use few oils in my kitchen. I prefer peanut oil for frying of any kind since it will withstand high temperatures without burning. Many doctors are now convinced that oils that burn at low temperatures cause great problems with our health. They may even be carcinogens. Olive oil is also great for cooking, but I use it only when I want that rich flavor of the Mediterranean regions. Peanut oil has no flavor. I also prefer butter to margarine, as I am not convinced that a hydrogenated vegetable oil is that much better for you than butter is; besides, I cannot abide the taste of margarine. So I use a little butter in cooking, and cut it with a bit of peanut oil. That way I have flavor but less butterfat. The peanut oil helps the butter withstand the high temperatures of cooking.

Green Bean and Potato Soup

I stole this soup from Peter, one of my cooks. His mother was from Eastern Europe, and you can see, right away, what *frugal*

means in those countries. This takes very little time to cook and
your family will love it.

Use a large soup pot for this one.

>   5 stalks celery, sliced thin
>   1 bunch green onions, chopped
>   ½ stick (¼ cup) butter
>   2 tablespoons flour
>   2 quarts water
>   ¾ cup powdered milk
>   3 medium potatoes
>   Salt and pepper to taste
>   ½ cup chopped fresh parsley
>   1 tablespoon dried dill weed
>   1½ cups sour cream
>   1 10-ounce package frozen French-style green
>   beans

Sauté the celery and green onions in the butter.

When the vegetables are not quite tender, add the flour, and
stir in. Add the water, and stir until blended. Add the milk, and
stir over medium heat until thickened.

Dice the potatoes, leaving the skins on. Add to the pot along
with some salt and pepper, parsley, and dill weed. Simmer, stirring often, until the potatoes are tender, about ½ hour.

Twenty minutes before serving, stir in the sour cream and
green beans. Simmer for 20 minutes, and enjoy.

MAKES ABOUT 3 QUARTS.

SERVES 10 TO 12.

Cuban Black Bean Soup

This one is spicy, hot, and hearty. I first tasted something like it
in the back streets of the Cuban section of Miami. It has taken
some time to work out the recipe because no one could give it to
me in English. See how my translation works out.

    1 **gallon water**
1½ **cups black beans, soaked in 2 quarts water
        overnight and drained**
    1 **pound bacon, chopped**
    1 **teaspoon dried, crushed red pepper flakes
        Salt and pepper to taste**
    2 **cloves garlic, crushed
        Pinch of oregano**
    2 **yellow onions, peeled and chopped**
    1 **tablespoon prepared mustard
        Handful of chopped parsley
        Handful of chopped celery**

Add fresh water to beans. Simmer for 5 hours.

Add the remaining ingredients. Simmer for another 2 hours. Watch that you don't burn this great soup!

SERVES 10 TO 12.

■ HINT: On Cooking One Day a Week

Frugal cooking means that you don't waste time or food. For that reason you need to think about planning a week of menus and then cooking as much as possible one day a week. On that chosen day do little else. Make brown soup stock, omelet fillings, crepes, a roast chicken or two, or perhaps a boiled chicken, Chinese style. You will need tomato sauce, salad dressings, a mirepoix of vegetables. Sauté some yellow onions so that you are ready with French onion soup in no time. A good beef stew or a grain casserole would also be helpful. Do as many of these as you can. And then relax during the week. Dinner is already half-done before you get home.

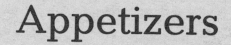

Appetizers

The Hors d'Oeuvres Buffet

The cocktail party is a very American thing. Of course, other cultures have appetizers. The Italians celebrate with antipasto, the Spanish with tapas, and the Lebanese with mezza. And on and on. However, we often do not use hors d'oeuvres as an appetizer at all. We Americans are wont to put out an entire snack buffet, offer too much alcohol, and then expect people to enjoy the dinner table. I don't believe that we should be trying to do both.

Appetizers are to be served as a first course at the dinner table. Serve a plate of good pâté, for instance, and then on with the meal. The meal should be long enough, and lovely enough, to make the evening. But we need not serve elaborate appetizers at the buffet before the meal. The hors d'oeuvres buffet should be a separate event, one at which you are trying to get a large number of people together at one time but not going to feed them dinner.

I rarely serve hard liquor at a dinner party, nor do I serve hors d'oeuvres. The liquor will burn out the taste buds, and the snacks will fill people up. If I have worked hard on a dinner party, then I serve my guests dry sherry and perhaps a few olives and a bit of cheese. Then I bring on the dinner. And please serve dinner no more than one hour after you have invited people. The wait for dinner is sometimes terrible!

The cocktail party is something else. Load up the buffet with little things that will hold up well for the evening, and you can feel free to serve people whatever it is that they want to drink. The point of the evening is not the food but the company and conversation. The following recipes will help with the hors d'oeuvres buffet.

Caviar Mold

This is a very easy dish that will add serious elegance to your party buffet.

> 6 eggs, hard-boiled and peeled
> 1 envelope gelatin
> 2 tablespoons cool water
> 2 tablespoons lemon juice
> ⅛ teaspoon salt
> ⅛ teaspoon Tabasco
> ½ small yellow onion, peeled and chopped fine
> 1 teaspoon Worcestershire sauce
> ¾ cup mayonnaise
> 1 3-ounce jar Danish black lumpfish caviar
> Chopped parsley for garnish

Grind or grate the eggs fine, and allow them to cool.

Dissolve the gelatin in the water. Place in a very small saucepan, and add the lemon juice. Stir over low heat until the gelatin dissolves completely.

Place the eggs, salt, Tabasco, onion, Worcestershire sauce, and mayonnaise in a bowl. Blend well, and then add the lemon and gelatin mixture. Mix again. Finally, very gently stir in the caviar. Do not stir much because you will discolor the mixture.

Pour into a 1-quart mold, and refrigerate. Unmold, and garnish with parsley.

Serve with crackers.

SERVES 12 TO 16 AT A COCKTAIL PARTY.

Piping Cheese

This simple soft cheese is to be used in the preparation of many fancy snacks. You can vary the herb blend as you wish.

  1 **pound cream cheese, at room temperature**
  ½ **cup mayonnaise**
  ¼ **cup sour cream or yogurt**
  ⅛ **teaspoon Tabasco**
  1 **teaspoon soy sauce**
  1 **teaspoon Worcestershire sauce**
  ½ **teaspoon dry mustard**
  ¼ **teaspoon whole oregano**
  ¼ **teaspoon whole basil**
  ¼ **teaspoon whole thyme**
  ¼ **cup fresh-grated Parmesan or Romano cheese**
     Salt and pepper to taste

Whip all ingredients together, and use to fill various snacks. Normally, this is done with a piping bag and tip, but you can fill many types of cracker and vegetable with a small knife or spoon.

MAKES 3 CUPS.

Stuffed Cherry Tomatoes

  1 **basket ripe cherry tomatoes**
     Piping Cheese (see above)
     Parsley for garnish

Pull off and discard the stems of each cherry tomato, and rinse tomatoes. Cut each three-quarters of the way across or through; cut across the grain of the tomato, not from the top to the bottom. Fill a piping bag with the piping cheese, hold the tomato open with one hand, and fill the "mouth" from the piping bag held in the other hand. Garnish with parsley.

MAKES ABOUT 25.

Smoked Clams and Parsley

> 1 **bunch parsley**
> 40 **small square crackers**
>   **Piping Cheese (page 64)**
> 1 **small can smoked baby clams**

Rinse the parsley, and prepare about 40 tiny parsley tips of trees
—that is, take a leaf of parsley from the stalk, leaving a small
stem on the leaf.

Arrange the crackers on a tray. Using a piping bag filled with
the piping cheese, pipe a little mountain of cheese on the
crackers. Place a tiny clam on top and a parsley tree in the side of
each mountain.

MAKES 40.

Artichoke and Curried Egg

I could sit down and eat this whole batch, but it is a little rich.
Don't chop the artichokes too fine because you want something
that you can heap on a small cracker.

> 6 **eggs, hard-boiled**
> 1 **16-ounce can artichoke hearts**
> ¼ **cup mayonnaise**
> ½ **cup sour cream**
>   **Salt and pepper to taste**
>   **Curry powder to taste**

Peel and chop the eggs. Drain and chop the artichoke hearts. Combine the eggs and artichokes into a very coarse spread. Mix the mayonnaise, sour cream, salt, pepper, and curry powder (make the curry flavor rather light. This is not to be hot but simply supportive of the eggs and artichokes. Why can I not tell you how much curry? Because I am not sure what kind you use, and curry powders vary in strength). Mix together, and refrigerate.

Mold into a mound on a lettuce leaf, and serve with crackers.

SERVES 16 TO 20 ON AN HORS D'OEUVRES BUFFET.

Salmon and Cream Cheese Ball

This one is from my mother, Emily Smith. She is the one who taught me the meaning of *frugal* as she is a tough Norwegian . . . and a fine cook. She is one of those people who can go into an empty kitchen and prepare a lovely meal for 8. This is great for an hors d'oeuvres buffet or as a first course at a nice dinner party.

1½ pounds fresh salmon roast *or* 1 pound canned
     salmon
½ teaspoon liquid smoke
1 tablespoon horseradish
1 tablespoon lemon juice
½ pound cream cheese, mashed
2 tablespoons mayonnaise
1 tablespoon dried parsley flakes

Steam the fresh salmon for about 45 minutes in a metal steamer (page 301). Cool the fish. Skin the salmon, remove the bones, and place the meat in a bowl. Add the remaining ingredients, and mix well.

SERVES 16 TO 20 ON HORS D'OEUVRES BUFFET.

SERVES 8 AS FIRST COURSE AT DINNER PARTY.

SERVES 1 IF JEFF SMITH IS PRESENT.

Marinated Baby Corn

I know that you can buy marinated baby corn from Germany, and it costs a fortune. Marinate your own!

1 16-ounce can baby corn from Taiwan*
Basic Fennel Dressing (page 00)

Drain the corn, and marinate in the dressing for several hours.
    Serve at room temperature.

SERVES 8 TO 10 ON HORS D'OEUVRES BUFFET.

Marinated Asparagus

1 package frozen asparagus spears or fresh
        asparagus
Basic Fennel Dressing (page 90)

Cut the frozen or fresh asparagus into 2-inch pieces, and marinate in the dressing for several hours.
    Serve at room temperature.

SERVES 8 TO 10 ON HORS D'OEUVRES BUFFET.

*Buy at gourmet shop or Chinese market.

Linda's Onion and Rye Snack

A good cook is able to produce something lovely from whatever is on hand. At least that is what our grandmothers told us. Few of us can do it, but Linda Settle, a dear friend who lives on Puget Sound, can do it every time. This is one of her creations for an hors d'oeuvres buffet.

    ½ **cup chopped peeled yellow onion**
    ½ **cup mayonnaise**
       Thin-sliced party rye or cocktail rye bread
       Fresh-grated Parmesan or Romano cheese

Mix the onion and the mayonnaise. Spread on a tiny bread slice, and top with a bit of cheese. Broil for a few minutes until the top is just a bit browned. Serve hot.

MAKES ABOUT 25.

Caponata
(Italy)

This lovely eggplant relish is a great beginning for any party.

    2 pounds eggplant
    1 tablespoon salt
    3 tablespoons olive oil
    2 cups celery, chopped into coarse pieces
    ¾ cup peeled, chopped yellow onion
    ⅓ cup wine vinegar
    4 teaspoons sugar
    3 cups canned tomatoes, mashed
    2 tablespoons tomato paste
    6 green olives, pitted and chopped
    2 tablespoons capers
    4 or 5 anchovies in oil
       Salt and pepper to taste

Cut the eggplant into 1-inch cubes. Dust with the 1 tablespoon
salt, and allow to drain in a colander. Meanwhile, in a little olive
oil, sauté the celery along with the onion for about 15 minutes;
and remove. Use a large frying pan so that the food won't be
crowded. In the same pan, sauté the drained eggplant for about
10 minutes in a little oil. Place all these in a heavy 2-quart kettle.
Add the wine vinegar, sugar, tomatoes, tomato paste, olives,
capers, and anchovies, and let simmer for 15 to 20 minutes. Add
salt and pepper. Chill, and serve.

    Serve it on a bed of lettuce, with a few brown crackers.

SERVES 10 TO 15 AS HORS D'OEUVRE.

Antipasto Plate
(Italy)

This dish is so dramatic that it will make any Italian dinner. Serve
it prior to the pasta course, which is served just before the main
course. It is a lovely mosaic of color and flavors.

Caponata (page 69)
Hard-boiled eggs, in wedges
Green onion
Italian salami
Tuna
Tomato Sauce (page 263)
Greek olives
Green or Italian dried olives
Romano cheese
Artichoke hearts
Cherry tomatoes
Canned sardines
Italian peperoncini (pickled small green
peppers)

On each plain glass plate arrange the following items so that every plate looks like every other: a little caponata, 2 or 3 wedges of hard-boiled egg, a green onion, 2 slices Italian salami, a little tuna mixed with some tomato sauce, a few Greek olives, a few green or Italian dried olives, a little cheese, a couple of artichoke hearts, a cherry tomato, a sardine, and a peperoncini. You don't need all of these, but use as many as you like.

Fish and
Shellfish

■ HINT: How Do You Check to See if Fish Is Fresh?

There are several things that you can check to be sure that fish is fresh: (1) The eye should be clean and bulging, shiny and bright; this is probably the most important test. (2) Lift the gills of the fish, and check to see that they are red and clean-looking, never brown or pale. (3) If the fish is fresh, the flesh will be elastic and firm, rather than soggy or soft. (4) The scales should be tight and bright, not falling off. (5) The fish should smell not "fishy" but fresh and clean.

Poached Salmon

I love the real King of the Sea. The salmon is very common in our diet here in the Pacific Northwest, and it is one of the reasons that I stay. Please don't overcook this glorious fish.

> 1 5- or 6-pound salmon, whole, cleaned
> 6 chicken bouillon cubes
>   White vinegar
>   Few black peppercorns
>   Pinch of dried dill weed

LEMON SAUCE
> 1 cup Béchamel Sauce (page 259)
> 3 tablespoons lemon juice
>   Nutmeg to taste

Remove the head and tail of the salmon. Reserve them.
Place the salmon in a fish poacher or any deep baking pan,

and cover it with water. *Remove* the fish, and add the chicken bouillon cubes to the water along with ⅛ cup vinegar to each 1 quart water. Add peppercorns and dill weed. Bring the water to a boil, and place the fish in the poacher. Cover, and barely simmer for less than 1 hour, or until the fish is flaky and tender.

Prepare lemon sauce by combining the béchamel sauce, lemon juice, and nutmeg.

To serve, arrange the whole fish on a giant bed of lettuce. Garnish with lemon wedges and cherry tomatoes, and serve with delight and pride. You may wish to peel off the skin on the side of the fish. Replace the head and tail, garnish with parsley, and if you are fussy, cover the eye with a slice of olive.

Serve with the lemon sauce. And salad, pasta, and wine, of course.

SERVES 10 TO 12.

Baked Stuffed Salmon

Who would have guessed that I would marry a woman from Brooklyn? When she saw her first 15-pound fresh salmon from Pacific Northwest waters, she wanted to go back home to Brooklyn. All she could think about was the flavor of that terrible canned salmon casserole that she had eaten in the grade school lunchroom. With this recipe I converted her. She is now a salmon lover.

> 1 5- to 6-pound whole salmon, cleaned
>   Salt and pepper to taste
>   Green pepper, sliced
>   Yellow onion, peeled and sliced
>   Carrot, grated
>   Parsley branches
>   Chicken Soup Stock (page 53)
>   Dry white wine
> 1 tablespoon dried dill weed

Choose a large baking pan into which you can fit the salmon and still have room for about an inch of liquid all around the fish. Salt and pepper the fish. Stuff it with green pepper, yellow onion, carrot, and parsley. Place in the pan, and add chicken broth and white wine with a little dill, so that the fish is sitting in a 1-inch-deep bath. Cover the pan with aluminum foil, and bake in a 325° oven for about 1½ hours.

Serve on a bed of lettuce.

This is great served with a hearty green salad with Basic Fennel Dressing (page 90) and a plateful of Broiled French Tomatoes (page 252).

SERVES 8 TO 10.

Salmon en Gelée

This dish will take some time and care, but the remarks that will issue from your friends or family are certainly worth the effort. After all, isn't that why we are cooking—to hear those sounds of joy and delight when our guests see the table?

> 1 5- to 6-pound salmon, poached (page 75) or
>   baked (page 76), then chilled
> 2 packages gelatin
>   Lemon juice
>   Carrot and turnip slices, cut into vegetable
>   flowers with tiny cookie cutter

Place the salmon on an oven rack. Place the rack over the sink, and remove the skin of the fish from the neck to the tail.

Prepare a clear gelatin with the lemon juice according to the recipe on the gelatin envelope. Chill the gelatin in the refrigerator until it is a little thicker than a very heavy cream.

Brush some of the gelatin on the fish, still over the sink, and working quickly, place the cut vegetable flowers on the back of the fish. (I use a little cookie cutter and cut flowers from slices of carrots and turnips.) Pour some more gelatin over the whole fish, and refrigerate until all is set.

Serve on a large bed of lettuce with garnishes of lemon wedges and cherry tomatoes. This dish will absolutely make any buffet dinner.

SERVES 10 TO 12.

Broiled Salmon Steaks

Simple, simple, simple, and delicious. That is what frugal cooking is all about.

- **2 10-ounce salmon steaks**
- **½ cup olive oil**
- **¼ cup Chinese light soy sauce**
- **½ teaspoon dried dill weed**
- **⅛ cup lemon juice**
-    **Ground clove**

Prepare a sauce of the olive oil, soy sauce, dill weed, lemon juice, and clove. Mix well, and brush over the salmon steaks. Place on a cookie sheet. Broil steaks on both sides until lightly browned and tender. Do not overcook. This will take very little time, so be careful.

Serve with Marilyn's Baked Potato with Bay Leaf (page 246) and a green salad.

This would also be great served with Italian Tomato Salad (page 94) or Green Beans with Oregano (page 220), and very crunchy French bread. A dry white wine would go well.

SERVES 8.

Seviche—Raw Fish Salad
(Mexico)

Some people are funny. Don't tell them that this fish is raw. Actually it is pickled or almost cooked by the action of the lime juice. Although this is now very "in" with the "nouveau" food crowd, try it at your own home. I stole this recipe from Dr. William Campbell, a dear friend and serious cook. When he is not checking out a glacier in the Arctic, he is cooking for friends and family. He likes this dish very hot . . . using lots of Chinese Red Chili Paste with Garlic (page 23).

- **1½ pounds fresh whitefish fillets***
- **1 cup (about 4 limes) fresh lime juice**

*I prefer red snapper or halibut, but I have enjoyed Arctic Cod as well.

DRESSING
- ½ cup olive oil
- 2 cloves garlic, crushed
- ½ teaspoon oregano
- ½ teaspoon whole thyme
- 1 teaspoon ground coriander
  Tabasco or Chinese red chili paste with garlic
  Fresh-ground black pepper to taste
- 1 green or red bell pepper, cleaned and chopped
- 4 green onions, chopped
- 2 tomatoes, diced

Cut the fish into very thin, small slices. Marinate in the lime juice for 1½ hours.

Mix together the olive oil, garlic, oregano, thyme, coriander, Tabasco or chili paste, and black pepper for the dressing.*

After the fish has marinated, blend in the pepper, green onions, tomatoes, and dressing. Stir gently to blend. Refrigerate for 1 hour before serving. I then like to place the salad on a big bed of lettuce and garnish it with avocado slices. Serve with a dry white wine and some dark bread, and you have a whole meal with great flavor, very little oil . . . and no additional salt is necessary.

Also try serving this unusual dish with pasta and a green salad.

White wine would go well.

SERVES 6 TO 8 AS APPETIZER OR FISH COURSE.

Baked Fish in Vinegar Sauce

This is actually fish in salad dressing, and it will startle the children in your house who claim that they don't like fish.

---

*I like my dressing a bit hot, and that is why I suggest you find a hot red chili and garlic paste from China. Any Oriental market will stock this for you.

>   2 or 3 pounds whitefish fillets
>   Flour
>   Salt
>   2 large yellow onions, peeled and sliced thin
>   Butter
>   ½ cup olive oil
>   ½ cup white wine vinegar
>   2 cloves garlic, crushed
>   1 teaspoon oregano
>   2 teaspoons dry mustard
>   Handful of chopped parsley
>   ½ teaspoon ground coriander
>   1 tablespoon lemon juice
>   ¼ cup dry white wine

Dredge the fish fillets in flour and a tiny bit of salt. Place them in a shallow baking dish so that they all fit snugly. Sauté the onions, in a bit of butter until they are tender and transparent. Spread the onions over the fish fillets. Prepare something akin to a good salad dressing as follows: Blend the olive oil, wine vinegar, garlic, oregano, mustard, parsley, coriander, lemon juice, and wine (you may wish to add some other favorite ingredients such as dill, in which case you could omit the coriander). Pour the dressing over the fish, and bake the fish, uncovered, in a 350° oven for about 45 minutes.

Serve a nice soup, followed by a pasta, then the fish with a salad on the side. Perfect dinnertime!

SERVES 5 TO 8.

Hangtown Fry

Don't ask me to authenticate the existence of an old down-and-outers' city outside San Francisco called Hangtown at the turn of the century. It seems to have existed. In any case this dish is attributed to that time. And whether you prepare it for the queen of England or for a citizen from Hangtown, I think you'll love it.

> **Butter**
> ¼ **cup oysters, drained**
> **White wine (¼ cup for 4 to 5 oysters)**
> **Green onion, chopped**
> 3 **eggs**
> **Salt and pepper to taste**
> **Dash of chopped parsley**

Heat a pan and add a bit of butter. Add the oysters, sauté for a moment, and then add the white wine. Be careful that you do no more than poach the oysters, because a cooked oyster is a lost oyster.

Remove the oysters to a heated plate, and add a bit of green onion to the liquor that remains in the pan. Reduce this mixture for a moment or two over high heat, and reserve.

Whip the eggs and 1 tablespoon water lightly. Pour into a preheated buttered omelet pan. When the omelet begins to form, add the oysters, salt, and pepper. Fold the omelet over, and pour the reserved liquor over the top. Add the parsley, and enjoy a classic.

I like to serve this with a green salad, a white wine, and Marilyn's Baked Potatoes with Bay Leaf (page 246).

SERVES 1.

■ HINT:

Always heat the frying pan before putting the oil into the pan. In that way you will not burn the oil while heating the pan. So heat the pan, add the oil, and the food immediately. This is an old Chinese rule. "Hot wok, cold oil, foods won't stick." It works!

Sole Italian Style

This is for that quick dinner party. Serve with a nice pasta and salad. Either a red or white wine will do because this dish is very rich in flavor.

   1½ **pounds fresh sole fillets**
       Salt and pepper to taste
       Butter for browning
    1 **teaspoon oregano, crushed**
   ½ **cup fresh-grated Parmesan or Romano cheese**
    4 **tablespoons olive oil**
   ¼ **cup Fish Stock (page 402) or bottled clam juice**
    2 **tablespoons fresh lemon juice**

Pat dry the sole and season with salt and pepper. Sauté the fish in a little butter in a heavy skillet until browned on both sides. Do not overcook. Sprinkle with the oregano and cheese, and top with the olive oil. Add the fish stock to the bottom of the pan (do not pour over the fish, but along the side), cover, and simmer over low heat for 5 minutes. Sprinkle with the lemon juice before serving.

SERVES 4.

Sole with Rosemary
(Italy)

I love the flavor and cleansing quality of fresh rosemary. The shrub is a perennial and will grow larger by the year. We can grow this herb in most areas of the country, so ask your garden man if you can grow it as well.

   1½ **pounds sole fillets**
    2 **tablespoons olive oil**
    1 **tablespoon lemon juice**
    2 **tablespoons white wine**
    1 **tablespoon fresh-chopped parsley**
   ½ **tablespoon fresh whole rosemary *or* 1 teaspoon**
        dried rosemary
       Salt and pepper to taste

Place the sole in a baking dish so that the fish fits snugly. Prepare a mixture of the olive oil, lemon juice, wine, parsley, and rosemary. Mix the above ingredients, and pour over the fish. Add salt and pepper, and bake for about 20 minutes, or until the fish barely begins to flake.

SERVES 4 TO 6.

My Favorite Quick Oysters

This is a first course that will simply stop your guests in the middle of their conversation.

> Per person
> 2 oysters
> 2 strips bacon
> 2 teaspoons chopped green pepper
> 2 teaspoons chopped green onion
> Dash of dry white wine
> Salt and pepper to taste

Shuck the oysters, reserving shell. Wrap each oyster in a strip of bacon and place it on the half shell. Top each with 1 teaspoon green pepper and 1 teaspoon green onion, and add a dash of wine. "A bit of salt and pepper is what we need and we can begin to feed." Broil these creatures for just a few moments until the bacon is hot and crunchy, and the oysters are tender, tender, tender.

Serve with a great deal of flamboyance as you march from the kitchen. This simple dish is a great favorite of mine.

SERVES 1.

Oysters Italian

This dish is served with the oysters broiled in their own half shell, though you can certainly buy fresh oysters in the fish market in the jar and use old shells over and over again.

>   1 dozen oysters
>   3 cloves garlic, crushed and cooked in 3
>   tablespoons butter
>   Salt and pepper to taste
>   1 cup bread crumbs
>   2 tablespoons olive oil
>   2 tablespoons chopped parsley
>   ½ teaspoon oregano

Shuck the oysters. Rub each shell with the garlic butter, and place the oyster back in it. Add salt and pepper. To the bread crumbs, add the olive oil, parsley, and oregano. Mix carefully, and sprinkle over the oysters. Place the shells on a baking tray, and broil for about 10 minutes. Serve on the half shell.

MAKES 12.

Oysters Florentine

This is a lovely dish that has had a great reputation but is very simple to prepare. This is a most elegant first course.

>   Oysters
>   Butter
>   Drained and defrosted frozen chopped spinach
>   Mornay Sauce (page 260)
>   Fresh-grated Parmesan, Romano, or Sardinian
>   cheese

Either shuck fresh oysters, or buy oysters in the jar and use old shells. I use the same shells over and over again for these dishes.

Butter the shells, and place about 1 tablespoon spinach in each. Add a little melted butter to each mound of spinach, and press one oyster into the mound. Top the oyster with the Mornay sauce and a bit of the cheese. Broil until everything is bubbling hot.

This can be served as a first course of an Italian meal. Follow with pasta and then a Frittata (page 111) and salad for the main course. Serve a white wine, very dry.

Salads

Salads Year Round

In Europe, salads are not seen as part of the main plate but as a separate course. What a lovely thing it is to offer a salad plate between an appetizer course and the entrée. It lengthens the dinnertime; it raises the event of the table; it refreshes the palate. So serve salads separately and enjoy!

■ HINT:

Keep salads moist on buffet with wet paper towels. When your guests arrive, remove the towels, and all will be crisp and fresh. This also works well with cold meat plates and many hors d'oeuvres.

Basic Greens

We are lucky our markets carry so many greens the year around. There are butter lettuce, romaine, endive, and the common iceberg. All these are good, but I prefer the beautiful red leaf. It is tender, light in flavor, and colorful. But it does not keep as well as the old iceberg, so be careful with it.

Basic Fennel Dressing

Bottled dressings are strong in flavor and high in price. *The Frugal Gourmet* suggests you prepare a basic dressing and leave it in your refrigerator. It keeps well.

½ cup olive oil
½ cup peanut oil
½ cup red wine vinegar
½ cup white vinegar
1 teaspoon sugar or more to taste
1 tablespoon dry mustard*
1 teaspoon fennel, ground
2 tablespoons lemon juice
⅛ cup dried parsley
Salt and pepper to taste

Blend the oils and the vinegars. Add a little sugar, mustard, and fennel. Add some lemon juice, parsley, salt, and pepper.

MAKES 2 CUPS.

*I like Colman's.

Greek Salad

This salad is common at good Greek restaurants, and it is a great favorite of my family. If you make a gigantic version, it will provide a grand summer evening meal. The wine should be white; the bread, crunchy. Or you can go to the Parthenon restaurant in Chicago and have a great salad . . . or to Pasparo's Taverna in Vancouver, British Columbia.

> **Cherry tomatoes, cut up**
> **White or yellow onions, cut into thin slices**
> **Green peppers, sliced**
> **Greek olives**
> **Feta cheese, chopped**
> **Salt and pepper to taste**
> **Oregano to taste**
> **Basic Fennel Dressing (page 90)**
> **Lettuce**

Mix the cherry tomatoes, white or yellow onions, and green peppers. Add some Greek olives and some feta cheese (both available in your delicatessen). Toss with salt and pepper, a little oregano, and the fennel dressing.

Serve over a bed of torn lettuce.

Hungarian Salad

Good Hungarian paprika has a lovely flavor, but most Americans have tasted only weak red powder that has sat on the grocer's shelf for much too long. Buy a fresh batch from a good spice shop.

> **Green peppers, sliced**
> **Cucumbers, peeled and sliced**
> **Basic Fennel Dressing (page 90)**
> **Hungarian paprika**
> **Lettuce**

Mix green peppers and cucumbers. Toss with the fennel dressing, to which you have added a little good Hungarian paprika.

Serve over a bed of lettuce tossed with the same dressing.

Spinach Salad

A good spinach salad is a marvelous thing. Try this one with any of the other salad dressings in this section. It is great with a mustard dressing, just great!

>   3 **bunches spinach, cleaned and torn**
>   6 **green onions, chopped**
>   6 **slices bacon, diced and fried crisp**
>   1 **cup fresh mushrooms, sliced**
>   1 **cup mung bean sprouts**
>   **Basic Fennel Dressing (page 90)**
>   **Fresh-grated Parmesan or Romano cheese**
>   **Salt and pepper to taste**

Toss the spinach with the green onions, bacon, mushrooms, and mung bean sprouts. Toss with the fennel dressing, and top with the Parmesan or Romano cheese, salt, and pepper.

My mother adds fresh sunflower seeds to this dish and creates a great hit!

SERVES 6.

■ HINT:

When making green salads, wash the greens, and then roll them up in a terry-cloth bath towel. Refrigerate the towel until serving time. The lettuce will be crisp and dry.

Japanese Cucumber and Crab Salad

A very delicate and unusual salad. Don't be put off by the salt, it is used to draw water from the cucumbers, and then the salt water is drained off. A most unusual and tasty salad.

> 4 cucumbers, sliced thin, unpeeled
> 1 tablespoon salt
> 1 6-ounce can of crab

DRESSING
> ¼ cup light soy sauce*
> ⅛ cup rice wine vinegar*
> ½ tablespoon sesame oil*
>   Pinch of sugar

Mix the cucumbers with salt. Place in a colander, and the salt and water will drain off. Drain for about 45 minutes. Mix with the crab. Make a dressing of the light soy sauce, rice wine vinegar, sesame oil, and sugar. Toss with the crab/cucumber mixture and serve.

SERVES 6.

My Special Salad

I might as well tell you the truth. I threw this one together 5 minutes before we went on the air one morning. I realized that we needed another dish, and I just grabbed what I could. That is not a bad method for creating salads.

*These ingredients are available in any Oriental food store.

  1 15-ounce can baby corn, drained*
  1 16-ounce can artichoke hearts, drained and
        quartered
  1 bunch asparagus, blanched, *or* 1 10-ounce
        package frozen asparagus, uncooked
     Salt and pepper to taste
     Basic Fennel Dressing (page 90)
  1 head green leaf or red leaf lettuce

Toss the baby corn with the artichoke hearts and cut asparagus.
Add salt and pepper and the fennel dressing. Serve over the
greens.

SERVES 6.

Italian Tomato Salad

Often, when I describe this salad, people seem nervous about
eating nothing but onions and tomatoes. Both are marinated, and
the flavors blend and become very mild.

  2 white Bermuda onions, sliced thin
  5 ripe tomatoes, sliced
  ¼ cup parsley, chopped
  1 tablespoon oregano
     Basic Fennel Dressing (page 90)
     Salt and pepper to taste

Mix the white onions with the tomatoes. Add the parsley, oregano, and fennel dressing. Add salt and pepper. Let this marinate
for a few hours before dinner, and then be ready to be sorry you
did not make more.

SERVES 6 TO 8.

*Available in Oriental food markets.

Bleu Cheese and Anchovy Dressing

This dressing is, of course, a child of the Caesar salad but is much quicker to prepare, and you will find it very rich. It is always popular at our dinner parties.

> 2 cups Basic Fennel Dressing (page 90)
> 3 or 4 small canned Spanish or Portuguese
>   anchovy fillets
> ¼ cup lemon juice
> 2 eggs, coddled*
> ⅛ pound bleu cheese
>   Salt and pepper to taste
>   Croutons

Place the fennel dressing in a food blender. Add the anchovies, lemon juice, eggs, and blue cheese. Blend for just a moment, and pour over your salad. (I like fresh-torn romaine lettuce.) Add salt and pepper. Add croutons, and serve.

MAKES 3 CUPS.

Cottage Cheese and Dill Dressing†

Simple, quick, and much lighter than the usual bleu cheese dressing.

> ½ cup cottage cheese
> ½ cup mayonnaise
> ½ cup milk
> 1 tablespoon olive oil
> 2 tablespoons wine vinegar or lemon juice
> ⅛ teaspoon sugar
>   Salt and fresh-cracked pepper to taste
> 1 clove garlic, crushed
> 1 teaspoon dried dill weed

*To coddle eggs, let them set in a bowl of hot tap water for 15 minutes.

†If you wish to make this into a low-fat/low-salt dressing, use a low-fat mayonnaise, a low-fat cottage cheese, and omit the salt.

Blend together all ingredients. Let sit for 1 day in the refrigerator before serving.

MAKES 1¾ CUPS.

Dijon Mustard Dressing

This one is my wife's favorite. It goes well with many vegetables and greens.

>   1 egg
>   ⅛ cup olive oil
>   ⅛ cup red wine vinegar
>   Salt and pepper to taste
>   1 tablespoon Dijon-style mustard*
>   Pinch of sugar

Coddle the egg by placing it in a bowl of very hot tap water. Let stand for 15 minutes.
   Place all ingredients in a food blender, and mix.

MAKES ¾ CUP.

Dill and Caper Dressing

This one is close to the dressing used in a salad Olivier, a Russian delicacy.

>   ¾ cup mayonnaise
>   ¾ cup sour cream, yogurt, or Mock Sour Cream
>   (page 276)
>   2 dill pickles, chopped
>   1 to 2 tablespoons capers
>   4 green onions, chopped
>   1 teaspoon dried dill weed
>   Salt and pepper to taste

Blend all ingredients together, and refrigerate for a few hours before serving.

MAKES 2½ CUPS.

*Grey Poupon is fine.

Whole-Meal Salads

The idea of a whole-meal salad is a simple one. It means that you use meats and vegetables in the salad so that one lovely dish offers a celebrative and satisfying meal—along with a glass of wine, of course.

This kind of cooking is a great help to working people, and that means that all of us qualify.

Broccoli and Chicken Salad

This will startle your children. "We're having only salad to-night." They will not be ready to accept such a thing until they taste this one. Also great for dinner parties in the summer.

- 2 **heads broccoli**
- 2 **tablespoons peanut oil**
- 2 **to 3 chicken breasts**
- 1 **cup parsley, chopped**
- 4 **green onions, chopped**
    Cottage Cheese and Dill Dressing (page 95),
        refrigerated

Clean the broccoli, and trim off the toughest parts of the stems. Cut the upper parts of the stems and the tops into small pieces or flowerets. Blanch in boiling water with the peanut oil. Simmer for about 5 minutes, and then drain and plunge into cold water. Drain, and chill.

Cook the chicken breasts by either roasting or poaching. Debone, cut up, and chill.

Assemble the salad, add the parsley and onions, toss with the dressing.

Serve with a dry white wine.

SERVES 4 AS DINNER, MORE AS SIDE SALAD.

Roast Beef Salad

A great way to use up the rest of the roast beef. Cut the meat thin, however, because cold roast beef is usually a bit dry. A thin slice will be able to absorb this great dressing.

> ½ roast beef, cut into thin strips
> 8 stalks celery, chopped
> 6 green onions, chopped
> 1 teaspoon capers, chopped
>   Dijon Mustard Dressing (page 96)

Place the meat and vegetables in a salad bowl. Chill.

Toss the dressing with meat and vegetables.

SERVES 3 OR 4.

Norwegian Spaghetti Salad with Shrimp

Don't ask me to prove that this is really Norwegian. I developed this salad and then decided it tasted like something a Norwegian would love . . . and I love it, and I am Norwegian. So it has to be genuine!

> ½ pound thin spaghetti
> 1 20-ounce bag frozen peas and carrots
>   Dill and Caper Dressing (page 96)
> ½ pound cooked salad or cocktail shrimp
>   Parsley

Cook the pasta, rinse in cold water, drain, and chill. Rinse the frozen peas and carrots in hot tap water until defrosted. Drain and chill. Mix the dressing with the pasta and peas and carrots. Garnish with the shrimp and parsley.

SERVES 8.

Steak Salad

This may appear a bit strange to you, but I assure you it is delicious. The steak is served warm with the dressing. This is very close to a great appetizer salad served at the Berghoff, an old German restaurant in Chicago.

> 1½ **pounds round steak, cut into 1¼-inch cubes**
>
> **DRESSING**
> ¼ **cup mayonnaise**
> ¼ **cup sour cream**
> 1 **tablespoon sweet pickle relish**
>   **Juice of ½ lemon**
> ⅛ **teaspoon sugar**
> ½ **tablespoon Dijon-style mustard***
>
>   **Lettuce**
> 2 **eggs, hard-boiled**
> 2 **tomatoes, cut into wedges**
>   **Salt and pepper to taste**

Fry the steak cubes over very high heat until done to your taste.

Mix the dressing. Combine the dressing with the warm steak cubes, and place on a bed of lettuce for each serving. Garnish with the eggs and tomatoes. Check salt and pepper.

SERVES 4.

Pea Salad with Bacon

A current craze with the restaurant luncheon crowd because it is satisfying, tasty, and not at all heavy.

---

*Grey Poupon is fine.

DRESSING

¼ cup sour cream
¼ cup mayonnaise
 2 tablespoons parsley, chopped
    Salt and pepper to taste
    Dried dill weed to taste (optional)

 1 20-ounce bag frozen peas
 8 slices bacon
¼ cup green onions, chopped
    Lettuce

Prepare the dressing by combining all its ingredients.

Rinse the peas in hot tap water until defrosted; drain and chill. Cook the bacon, and chop up. Mix all together with the onions, and serve on a lettuce bed.

SERVES 8 AS SIDE SALAD, FEWER AS WHOLE-MEAL SALAD.

Sausage Salad

I am so tired of three bean salad and three this and that salads, but I have developed a three sausage salad that will tickle your children. It is also great for summer picnics and warm-weather buffets. I have even served this for a luncheon menu in the middle of the winter.

½ pound knackwurst
½ pound bockwurst
½ pound Polish sausage
½ cup celery, chopped
¼ cup green onions
 2 tablespoons parsley, chopped
    Basic Fennel Dressing (page 90)
    Parsley or celery leaves for garnish

Simmer the sausages in 1 quart water for 15 minutes, cool, and slice. Or you could slice them first and then fry them a bit, but you will have a much oilier salad . . . and the color might be a bit too dark for you. (Yes, you can use any kind of cured or cooked sausages that you wish. I happen to like these three.)

Assemble the meats, celery, green onions, parsley, and dressing. Serve it on a great platter with a parsley or celery leaf garnish.

SERVES 4 TO 6.

Cold Pasta Salad—Pasta Fredda
(Italy)

Typical of the new lighter Italian cuisine. I found this salad, or one very close to it, in a fine antipasto restaurant in San Francisco called Prego.

   ½ **pound corkscrew pasta, cooked, chilled in cold water, and drained**
   ¼ **cup pesto sauce (page 147)**
   2 **tomatoes, chopped**
      Black pepper
   2 **cloves garlic, crushed**
   2 **tablespoons pine nuts**
   3 **tablespoons parsley, chopped**
   ¼ **cup olive oil**
   ¼ **cup fresh lemon juice**

Toss all ingredients together, and refrigerate before serving.

SERVES 4 TO 6.

Eggs

The Classic Omelet

During the years that I have conducted cooking classes I have always been surprised that my students seem so delighted to be able to make an omelet. I consider it a glorious dish, and certainly simple, if you know a few basic rules. You have nothing to learn from restaurants that serve a tough, worn-out egg pancake and call it an omelet. Your omelet should be light and fluffy, barely browned, and filled with wonderful things. Inexpensive and easy, but first the pan.

■ HINT: The Omelet Pan

Please do not buy a fold-over pan, hinged in the center so that you can layer, rather than fold, the omelet.

Choose an aluminum pan with sloping sides, preferably covered with SilverStone. The pan should have a metal handle so that it can be put under a broiler if you wish. Any good restaurant supply house or gourmet shop will have one of these for you. Use it for nothing but omelets, and once you have cured it, don't ever wash it with soap. Just swish it out with hot water, and put it away.

The recipes given here all call for a 10-inch pan. You can use such a pan for either 2-egg or 3-egg omelets.

■ HINT: The Basic Rules for a Good Omelet

1. Use butter and peanut oil in your cooking. The blend of the two will prevent the butter from burning and will give the eggs fine flavor and color.
2. Have the eggs at room temperature. Always have a dozen eggs sitting in a bowl on the counter. They will

keep fine for two weeks in the refrigerator and for several days on the counter.

3. Never put salt in the egg mixture. It toughens the eggs. Add the salt just before folding.

4. Never use milk in the egg mixture. Use only water. Milk makes your omelet watery since it will not blend with the eggs. Water blends and helps keep the omelet high.

5. Heat the pan before you put in the peanut oil and butter. When the butter stops foaming, add the eggs.

Basic Omelet

> 3 eggs, at room temperature
> 1 tablespoon water
> ½ tablespoon peanut oil
> ½ tablespoon butter
>   Salt and pepper to taste

Heat the pan on medium high.

Whip the eggs with a table fork in a small bowl. Add the water, and whip again.

Place the oil and butter in the pan at the same time. When the butter stops foaming, whip the eggs a couple of times, and pour them into pan. When the omelet begins to set, you may have to lift the edge with a wooden spatula and allow the wet portion of the mixture to run under the omelet. Add salt and pepper if you wish.*

*Before salt and pepper are added, any filling may be added. Place it on the front half of the omelet (the handle of the pan is considered the back portion).

Slide the omelet onto a plate, and holding the handle back-hand, fold the omelet over in half, using the pan. Garnish with parsley or some of the filling and serve hot.

SERVES 1.

French Potato and Garlic Omelet

True, this looks like French peasant food, and I suppose it is. But it is just delicious, so bring on the French peasants and enjoy.

> 1 slice bacon, diced
> 2 green onions, chopped
> ½ clove garlic, crushed
> ½ cup cold cooked unpeeled new potatoes
> Basic Omelet (page 106)
> Salt and pepper to taste
> Fresh-grated Parmesan or Romano cheese for
>   garnish

Sauté the bacon in a small frying pan—*not your omelet pan*. When the bacon is crisp, add the green onions, garlic, and potatoes. Cook until hot, and use for filling in the omelet. Add salt and pepper last. Garnish with cheese on top.

Serve with a green salad with Dijon Mustard Dressing (page 96) and a dry red wine.

SERVES 1.

Cheese and Tomato Omelet

For a nice Italian meal, first serve Antipasto Plate (page 70). Then follow it with a pasta dish such as Pasta Carbonara (page 149). The main course then consists of a salad and an omelet.

¼ cup your favorite spaghetti sauce, heated
¼ cup cottage cheese
    Basic Omelet (page 106)
½ tablespoon fresh-grated Parmesan or Romano
        cheese
    Salt and pepper to taste
    Sliced tomato for garnish

Heat the spaghetti sauce. Place the cottage cheese in the omelet, ladle the sauce over the cheese, and sprinkle with the cheese. Add salt and pepper. Fold, and serve. Garnish with tomato slices.

SERVES 1.

Swiss Cheese and Sour Cream Omelet

Simple, but very rich!

3 tablespoons sour cream
2 slices Swiss cheese, chopped
    Basic Omelet (page 106)
    Salt and pepper to taste
1 tablespoon parsley, chopped

Place the sour cream and Swiss cheese in the omelet. Add salt, pepper, and parsley. Fold, and serve.

SERVES 1.

Mushroom Omelet

It is the vermouth that does it for this one. Or you can try a Marsala for a very Italian taste.

 1 tablespoon yellow onion, peeled and chopped
½ cup mushrooms, cleaned and sliced
½ tablespoon butter
    Salt and pepper to taste
    Pinch of ground nutmeg to taste
 1 tablespoon dry vermouth
    Basic Omelet (page 106)
 1 teaspoon lemon juice

Sauté the onion and mushrooms in the butter. Add the salt, pepper, nutmeg, and vermouth. Sauté for a moment to reduce the moisture, and place in the omelet. Add the lemon juice, and fold.

SERVES 1.

Two-Mushroom Omelet

The sweet vermouth gives the mushrooms a very Italian flavor. Any mushroom lover will think this is heaven.

 2 dried European mushrooms (page 231)
 1 cup tepid water
 1 tablespoon butter or oil
½ cup white mushrooms, sliced
 1 green onion, chopped
    Salt and pepper to taste
 2 tablespoons sweet vermouth
    Basic Omelet (page 106)

Soak the dried mushrooms in the water for 1 hour. Drain, squeeze dry, and chop. Sauté in the butter or oil along with the white mushrooms and the green onion, just until barely tender. Add the salt, pepper, and sweet vermouth. Toss, and use for a filling for the basic omelet.

SERVES 1.

Channing's Apple Omelet

Channing is my oldest son. He has an ability to taste that puts me to shame, and often I will find him in the kitchen, pans hot, and this omelet on the stove.

- ½ cup sliced apple
- 1 tablespoon butter
- ½ teaspoon sugar
   Sprinkle of cinnamon
- ½ tablespoon brandy or dry sherry
   Basic Omelet (page 106)
   Salt (optional)

Sauté the apple slices in the butter until tender. Add the sugar and cinnamon, and toss a bit. Finally, add the brandy or sherry. Fold into the omelet. Add salt if you wish.

SERVES 1.

Other Fillings

Sautéed mushrooms
Ham and Swiss cheese
Sautéed vegetables (such as green onions, green
   peppers, tomatoes, along with a bit of basil
   or oregano)
Strawberry jam and sour cream for dessert
   omelet
Stews and leftover spaghetti

Note

These recipes can be adapted to a 2-egg omelet easily. Just cut down on the filling, and use 2 eggs with ¾ tablespoon water.

Frittata
(Italy)

A frittata is a broiled omelet from Italy. It is very dramatic and very delicious. Once you catch on to this, try mixing other vegetables or even meats in the frittata.

        1 **zucchini**
        2 **tablespoons bread crumbs**
        2 **tablespoons milk**
        ½ **teaspoon fresh-grated lemon peel**
        6 **eggs**
        2 **tablespoons water**
           Butter
           Peanut oil
           Salt and pepper to taste
        3 **tablespoons fresh-grated Parmesan or**
           Romano cheese

Slice the zucchini, and blanch it for 5 minutes in boiling water; drain. Mix the bread crumbs, milk, and lemon peel together. Blend with the zucchini.

Whip the eggs, and add the water; whip again. Pour into hot omelet pan greased with butter and peanut oil. When eggs begin to set, top with the zucchini mixture. Add salt and pepper. Add the cheese, and place under a hot broiler until the top browns and is set.

Slice as a pie and serve with salad.

SERVES 4.

Crepes

What is the history of the pancake? It was probably the very first kind of bread that we knew. Its ancestors were the flat loaves of unleavened bread baked on hot rocks in the desert. Its relatives include the crepe from France, the American pancake, the thin Swedish pancake, the German potato pancake, the Jewish latke, the Russian blini, the Jewish blintz, the Chinese pancake, and the Mexican tortilla. In our time we can enjoy all these, in a hundred variations.

Basic Crepes

The pan is very important to a good crepe. I use my omelet pan (page 105). No, you do not need an upside-down crepe cooker; I consider it a gimmick that has little use in the kitchen.

> 2 eggs, at room temperature
> ¾ cup milk
> ⅔ cup beer
> 1 cup flour
> ¼ teaspoon salt
> 2 tablespoons peanut oil

Place the eggs, milk, and beer in a food blender, and then the flour and salt. Blend for 30 seconds, and then scrape down the sides of the container. Blend for 1 minute more, or until the mixture is smooth. Cover, and refrigerate for at least 2 hours.

Fry the crepes in a medium-hot 10-inch pan lubricated with the peanut oil. Pour in 2 ounces batter for each crepe. Tip and turn the pan until the batter covers the bottom. Cook until the top appears dry and the bottom has just begun to brown. Turn with a wooden spatula, and brown the other side very lightly; you should have only little specks of brown. Stack with a piece of wax paper between each.

MAKES ABOUT 12.

Cold Chicken Crepes

Fill crepes with cold cooked chicken. Add a dash of salt and pepper and perhaps a bit of fresh-grated Romano or Parmesan cheese. Roll, and top with sour cream or yogurt. Garnish with parsley. Serve cold with a green salad and white wine.

Stuffed Crepes Italian Style

Once you catch on to the fact that a cannelloni is simply a rich crepe, you will be baking these regularly for your guests and family. Think up other fillings, and have a party.

> 1 **pound cottage cheese, well drained**
> 1 **egg, at room temperature**
> ½ **cup coarse-grated Swiss cheese**
> **Fresh-grated Parmesan or Romano cheese**
> 1 **clove garlic, crushed**
> **Fresh-ground black pepper to taste**
> **Basic Crepes (page 112)**
> **Tomato Sauce (page 263) or spaghetti sauce**

Mix the cottage cheese, egg, Swiss cheese, 2 tablespoons Parmesan or Romano, garlic, and pepper well.

Lay out 8 crepes. Fill each with the cheese mixture, and roll up. Place in a greased baking dish with the seam sides down. Top with tomato or spaghetti sauce along with a little more grated Parmesan or Romano. Bake at 350° for about 15 minutes.

Serve with an Italian Vegetable Sauté (page 220), a green salad with Bleu Cheese and Anchovy Dressing (page 95), and a very dry red wine for a totally meatless meal that will be superb.

MAKES 8.

Stacked Dessert Crepes

Spread Basic Crepes (page 112) with raspberry jam, peach jam, or vanilla pudding (I use all three). Stack the crepes, and add a slosh of brandy. Top with powdered sugar and then a bit of whipped cream. Cut into pie-shaped wedges to serve.

Swiss Cheese and Bacon Crepes

I like an unusual starch dish for a dinner party, and this one is perfect. It will go with anything.

> 4 slices bacon, diced
> 6 slices Swiss cheese
> 6 Basic Crepes (page 112)
> Butter or peanut oil for pan frying

Fry the bacon until crisp; drain the fat.

Place 1 slice Swiss cheese on a quarter of each crepe so that the crepe can be folded up into one-quarter of its original size. Place some bacon on the cheese, and fold up the crepe.

Lightly brown the crepes in the butter or oil on one side, and serve, browned side up, as a side dish for dinner.

SERVES 6.

Chicken Dinner Crepes

This dish is inexpensive and very elegant. When you serve it to your guests, they will make all kinds of marvelous noises as they smell and anticipate. For me that's half the joy of cooking.

½ pound mushrooms
   Butter or peanut oil
1 cup frozen green beans, defrosted
1 tablespoon green pepper, chopped
¼ tomato, chopped
2 cups cooked and deboned chicken
1 cup Béchamel Sauce (page 259)
   Salt and pepper to taste
8 Basic Crepes (page 112)
   Fresh-grated Swiss cheese

Sauté the mushrooms in a bit of butter or oil, and set aside. Sauté the green beans just until hot. Add the green pepper and tomato, and sauté until all is tender. Add the chicken and the mushrooms, and blend in the béchamel sauce. Add salt and pepper. Fill the crepes with this mixture, and roll up. Place on a greased baking sheet, and top with grated Swiss cheese. Bake at 375° until cheese is melted and filling is hot.

MAKES 8.

Crepe Soup Noodles
(Austria)

Use your leftover crepes by rolling them up and cutting them up like noodles. Use with chicken soup to make what the Austrians call Pancake Soup.

Asparagus- and Carrot-Filled Crepes

Why not a vegetable-filled crepe instead of the usual vegetables on the side? It is a little rich, but in this way you can cut down on the amount of meat that you would normally serve.

> 3 **carrots, grated**
> 2 **tablespoons butter**
> 1 **10-ounce package frozen asparagus**
> **Salt and pepper to taste**
> 6 **Basic Crepes (page 112)**
> **Fresh-grated Swiss cheese**

Sauté the carrots in the butter over medium-high heat until they begin to brown. Add the asparagus to the pan, and cook just until hot. Season with salt and pepper.

Fill each of the crepes with the filling, and place, seam sides down, on a greased baking sheet. Top with Swiss cheese, and place under broiler until the cheese is bubbling hot. Top with a bit of sour cream.

SERVES 6.

Other Fillings

For breakfast: Fill with jam, and dust with powdered sugar.

For lunch: Fill with chicken and mushrooms.

For dinner: Fill with hot fresh asparagus and Béchamel Sauce (page 259). Or fill with any sautéed vegetable. Or fold a crepe into a quarter and stuff one pocket with Swiss cheese and gently fry again in butter; or fill with leftovers such as stew.

For dessert: Fill with whipped cream and strawberries. Or dip crepes into a syrup made of the grated peel of 1 orange fried for a moment in butter; add the juice from the orange, and allow most of the moisture to evaporate; add 3 or 4 stiff shots, or 3 or 4 tablespoons, of brandy; heat thoroughly; dip the crepes into the syrup, and fold; dust with powdered sugar.

Quiches

The quiche is one of my favorite foods because it is easy to prepare and is not expensive, and you can be as elaborate or as simple with its preparation as you wish.

The history of the "egg pie" called a quiche is French. It actually comes from northeastern France in the area called Lorraine. The old classic, quiche Lorraine, is simply a bacon and egg pie. Often onions are included. Some claim that since this region is so close to Germany the egg pie could have come from the German kitchen; certainly the Germans have eaten egg and onion pies for years. In any case, we can fall back upon both cultures for recipes and then add a few ingredients of our own.

■ HINT: Rules for a Good Quiche

1. Always precook the pastry shell a bit. This prevents that soggy bottom that we all dislike.
2. Remove unnecessary moisture from vegetables by cooking them a bit before they are placed in the egg mixture. Usually I sauté my vegetables. You could also salt all of the vegetables and let them drain, but I prefer that we leave the salt alone.
3. Have your eggs at room temperature. They will blend much more easily.

Equipment

Y ou can find all kinds of quiche pans on the market. The most common is simply a pie plate, but your quiche will be rather thick. A wider plate for quiche can be found in glass, tin, or expensive French porcelain. You will be happiest with the results if you use a traditional quiche pan.

Quiche Crust

Most of us have trouble making good crusts for pies or quiches. The following recipe belongs to my mother, Emily. Everything she does is very delicious and very healthy. Note that there is no salt or animal fat in this crust. If you need salt, add it sparingly.

>   2 cups flour
>   2 teaspoons baking powder
>   Salt (optional)
>   ½ cup vegetable oil
>   ¼ cup milk

Mix the flour and the baking powder together. Add salt if you wish. Mix the oil and milk together, and then pour into the flour. Stir only until mixed. The mixture will be rather coarse and granular, but it will roll out well. Do not overmix. Mold into two balls, and wrap with plastic. Allow to sit for 15 minutes.

Each ball will make one 9-inch piecrust. If you are using a larger French quiche pan, then use a bit more of the dough. Roll out between two sheets of wax paper.

Place the pastry in the quiche pan or pie plate, and prick the bottom with a kitchen fork. Line the inside with wax paper or aluminum foil. Put two cups of dry beans into the piecrust, and bake at 400° for 12 minutes. Save the beans for the next piecrust session. The shell is now ready for filling and cooking.

MAKES 2 9-INCH CRUSTS OR 1 LARGER CRUST.

Asparagus Quiche

I like this best with fresh asparagus. During asparagus season our family enjoys this lovely vegetable daily, and this is a favorite dinner.

   1 **pound fresh asparagus** *or* **1 package frozen**
         asparagus spears
   2 **tablespoons butter**
   1 **Quiche Crust (page 118), baked and cooled**
   4 **eggs, beaten**
   ¾ **cup cream**
   1¼ **cups milk**
   ¼ **teaspoon dried dill weed**
      Salt and pepper to taste

Clean the asparagus, or defrost and drain the frozen asparagus. Cut up into inch-long pieces, and sauté in the butter to remove some of the moisture. The asparagus should be tender and green, not soft.

Place the asparagus in the bottom of the crust. Mix the eggs, cream, milk, dill weed, salt, and pepper. Fill the crust, and bake at 375° for 30 to 40 minutes, or until a knife inserted into the center of the pie comes out dry. Cool for 10 minutes before cutting. Can also be served at room temperature.

This one makes a great lunch dish. Serve it with a salad and very dry white wine.

SERVES 6.

Broccoli and Swiss Cheese Quiche

Even frozen broccoli is good in this one.

> 1   **pound broccoli**
> 1   **medium yellow onion, peeled and sliced**
> 2   **tablespoons butter**
> 1   **Quiche Crust (page 118), baked and cooled**
> 4   **eggs, beaten**
> ¾   **cup cream**
> 1¼   **cups milk**
>   **Salt and pepper to taste**
> ½   **pound Swiss cheese, grated into coarse pieces**

Clean the broccoli, and cut into flowerets. Sauté the onion and the broccoli in the butter until tender but not soft.

Place the vegetables in the bottom of the quiche crust. Mix the eggs, cream, milk, salt, and pepper. Fill the shell, and top with the Swiss cheese.

Bake at 375° for 30 to 40 minutes, or until a knife inserted in the center of the pie comes out dry. Cool for 10 minutes before cutting. Can also be served at room temperature.

SERVES 6.

Seafood Quiche

Make as in Broccoli and Swiss Cheese Quiche above. Substitute ½ pound cooked crab or cooked shrimp for the broccoli. If you can afford more than ½ pound of seafood for this one, go ahead. It will be heaven!

SERVES 6.

Leek Quiche

This one will be the favorite of your onion lovers. It is very attractive and not at all difficult.

    1 pound leeks
    2 tablespoons butter
    4 eggs, beaten
    ¾ cup cream
    1¼ cups milk
    ½ pound Swiss cheese, grated into coarse pieces
      Salt and pepper to taste
    1 Quiche Crust (page 118), baked and cooled

Trim 1 leek, and carefully remove three or four attractive leaves for decoration. Trim the leaves so that they will fit the top of the pie as if a leek had been baked whole in the pie. Blanch the leaves for a few minutes in boiling water, drain well, and set aside to cool.

Cut each of the remaining leeks just above the spot where it begins turning green from white. Slice each down the center, or lengthwise, and then cut into 1½-inch pieces. Wash thoroughly in cold water to remove the dirt and grit. Drain well, and sauté in the butter. Do not overcook; these should not be discolored but rather bright and tender.

Combine the eggs, cream, and milk, and stir in the Swiss cheese along with the salt and pepper. Fill the quiche crust by adding the sauteed leeks and covering with the egg mixture. Lay the reserved leek leaves on the top as if they were growing to-gether—i.e., place the bottoms together, and fan out the tops into an attractive pattern.

Bake at 375° for 30 to 40 minutes, or until a knife inserted in the center of the pie comes out dry. Cool for 10 minutes before cutting. Can also be served at room temperature.

Serve with a bit of beef, perhaps Boiled Beef Brisket with Green Sauce (page 177), cold tomato slices, and a light white wine. Or this dish will do nicely by itself with a salad and wine.

SERVES 6.

Spinach and Feta Cheese Quiche

This will taste very Greek to you. Be sure that you drain the spinach well.

    1 10-ounce package frozen chopped spinach,
          defrosted
    4 eggs, beaten
    ¾ cup cream
    1¼ cups milk
       Salt and pepper to taste
    2 tablespoons lemon juice
    2 tablespoons parsley, chopped
    ¼ pound feta cheese, crumbled
    1 Quiche Crust (page 118), baked and cooled
    3 tablespoons fresh-grated Parmesan or Romano
          cheese

Drain the spinach, and squeeze out as much moisture as possible; it should be fairly dry. Mix the eggs, cream, and milk. Add the salt, pepper, lemon juice, and parsley. Stir in the spinach and feta cheese. Fill the quiche crust, and place the Parmesan or Romano on top.

Bake at 375° for 30 to 40 minutes, or until a knife inserted in the center comes out dry. Cool for 10 minutes before serving. Can also be served at room temperature.

SERVES 6.

Crustless Quiches

This is a very easy and creative way of cooking, though it should not be called a quiche at all. It is, rather, a very heavy egg and cheese filling, without the crust. I enjoy this dish and have served it in one of my restaurants with many variations. Since this filling is so much heavier than a normal quiche, you don't have to precook all the vegetables. Think up some of your own combinations.

Basic Crustless Quiche

½ cup (¼ pound) butter
10 eggs
½ cup flour
1 teaspoon baking powder
¼ teaspoon salt
1 pound large-curd cottage cheese
1 pound jack cheese, shredded

Melt the butter. Whip the eggs until fluffy, and add the flour, baking powder, salt, cottage cheese, melted butter, and half the jack cheese.*

Place the mixture in a greased 9- by 13-inch baking dish. Top with the remaining jack cheese. Bake at 400° for 15 minutes. Then reduce temperature to 350°, and continue to bake for 35 to 40 minutes, or until the top is lightly browned.

Cool, and cut into squares for serving.

SERVES 8 TO 10.

*At this step add any special ingredients you like.

Onion and Caraway Crustless Quiche

Sound like a strange combination? In Germany they make a Zwiebel Kuchen, or onion and caraway egg pie. It is delicious, and this is very close in flavor.

        3 large yellow onions, peeled and sliced
        3 tablespoons butter or peanut oil
        1 batch Basic Crustless Quiche filling (page 123)
        1 tablespoon whole caraway seeds

Sauté the yellow onions in the butter or oil until barely browned, but tender. Add to the crustless quiche filling along with the caraway seeds.

Bake as on page 123.

SERVES 8 TO 10.

Garden Quiche, Crustless

This form of crustless quiche is great for getting rid of leftovers. One of my cooks in Tacoma used simply to clean out the refrigerator and then give the luncheon quiche a crazy name. One day he served Synopsis Quiche because it was a brief synopsis of the week. Another day he came up with this one.

Add some oregano to this dish to give it a bit of an Italian flavor.

        2 yellow onions, peeled and chopped
           Butter
        1 batch Basic Crustless Quiche filling (page 123)
        8 green onions, chopped
        4 small zucchini, sliced
        ½ cup parsley, chopped
        3 tomatoes, sliced very thin

Sauté the yellow onions a bit in butter. Add it to the crustless quiche filling along with the green onions, zucchini, and parsley. Top with the remaining jack cheese (see page 123) and then with the tomato slices. Bake as on page 123.

SERVES 8 TO 10.

Individual Crustless Quiches

Both my sons think that private little anythings are a great delight. They always have thought this, and I suppose it stems from my letting them know from the beginning that their presence at our table was very important. Even at very formal dinner parties they have been with us at the table. Oh, it took some doing and some training, but it has certainly been worth it.

These little individual portions are perfect for a normal dinner, are a compliment to your children, or would help create a more formal affair.

> 1 10-ounce package frozen peas and carrots
> 2 leeks
> 1 batch Basic Crustless Quiche filling (page 123)

Defrost the vegetables, and drain. Clean and sauté the leeks as in the Leek Quiche (page 121). Mix half the leeks and the peas and carrots with the crustless quiche filling, reserving the other half of the leeks for the decoration of the small custard dishes.

Butter several 6-ounce custard or soufflé cups* (you can find some nice ones in glass that are not expensive). Place 2 or 3 pieces of leek in the bottom of each in a nice pattern that will look attractive when you invert the dish and remove the contents. Add filling until evenly distributed among cups.

Place the dishes in a baking pan, and fill with enough water to come up to one-third of the height of the cups.

Bake at 375° for 30 minutes, or until a knife inserted into the center comes out dry. Cool the cups for 5 minutes, and then invert and remove the eggs from their baking cups. Serve upside down on the plate.

SERVES 12.†

---

*You can add any number of good things to these little pots and have a very flamboyant meal. Seafood, mushrooms, fresh fruit—all will work well.

†You can make fewer cups and then bake the rest of the mixture in a larger dish for a later party.

Shirred Eggs

For a fancy breakfast, this is the dish. You can teach the kids to make it by themselves and then sit in bed and wait for the results. Why not?

> **Butter, melted**
> 2 **eggs**
> **Salt and pepper to taste**
> **Fresh-grated Parmesan or Romano cheese**

Put a little melted butter in the bottom of an individual ovenproof casserole. Break in the eggs. Top with salt, pepper, and a little cheese. Bake at 325° until eggs just begin to set, about 10 to 15 minutes.

SERVES 1.

Beans, Grains, and Pasta

Beans

The use of dried legumes predates written history. We do know that many dried beans were popular by the time of ancient Egypt, but we cannot even trace the beginnings of garbanzos (chick-peas) or lentils. There is a grand story of Esau in the Bible in which he sells his birthright for a bowl of pottage, and I have the original recipe. You will find it here, and thus you will know that I go to all ends to do research for you . . . and for me.

The word *legume* comes from the French word for vegetable —any vegetable. In this country, however, the word refers to beans and seeds from beanlike pods. The following recipes will be helpful not only in terms of your budget but in terms of your creativity.

Cuban Black Beans

I hope you don't have trouble finding these beans. They are worth the effort, I promise. If you serve them over rice with a green salad on the side, you have a complete and interesting meal. I had this dish in Miami one evening, and I have made it often since.

    ½ pound black beans or turtle beans, soaked
            overnight
    4 stalks celery, chopped
    1 large yellow onion, peeled and chopped
    1 pound ham hocks, cut into 2-inch pieces
    1 teaspoon crushed red pepper flakes
    2 bay leaves
    ¼ cup parsley, chopped
       Tabasco to taste
       Salt and pepper to taste

Drain the water from the beans, and place all the ingredients in a cooking pot with a tight-fitting lid. Barely cover with fresh water, and simmer for 1 hour, or until tender. Remember that you should not add salt to this dish until it is ready to serve because the ham hocks add salt to the dish.

Serve over cooked long-grain white rice.

SERVES 4.

Black-Eyed Peas
(Texas)

Harriet, my friend from Texas, is a great cook, and she loves this dish. When she makes it, however, she puts in so much red pepper flakes that I can feel the heat of the Texas summer sun. You adjust it to your liking.

> ½ **pound black-eyed peas, soaked for 4 hours and drained**
> 2 **stalks celery**
> 1 **yellow onion, peeled and chopped**
> 1 **teaspoon crushed red pepper flakes**
> **Salt and pepper to taste**
> ½ **pound smoked ham, cubed**

Place all the ingredients in a pot, and do not quite cover with water. Simmer, covered, for about 30 minutes, or until tender.

SERVES 4.

Pizza Pinto Beans

The name for this dish is terrible, but the crew in the television studio named the dish when they first tasted same. I was just trying to feed them, but they liked the result, and thus we offer it to you.

This is a kid's dish, without apology. (I like it, too!)

½ **pound pinto beans, soaked overnight, drained**
½ **pound hamburger**
2 **yellow onions, peeled and chopped**
½ **cup spaghetti sauce**
¼ **pound pepperoni, sliced**
½ **cup fresh-grated Swiss cheese**
1 **teaspoon oregano**

Cook the beans in 1 quart water until barely tender, about 1 hour.
Drain, and place in casserole. In a frying pan, cook the hamburger with the onions until the onions are clear and drain the fat.
Add the meat and onion mixture to the casserole along with the spaghetti sauce and pepperoni. Top with the cheese and the oregano.

Bake at 375° for about 25 minutes, until hot and lightly browned.

SERVES 4 OR 5.

Beans with Tomato Sauce, Greek Style

Simple and genuine. I cannot remember from which Greek restaurant I stole this one. Do you do that? Taste something and then decide you are going to duplicate the dish, only to have it become a family favorite and you cannot even remember the source?

1 **yellow onion, peeled and chopped**
   Peanut oil
½ **pound small white beans, soaked overnight and**
   cooked, drained
½ **cup tomato sauce**
   Ham, beef, pork, etc., scraps, cooked
2 **cloves garlic, crushed**
½ **teaspoon oregano**
¼ **cup red wine**
   Salt and pepper to taste

Sauté the onion in a bit of oil until limp. Blend all ingredients together, and simmer for 20 minutes.

This makes a very nice side dish for the family that is tired of potatoes or grains.

SERVES 4 OR 5.

Red Beans with Peas and Pasta
(Italy)

Americans often think that such a dish is a repeat of starch. Nonsense. It is good Brooklyn cooking!

- ½ pound red beans, soaked overnight, drained
- ½ pound pasta
- ¼ cup olive oil
- ⅛ cup white wine vinegar
- 2 tablespoons fresh lemon juice
    Salt and pepper
    Oregano to taste (optional)
    Sugar to taste
- 1 10-ounce size package frozen green peas
    Parsley for garnish

Cook the beans in 1 quart fresh water for 1 hour. Drain. Be sure that they are not overdone. Let cool.

Cook the pasta, drain, and chill in cold water.

Prepare dressing of the oil, vinegar, lemon juice, salt and pepper, and oregano if desired. Add sugar to taste.

Drain the pasta, and place in bowl with beans. Rinse the defrosted frozen peas, and drain. Add to the bowl with the dressing, and toss. Garnish with parsley.

This is served as a starch or vegetable dish. It goes with just about any menu.

SERVES 6 TO 8.

Garbanzo Salad
(Italy)

These little beans are sometimes called chick-peas or *ceci*. You can use canned garbanzos for this dish, but dried are much cheaper, though they may be a bit discolored.

   ½ pound garbanzos, soaked overnight, drained
   1 green pepper, sliced
   4 green onions, chopped
   ½ yellow onion, peeled and sliced thin
      Chopped parsley
      Salt and pepper to taste
   ¼ cup olive oil
   ⅛ cup white wine vinegar
   2 tablespoons lemon juice
   ¼ teaspoon basil
   ¼ teaspoon oregano
      Sugar to taste

Cook the garbanzos in water to cover for 1 hour. Do not overcook; they need to be firm but tender for the salad. Drain and chill.

Combine all ingredients, and toss in steel bowl.

Allow the salad to marinate in the refrigerator for several hours before serving it.

SERVES 4 TO 6.

Black-Eyed Pea Salad

Black-eyed peas have a bit of a smoky flavor, and they make a great salad.

½ **pound black-eyed peas, soaked overnight,
   drained**
4 **green onions, chopped**
¼ **cup olive oil**
⅛ **cup white wine vinegar**
2 **tablespoons lemon juice**
 Tabasco to taste
 Salt and pepper to taste

Cook the black-eyed peas in fresh water until tender but firm, about 45 minutes. Drain. Combine all ingredients, chill, and marinate in the refrigerator for several hours before serving.

SERVES 4.

Lima Bean and Mushroom Salad

For something a bit more elegant, use frozen limas. This salad is just delicious, and your children might just begin to like lima beans.

½ **pound dried lima beans, soaked overnight,
   drained**
½ **pound mushrooms, cleaned and sliced**
¼ **cup sour cream**
¼ **cup mayonnaise**
 Salt and pepper to taste
¼ **teaspoon dried dill**
 Chopped capers (optional)
 Parsley for garnish

Cook the beans in fresh water until tender, about 1 hour. Drain and chill. Place the beans and mushrooms in a bowl. Prepare a dressing of sour cream, mayonnaise, salt, pepper, dill, and capers

if desired; toss with beans and mushrooms. Chill before serving.
Garnish with parsley.

SERVES 4 OR 5.

Chicken and Lentils
Middle Eastern Style

Lentils are the most nutritious legume in the world. Couple these
little disk-shaped beans with chicken and you have a whole meal
at little expense.

> 2 cups lentils
>   Salt to taste
> 2 cloves garlic, crushed
> 1 bay leaf
> 2 teaspoons oregano
> 1 teaspoon dill weed, dried
> 4 tablespoons fresh lemon juice
> 1 3-pound frying chicken, cup up and pan
>   browned
> ½ cup fresh-grated Parmesan or Romano cheese
> 2 cups plain yogurt

Soak the lentils in 8 cups of water in a bowl for 5 to 6 hours.
Place the lentils, along with the water, in a pot with the salt,
garlic, bay leaf, oregano, and dill weed. Simmer for about 1
hour, covered, until tender but not mushy.

Add the lemon juice to the lentil mixture. Place the chicken
pieces in a casserole and pour the lentil mixture over them. Top
with the cheese. Bake, covered, at 350° for about 1 hour 15
minutes. You may need to add additional water during the baking. Top with the yogurt before serving.

Serve with a very crunchy bread and a Spinach Salad (page
92). A heavy red wine goes well with the rich flavor of the
chicken and lentils.

SERVES 4 TO 6.

Esau's Pottage

Lentils are a very old vegetable, going back to pre-biblical times. In the Book of Genesis, Esau comes upon his brother Jacob, who is cooking a pottage of lentils. Esau is hungry, and in order to get to the lentils, he agrees to give Jacob his birthright. I assume that must have been some dish of lentils! This is the recipe that Esau gave me . . . so it is genuine.

    2 cups lentils
    4 chicken bouillon cubes
       Salt to taste
    1 cup sautéed yellow onions
    3 tablespoons sesame oil

Soak the lentils in 1 quart water for 3 hours. Place lentils and water in a pot, and simmer for about 1 hour, or until barely tender.

Add the bouillon cubes, salt, yellow onions, and sesame oil. Place all this in a baking casserole, and bake at 325° for about 1 hour.

Serve as a side dish with almost any menu.

SERVES 6 TO 8.

Grains

Bulgur Wheat

So many marvelous things have come to us from the desert. Bulgur wheat has been made in desert communities in the Middle East for centuries, and it is simply wheat that has been soaked until tender, cut up into small grains, then spread on a cloth in the sun to dry. The product cooks up like rice, and that is how it is eaten. Any good delicatessen should have this for you in the bulk, or try a Middle Eastern store. It will be cheaper there. Note that there are three grinds: coarse, medium, and fine.

    2 cups medium-grind bulgur wheat
    2 tablespoons olive oil
    2 tablespoons butter
    6 green onions, chopped
    4 cups chicken broth
      Salt and pepper to taste
    ½ teaspoon oregano

Brown the bulgur in a frying pan in the oil and butter. Add the green onions, and cook for another moment. Place in a pan with the chicken broth (you may use instant chicken broth). Season with a little salt, pepper, and the oregano. Simmer for about 20 minutes just as you would rice.

Sautéed mushrooms added to this dish are also good. Serve in place of the bulk and boredom of potatoes!

SERVES 6 TO 8.

Rice and Noodle Pilaf
(Lebanon)

This dish is actually from Lebanon. I ate it often as a child, and I am sorry to see on the market an instant version that claims to have come from San Francisco. Ah! You don't need instant packages to prepare something this simple. My version is cheaper and much more flavorful, and it has no chemicals or additional salt. So there!

1 8-ounce package thin, flat, dried Chinese egg
   noodles, broken into 1-inch pieces, or rice-
   shaped pasta
2 tablespoons olive oil
2 tablespoons butter
2 cups Chinese long-grain rice or Texas long-grain
   rice, washed and drained
4½ cups water
   Salt to taste

Brown the egg noodles or pasta in the oil and butter. When they are lightly browned, add them to a pot containing the rice and water. Bring to a boil; then cover, and move to another burner, which you have already heated to very low. Cook for 20 minutes, and you will have perfect Middle Eastern pilaf. Add salt.

SERVES 8.

Baked Barley Casserole

Barley is amazing because it swells larger than any other grain. One cup will feed the house, I promise. Of course, if you use good beef stock that you have made yourself, you will have a dish that is so delicious the family will leave the roast beef and simply eat the barley.

1 **cup barley**
Butter
3 **tablespoons olive oil or peanut oil**
2 **or 3 yellow onions, peeled and chopped**
Salt and pepper to taste
6 **cups chicken or beef broth***

Brown the barley in a little butter and the oil. Place in a casserole. Brown the yellow onions in butter, and add them to the barley. Add salt and pepper. Add 3 cups chicken or beef broth, cover, and place in 350° oven for about 1 hour, or until moisture is almost absorbed. Add another 3 cups broth, and cook, covered, until absorbed. (Yes, that is right: 1 cup barley to 6 cups broth.)

SERVES 4 TO 6.

*If you use your own beef stock, made according to the directions on page 47, you need to use less stock and more water; your homemade stock is so rich in gelatin that water must be added so that the barley will cook properly. So, if you use homemade stock for this recipe, use 4 cups of stock and 2 cups of water instead of the 6 cups stock called for.

Pasta

Pasta of every form and origin is becoming more popular every day. I suspect the reasons may be complicated, but it looks as if we have gotten into pasta because it is cheap and quick and can be as flamboyant as we like.

While I prefer fresh pasta, don't stop serving pasta simply because you cannot purchase it fresh or don't have time to make your own. Buy a good-quality pasta made with durum wheat or semolina. It will be less likely to get soggy. Do not overcook pasta, and never rinse it in cold water after cooking it unless you are making a cold pasta salad.

Pasta with Clam and Vegetable Sauce

I really prefer this with fresh clams, but on occasion I have been known to make this dish in the middle of the night . . . using canned clams.

 5 cloves garlic, crushed
 5 tablespoons olive oil
 6 stalks celery, chopped
 2 small zucchini, sliced thin
 4 green onions, chopped
 ¼ pound mushrooms, sliced
 2 ripe small tomatoes, chopped into coarse pieces
 3 tablespoons parsley, chopped
 1 6½-ounce can clams
 ¼ cup white wine
    Salt and pepper to taste
 1 pound pasta, cooked
    Fresh-grated Parmesan or Romano cheese

Sauté the garlic in the oil for a few minutes; do not brown the garlic too much. Add the celery, zucchini, green onions, mushrooms, tomatoes and parsley, and sauté until all is barely tender. Add the clams, juice and all, the wine, salt, and pepper (I like lots of pepper in this dish). Simmer for a few more minutes. If there is too much juice in this for you, remove the solids from the pan and reduce it over high heat very quickly. Blend in the solids again, and serve over hot pasta. Top with the cheese.

SERVES 8 AS FIRST COURSE.

Fettucine with Salami and Zucchini

When I was a child, I thought my uncle Vic was very wealthy because he always had a stick of Italian salami in his refrigerator. I decided that I wanted to have the same. Now that it has happened, I am not wealthy, but I do enjoy that salami stick. I put it into dishes on occasion. This one is very good.

2 small zucchini
2 cloves garlic
2 tablespoons olive oil
¼ pound Italian wine-cured salami, sliced thin,
    cut matchstick-style
1 tablespoon capers, chopped
    Peppercorns, fresh ground
½ cup whipping cream
    Salt to taste
½ pound fettucine, cooked
    Fresh-grated Romano or Parmesan cheese

Slice the zucchini. Put several slices together, and slice again into matchsticks. Slice the garlic very thin.

Sauté the garlic in the oil until barely browned. Add the zucchini, and sauté for 3 minutes. Add the salami, capers, pepper, and cream. Simmer until all is very hot. You will need little or no salt in this dish.

Serve over the hot pasta. Top with the cheese.

SERVES 3 OR 4.

Angel Hair Pasta with Broccoli and Three Cheeses

I have fallen in love with a restaurant just off Michigan Avenue in Chicago. It serves northern Italian food and is called Avanzare. The pasta is made fresh on the premises, and the chef is very creative. This dish came as an inspiration after I had tasted most of his menu.

2 **cloves garlic, crushed**
2 **tablespoons olive oil**
½ **yellow onion, peeled and chopped**
½ **pound broccoli, flowerets only**
⅓ **cup whipping cream**
   Fresh-ground pepper to taste
   Salt to taste
½ **pound angel hair pasta**
¼ **pound Swiss cheese, grated**
4 **tablespoons Romano cheese, grated**
3 **tablespoons Mizithra cheese, grated**
   Chopped parsley for garnish (optional)

Sauté the garlic in the oil until it just begins to brown. Add the yellow onion and the broccoli flowerets (i.e., the tops of the spears), and sauté until the broccoli is barely tender.

Add the cream and pepper. You may add salt if you wish.

In the meantime, cook the angel hair pasta for just a few minutes in salted boiling water. Watch this carefully because the pasta cooks in very little time. Drain the pasta, and toss with the three cheeses. Add the cream and the vegetables, toss, and serve.

You may wish to garnish this with more cheese on top. Some parsley might be nice as well.

SERVES 3 OR 4.

Pasta Primavera
(Italy)

This dish is so named because it uses vegetables that come with the spring. However, in our time we can purchase these items all the year round, so you can enjoy this spring dish in January.

Al Cribari, from the Cribari Wine Company in California, gave me this one.

2 cloves garlic, minced fine
1 tablespoon olive oil
1 small yellow onion, peeled and diced
2 ripe tomatoes, chopped
   Salt and pepper to taste*
½ teaspoon basil
½ teaspoon oregano
2 medium zucchini, grated into coarse pieces
½ cup dry red wine
1 egg, beaten
¼ cup grated Parmesan or Romano cheese
1 pound pasta, cooked

In a large frying pan, sauté the garlic in the oil until it is lightly browned. Add the onion, and sauté until it is clear. Add the tomatoes, salt, pepper, basil, and oregano. Simmer for a few minutes, and add the zucchini. Cook for about 5 minutes on high heat, or until the moisture is almost gone.

Add the wine, and simmer to reduce moisture. Add the egg and the cheese. Pour over the pasta, and enjoy.

You can use this sauce over meats, fish, even poultry. It is also good over rice or bulgur wheat. Mr. Cribari's mother served it to him as a vegetable dish when he was a child.

SERVES 6 TO 8 AS FIRST COURSE.

Noodles with Bleu Cheese

This delicious dish can also be served using Gorgonzola, a bleu goat cheese from Italy, or French Roquefort.

10 ounces noodles or fettucine
¼ pound bleu, Gorgonzola, or Roquefort cheese,
   at room temperature
¼ cup whipping cream *or* Half-and-Half
   Fresh-ground black pepper
¼ cup fresh-grated Parmesan or Romano cheese

While the pasta is cooking in boiled salted water, crumble the cheese, and mix it with the cream and pepper.

Drain the pasta, and place it in a frying pan. Add the cheese

*If you use little salt, this dish is a low-sodium and low-calorie dish.

mixture and cook for 2 to 3 minutes. Serve hot with grated-cheese topping.

SERVES 4 AS FIRST COURSE.

Spaghetti with Two Mushrooms
(Italy)

For this one you need dried mushrooms. They need not be the expensive Italian dried mushrooms, as the note on page 231 will explain.

- **3 ounces dried mushrooms**
- **1 pound fresh mushrooms**
- **3 cloves garlic, sliced very thin**
- **4 tablespoons olive oil**
- **¼ cup whipping cream**
  Salt and pepper to taste
- **1 pound spaghettini, cooked**
  Fresh-grated Romano or Parmesan cheese

Soak the dried mushrooms in warm water for 1 hour; drain, and chop into coarse pieces. Slice the mushrooms.

Sauté the garlic in the oil until it barely begins to brown. Add the two mushrooms, and sauté for 6 minutes. Add the cream, salt, and pepper, and simmer for a few minutes.

Serve over the hot pasta. Top with the Romano or Parmesan cheese.

SERVES 8 AS FIRST COURSE.

Baked Pasta with Sautéed Vegetables

This dish is simple, and if you keep a mirepoix on hand, as I have urged you, the dish can be made in very little time.

  10 ounces pasta
   3 tablespoons melted butter
  ½ cup fresh-grated Parmesan or Romano cheese
 1½ cups Mirepoix of Vegetables (page 278)
      Parmesan or Romano cheese and butter or olive
        oil for topping

Boil the pasta in salted water, drain, and toss with the melted
butter, Parmesan or Romano cheese, and the mirepoix. Place in a
buttered baking dish, and sprinkle more cheese on top. Some
people like to drizzle more butter or oil on top.

Bake in a 375° oven until browned on top, about 20 minutes.

SERVES 4 AS FIRST COURSE.

Pasta with Chicken Livers
(Italy)

Talk about rich! Any chicken liver lover will linger at the table if
you prepare this dish.

  ½ cup Velouté Sauce (page 262)
  ½ pound chicken livers
   2 tablespoons olive oil
  10 ounces pasta*
   3 tablespoons melted butter
  ½ cup fresh-grated Parmesan or Romano cheese
      Salt and pepper to taste
      Pinch of nutmeg

Prepare the velouté sauce.

Sauté the chicken livers in the olive oil for a few minutes, or
just until browned and tender.

Cook the pasta, and drain.

Toss with the butter, cheese, salt and pepper, and nutmeg.

Chop the livers, and add to the velouté sauce. Toss with the
pasta, and serve immediately.

SERVES 4 AS FIRST COURSE.

*I prefer thin fettucine.

Homemade Pasta or Noodles

While I certainly prefer fresh pasta, don't feel bad if you don't have time to make your own. Many good dry pastas are on the market, and they work well. Buy a brand that is made primarily of durum or semolina wheat. Or make your own. I go to this much work only occasionally.

> 2 cups flour
> 2 eggs
> 2 tablespoons olive oil
> Water

Place the flour in a large bowl, and make a well in the flour. Add the eggs and oil. Pinch, pinch, pinch until the flour is blended with the eggs and oil. You may have to add a couple of tablespoons water to get a very firm dough. Knead on a table until elastic and smooth. Let rest, covered, for 30 minutes. Roll out, and cut in desired shape.

SERVES 4.

Pasta al Pesto
(Italy)

This is one of my favorite pasta dishes. When I don't have the time to grow my own basil, I buy it by the bagful at the Pike Place Farmers Market, a Seattle institution. Buy the basil in the summer, when it is cheap, and prepare and freeze the sauce.

    4 cups basil
    ½ cup olive oil
    2 cloves garlic
    6 sprigs parsley
       Salt and pepper to taste
    ¼ cup pine nuts, walnuts, or almonds
    ½ cup fresh-grated Parmesan or Romano cheese

Place the basil in a blender (don't bother trying this with dried basil; it won't work). Add the oil, garlic, parsley, salt, pepper, and pine nuts, walnuts, or almonds. Blend until all are chopped very fine. Remove from the blender, and add the Parmesan or Romano cheese.

Toss a little of this great sauce with hot thin spaghetti, and top with a little more cheese. Superb!

SERVES 10 TO 12 AS A PASTA SAUCE.

MAKES ABOUT 2 CUPS.

Cannelloni
(Italy)

This is so much easier than trying to stuff dried noodle tubes. A good Italian restaurant makes them this way, and you should, too.

    NOODLES
    3 eggs
    1 cup water
    1 cup flour
       Salt to taste
       Peanut oil

    FILLING
    1 pound small-curd cottage cheese
    1 egg
    2 tablespoons chopped parsley
       Salt and pepper to taste
    2 tablespoons fresh-grated Parmesan or Romano
          cheese

    TOPPING
    1 cup Tomato Sauce (page 263)
       Fresh-grated Parmesan or Romano cheese

To make the noodles: Place the eggs in blender. Add the water, flour, and salt. Blend until smooth. Place 2 or 3 tablespoons of this batter in a heated crepe or omelet pan that has been oiled. Cook on one side only until dry on the top. These should not be at all browned or too dry, so pan should not be too hot. Separate the cooked noodles with wax paper.

To make the filling: Drain the cottage cheese. Mix with the egg, parsley, salt, pepper, and Parmesan or Romano cheese.

To finish: Lay out noodles, uncooked side up. Place filling in noodle as if rolling a burrito. Roll up and place, seam side down, on oiled baking sheet. Spoon some of the tomato sauce on top along with a little grated cheese. Bake at 350° for about 15 minutes, or until hot and bubbling.

MAKES 8 TO 10.

Pasta Carbonara
(Italy)

This classic bit of peasant cookery gets its name from the fact that the meat was first cooked over charcoal in the old days. It is another one of those marvelous dishes that help us understand that tomato sauce is not the common sauce for pasta in Italy.

> ¼ pound bacon
> 1 stick (¼ pound) butter
> 1 cup milk
> 2 tablespoons wine vinegar
> 1 pound pasta
> 2 eggs, whipped
> ⅓ cup fresh-grated Parmesan or Romano cheese
>   Salt and pepper to taste

Cut the bacon into little pieces, and cook in the butter until clear. Heat the milk in a small saucepan, and add the bacon and butter. Add the vinegar; this will turn the milk to cheese. Simmer for about 15 minutes, or until the sauce cooks smooth.

Boil your favorite pasta al dente. Drain, and return to the pan. Immediately throw in the eggs, the bacon sauce, and the Parmesan or Romano cheese. Add salt and pepper, toss, and serve.

SERVES 8 TO 10 AS A FIRST COURSE.

Poultry

Chicken

While each of us in this country assumes that the chicken is really ours, we must give credit to the Chinese. Again! The chicken was common food as early as 3000 B.C., but the Chinese were the first to domesticate the bird around 1200 B.C. Prior to its domestication, that old fowl of the wild jungle must have been one tough creature, a toughness which it seems to have maintained. Even today it is the national symbol of France; the French admire the courage of an animal that will fight to the death.

The chicken was not known in Europe until about A.D. 600, but by the time explorers were out searching for the edge of the world it had become a common food source. We are sure that the bird came to the New World aboard the decks of ships such as those commanded by Columbus. I cannot imagine the mess on the decks of those ships, in view of the chickens' running about, and who knows what else. In any case, we are thankful that the bird is with us now, and we certainly can give up on the old Sunday chicken dinner routine, and enjoy the fowl much more often.

There just have to be some more new ways of serving chicken. The meat is versatile and inexpensive, and everyone loves chicken. If you remove the skin from the bird, it is also low in fat, so experiment with these recipes. You'll get great reviews!

Chicken Stuffed with Potatoes and Olives
(Italy)

Sounds strange to you? This is a dish from Italy, where originally, I suppose, it was another peasant dish. Now it is far from that.

3 or 4 medium red or new potatoes, unpeeled,
   cooked, and cubed
8 to 10 stuffed green olives, chopped
   Rosemary to taste*
3 to 4 tablespoons chopped parsley
2 cloves garlic, crushed
3 canned flat anchovies, mashed (optional)
1 tablespoon chopped capers (optional)
3 tablespoons olive oil
   Salt and pepper to taste
1 3-pound chicken

In a large bowl, place the potatoes, olives, rosemary, parsley,
garlic, anchovies if desired, capers if desired, and olive oil.
(While the capers and anchovies are optional, they do add a lot to
this dish. Omit them, and you will still enjoy the results.)

Salt and pepper the chicken inside and out.

Toss the ingredients in the bowl together gently, and use to
stuff the chicken. Do not stuff too tightly. Bake at 375° for 70 to
80 minutes. Quarter, and serve the bird with the dressing.

I would add only fresh fruit to the table, along with a grand
salad, perhaps Italian Tomato Salad (page 94). Any dry wine will
do well.

SERVES 4.

Chicken Piccata
(Italy)

The term *piccata* simply means "sharp," and it refers to the flavors of lemon juice and capers found in this dish. Traditionally,
this recipe is made with veal, not chicken, but veal is so expensive that I have learned to enjoy chicken breast as a replacement.

*I use 1 tablespoon of whole rosemary.

1 small yellow onion, peeled and chopped
2 cloves garlic, crushed
4 green onions, chopped
2 tablespoons olive oil
8 chicken breasts
½ cup flour
   Salt and pepper to taste
2 tablespoons butter
2 tablespoons dry sherry
2 tablespoons fresh lemon juice
1 tablespoon capers, chopped
2 tablespoons chicken stock (optional)
8 thin lemon slices
2 tablespoons chopped parsley

Sauté the yellow onion, garlic, and green onions in the olive oil just until tender. Remove from the pan, and set aside.

Remove the skins and bones from the chicken breasts, and pound them flat with a fancy meat pounder or with two pieces of wax paper and a two-by-four. Mix the flour, salt, and pepper together, and place in flat bowl. Dip the chicken slices into the flour mixture. Lightly brown chicken slices in butter, 2 to 3 minutes per side. Add the sautéed onions and garlic. Over high heat add the sherry, lemon juice, and capers. This should thicken to make a nice gravy for the chicken; if the gravy becomes too thick, add a bit of chicken stock.

Garnish with thin slices of lemon and the chopped parsley.

Begin the meal with Pasta Primavera (page 143), and then move on to the chicken, along with a salad and perhaps Zucchini with Fresh Rosemary (page 223). A dry white wine will help the celebration.

SERVES 8.

Stuffed Chicken Thighs

You will have to invest a little time in this dish, but the results are dramatic, moist, and tasty.

   8 **chicken thighs**
   1 **teaspoon thyme**
   3 **tablespoons parsley**
   ¼ **cup white wine**
   2 **tablespoons lemon juice**
   ¼ **pound smoked ham, cut into long sticks**
   4 **green onions, cut in two**
      Salt and pepper to taste
   2 **tablespoons white wine**
      Roux of 1 tablespoon flour browned in 1
         tablespoon butter
   1 **tablespoon lemon juice**

Simmer the chicken thighs in 3 cups water, along with the thyme, parsley, white wine, and lemon juice. Or simply steam the thighs for 25 minutes; remove from steamer, and cool (see page 301 for steaming methods).

When chicken is barely tender, remove it and let it cool.

Gently push the bone from the center of each thigh. Take care not to tear up the thigh.

Insert one long sliver of smoked ham and one piece of green onion in each thigh. Place in flat bowl along with salt and pepper and the 2 tablespoons white wine, and steam for 20 minutes. Prepare a sauce for the chicken by thickening the juices in the dish with a bit of roux. You may wish to add 1 tablespoon lemon juice. Serve the sauce over the chicken thighs.

SERVES 4.

Pan-Fried Chicken Strips
(Italy-China-San Francisco)

This dish is a snap to prepare and delicious. Prepare everything ahead of time, and throw it together at the last minute while your guests or family are finishing their sherry.

2 tablespoons olive oil
2 pounds chicken breasts, skinned, boned, and
       cut into ½-inch-wide strips
2 cloves garlic, crushed
6 green onions, chopped
4 tablespoons Marsala wine
2 tablespoons lemon juice
   Salt and pepper to taste

Heat a large frying pan. Add the oil, chicken strips, garlic, and green onions. Sauté over high heat until the chicken is lightly browned and tender. Remove from the pan. Add the Marsala and lemon juice, and allow the liquid to reduce for a moment. Return the chicken to the hot pan, and add salt and pepper. Do not overcook this dish. Serve immediately.

Go all the way with the chicken thing, and serve this delicious dish along with a Frittata (page 111) and a fresh green salad. Red or white wine will do well, as long as it is dry.

SERVES 4 TO 6.

Chicken Pieces with Lime

This dish came about while I was trying to find new ways to enjoy chicken without salt. You will be surprised at what a little lime juice . . . and no salt . . . will do for your poultry.

1 chicken, cut up
2 tablespoons olive oil
½ teaspoon whole thyme
2 tablespoons lemon juice
   Fresh-cracked pepper to taste
2 limes, cut into wedges

Place the chicken pieces in an oiled baking dish, and mix with the olive oil, thyme, lemon juice, and pepper. Bake at 375° for 45 minutes to 1 hour, or until the chicken is golden and tender.

Garnish with the wedges of lime so that each guest may soak his chicken in lime juice and enjoy. You will not even miss the salt!

SERVES 4.

Boiled Chicken, Chinese Style

The idea of a boiled chicken hardly causes great excitement. That is because we are in the habit of boiling a chicken until there is no longer any flavor in the bird itself, but the boiling solution tastes great!

In this recipe we do not actually boil the bird at all but rather place it in boiling water and then leave it alone. Please read the instructions carefully. This dish is so simple and so delicious that you will think the instructions are incorrect.

Fill a large kettle with water, and bring to a boil. (An 8-quart pot two-thirds filled with water works great for a 2½- to 3-pound bird.) When the water boils, place the whole cleaned chicken into it. When the water stops boiling, take the chicken out. Cover the pot, and when the water again boils, place the chicken back in the pot. Cover the pot, and turn off the heat. Leave the chicken in the pot and the pot on the burner. After 1 hour the chicken is done. Remove, and cool.

You can debone this chicken in very little time. If you are on a low-salt/low-fat diet, be sure to remove the skin. Save the juices that flow from the bird when deboning because this liquid contains a great deal of natural gelatin and will help keep the bird moist if you should decide to store the meat in the refrigerator.

The chicken is ready to serve or use.

Chicken Salad

Chicken salad is so easy to prepare when you have on hand the lovely moist chicken prepared according to the directions above.

Cooked chicken
Celery, chopped
Mayonnaise or sour cream or yogurt
Lemon juice
Salt and pepper
Green onions, chopped (optional)
Capers, chopped (optional)
Lettuce

Chop the chicken, and mix with all the remaining ingredients, except the lettuce. Serve it on a bed of lettuce.

Chicken and Egg Terrine

Your children will like this dish because it asks the question "Which came first, the chicken or the egg?"

- 1 3-½ pound chicken, boiled, skin and bone
        removed and 1 cup broth reserved (page 158)
- 1 envelope unflavored gelatin
- 2 tablespoons white wine vinegar
- 2 tablespoons lemon juice
- 10 stuffed green olives, sliced
- ¼ cup parsley, chopped
- 4 green onions, chopped
- 1 tablespoon capers, chopped
    Pepper and very little salt
- 8 eggs, hard-boiled

Make this the day before serving.

Tear the chicken up into small pieces. Dissolve the gelatin in the broth, and add the vinegar and lemon juice. Warm until all is dissolved. Add the chicken meat, and set aside.

Mix the olives, parsley, green onions, capers, pepper, and salt in a large bowl. With a slotted spoon remove the chicken from the gelatin, and add it to the bowl; reserve the gelatin. Place one-half of the chicken mixture in a 1-quart terrine or loaf mold. Cut the ends from the eggs until you can see a bit of the yolk. Arrange the eggs, end to end, down the center of the mold. Fill the mold with the remaining chicken mixture. Press down with your hand, and then pour in the gelatin until it just comes to the top of the meat.

Refrigerate the mold overnight.

To serve, remove and slice across the mold so that the egg is sliced and attractive. Serve as a first course or as a summer salad.

SERVES 6 TO 8.

Chicken with Leeks and Cream

This is one of my favorite dishes. Use the Boiled Chicken, Chinese Style (page 158), so that the dish will be moist and flavorful. True, it is a little rich, but now and then I have to make it.

> 1   3- to 4-pound chicken, cooked, skinned, and
>   deboned
> 3   to 4 leeks
> 1   tablespoon olive oil
> 1   clove garlic, chopped (optional)
>   Salt and pepper to taste
>   Pinch of nutmeg
> ½   cup whipping cream
>   Parsley for garnish

Tear up the chicken meat into bite-size pieces.

Cut the leeks into 2-inch pieces up to the point where the leek begins to turn green. Slice the piece once lengthwise, and divide the leaves. Rinse if dirty.

Sauté the leek leaves in the oil along with the garlic if desired. Do not allow the leaves to discolor; you simply want to cook them until they are barely tender.

Add the chicken to the pan, and cook it until hot. Add the salt, pepper, and nutmeg. Mix well, and add the cream. Heat, and serve. Decorate with parsley.

This is a very rich dish. I like it with plain white rice on the side because the sauce is just wonderful.

SERVES 6.

Roast Chicken and Parsley
(Italy)

In the mountains of Italy you will find people cooking herb-filled chickens on spits. The results is a very moist and flavorful bird.

- 1 3- to 4-pound chicken
  Salt and pepper to taste
- ½ cup olive oil
- ¼ cup lemon juice
- 1 teaspoon ground thyme
- 1 bunch parsley

Wash and dry the chicken. Salt and pepper it inside and out. Rub the bird well, inside and out, with a dressing made of the oil, lemon juice, and thyme. Stuff the bird loosely with the fresh parsley, and bake, uncovered, in a 350° oven for about 1¼ hours.

SERVES 3 OR 4.

Chicken with Rosemary
(Italy)

I hope you can find fresh rosemary for this one. Rosemary grows as a shrub here in the Northwest, and I expect that you can get some growing in your yard. Try it. If not, use dried.

 1 **3- to 4-pound chicken, cut up***
 3 **slices bacon, chopped**
 1 **tablespoon butter**
 1 **tablespoon olive oil**
    Salt and pepper to taste
 1 **or 2 cloves garlic, crushed**
 ½ **cup white wine**
 ½ **tablespoon dried rosemary** *or* **1 tablespoon fresh**
       rosemary
 2 **tablespoons tomato paste**
 ½ **cup chicken broth**

Fry the bacon until barely crisp, pour off the fat, and remove the
bacon. Add the butter and olive oil to the pan, and brown the
chicken pieces. Add salt, pepper, and garlic to the pan when
the chicken is almost browned. When it is browned, add the
white wine and rosemary to the pan. Add the bacon, cover, and
cook for 15 minutes. Mix the tomato paste with the chicken
broth, and add to the pan. Cover, and cook for about 30 minutes,
or until the chicken is tender.

SERVES 3 OR 4.

*For a more elegant dinner, use just chicken thighs.

Duck

Duck with Curry and Honey

We eat very little duck in this country, and I cannot figure out why. The bird is easy to cook, very rich, and not expensive. In China every family has its own little family of ducks. I would love to live with ducks in the backyard—but the cat has voted no.

    1 2½- to 3-pound frozen duck, defrosted
        Salt and pepper to taste
    1 yellow onion, peeled
    2 cloves
    4 tablespoons honey
  1½ tablespoons curry powder

Rinse the duck, and pat dry. Salt and pepper the duck, inside and out. Place the yellow onion stuck with the two cloves in the cavity. Roast the duck at 325° for 1 hour. Then begin basting duck every 10 minutes with a mixture of the honey and curry powder. The duck should cook for a total of 1½ hours. Cut into large chunks, and serve.

SERVES 4.

Turkey

Simmered Turkey

I know this sounds a bit strange to you, but let us consider the fact that the turkey is generally very inexpensive, has little fat that cannot be removed easily, and is terribly versatile. So we should use it much more often than we do.

Be sure that the turkey, if frozen, is completely defrosted. Remove the neck and giblets.

Place a large pot on the stove, and put the whole turkey into it. Cover completely with cold water, and then remove the bird, leaving the water in the pot. (In this way we know how much water to use for the cooking. It will take about a 20-quart pot to simmer a 10-pound bird.)

Bring the water to a boil. Remove the wings and legs from the bird, and set aside. Place the body of the bird in the pot, and bring the water back to a boil. Turn down the heat, cover the pot, and keep the water at a light simmer for 45 minutes. Then add the wings and the legs to the pot. Cover the pot again, and simmer for an additional 45 minutes. Then leave the lid on the pot and the pot on the burner. Turn off the heat, and let the bird stand in its own liquid for 2 hours. It is now ready to remove and be served or used. At the end of the 2-hour period you may place the whole works in the refrigerator and chill for the next day. Do not store the turkey in aluminum, but stainless steel ware is fine.

Please do not season the bird while cooking. Salt dries out the bird. If you must add salt, add it later just before serving.

Low-salt/low-fat eaters will find this turkey to be just the thing. Simply remove the skin from the bird after cooking (this contains most of the fat) and eat without guilt!

Remove the meat from the bone, and serve with a light gravy for a lovely dinner. The meat will be very moist and fresh in flavor.

Prepare Giblet Gravy by cooking the chopped giblets in some of the stock for about 1 hour before the bird is to be served. Season to taste. Add Kitchen Bouquet to color, if you wish, and perhaps a bit of sage or thyme. Thicken with roux, and serve.

Chill the bird in its juice, and slice it the next day for a light dinner.

Turkey and Dumplings

Sauté carrots, celery, yellow onion, and perhaps some zucchini well so that they do not have to cook in the stock long. Add the cooked meat and vegetables to the stock along with seasonings (I like a bit of fresh parsley, some thyme and sage, and a bit of black pepper), and bring it to a light simmer. Cook the dumplings over the stew.

Pasta Salad with Turkey is simple because the meat is so moist. (See Norwegian Spaghetti Salad with Shrimp, page 98, and substitute turkey for the shrimp.)

Green Salad with Turkey makes an unusual evening meal.

Turkey Soup

Save the bones and the stock of Simmered Turkey (page 164), and cook a second time for great soup. Add a bit of celery, carrots, and onion to the pot along with all the bones and some additional pepper. A little rice added after the soup is finished is just delicious.

Cold Turkey with Dill Sauce

Slice the cold meat of Simmered Turkey (page 164), which you have kept in the broth in the refrigerator, and serve it with Cucumber and Dill Sauce (page 276). Garnish with a bit of parsley.

Turkey and Rice

Add cooked meat of Simmered Turkey (page 164) to hot cooked rice along with a bit of butter and your own blend of herbs. (I prefer fresh parsley and perhaps sage and thyme, as well as a little chopped celery. A few spoons of fresh-grated Parmesan or Romano cheese completes the dish.)

Turkey with Mushrooms and Marsala

Turkey with class! I developed this dish for Jason, my turkey-loving son. It has an Italian flair, and it is a great way to use up the leftover holiday bird.

- ¼ pound mushrooms, sliced
- 2 tablespoons butter
- 1 pound sliced cooked turkey
- ¼ cup Marsala wine
  Salt and pepper to taste
- ¼ cup broth from Simmered Turkey (page 164) or chicken broth
- 2 tablespoons chopped parsley

Sauté the mushrooms in the butter. When the mushrooms are browned a bit, add the turkey slices. Sauté only until hot. Add the remaining ingredients, stir about for a minute, and remove the turkey and mushrooms to a heated platter. Reduce the sauce, and pour over the turkey.

Serve with rice or noodles, a green salad, and sautéed zucchini slices with herbs.

SERVES 3 OR 4.

Turkey Pasta with Cream Sauce

The flavors of garlic, turkey, and cream really do belong together. This recipe will prove my point.

   1 tablespoon butter
   1 tablespoon flour
   ¾ cup heavy cream
      Salt and pepper to taste
      Pinch of nutmeg
   1 pound pasta
   2 cloves garlic, sliced thin
   2 tablespoons olive oil
   2 zucchini, sliced thin
   1 pound cooked turkey, cubed
      Fresh-grated Parmesan or Romano cheese

Prepare the roux by heating the butter in a small saucepan and adding the flour. Over medium heat, stir until the flour just begins to turn a very light brown. In another pan heat the cream. When it is hot, add the roux to the cream, stirring carefully until the sauce is thickened. Add the salt, pepper, and nutmeg. Remove from the heat.

Cook the pasta. Drain when finished.

Sauté the garlic in the olive oil until just lightly browned. Add the zucchini and the turkey, and sauté until all is hot. Add a bit of pepper to taste.

Toss the turkey and zucchini with pasta, and add the sauce. Top with Parmesan or Romano cheese.

SERVES 8 AS FIRST COURSE.

Turkey and Spaghetti Sauce

Try adding some of the cooked turkey to your favorite spaghetti sauce and serving it over pasta. Add lots of cheese, and enjoy!

Turkey on a Muffin

Put a few thin slices of cooked turkey on a toasted English muffin. Add a tomato slice. Top with a cheese sauce, and broil until bubbly and browned a bit.

Chicken Wings

Our whole family is fond of chicken wings. They are inexpensive, easy to handle, very versatile, and delicious. Wings contain a great deal of natural gelatin, so they are moist and juicy.

Cutting the Chicken Wings

Cut each wing into three pieces. Cut at each of the two joints, and you wind up with the wing tip, which I generally use for soup, the middle portion, and the thickest part of the wing, that part which is closest to the bird, literally the upper arm of the bird. The upper arms make marvelous little drumsticks.

Steamed Chicken Wings
(China)

The Chinese have long enjoyed chicken wings because of the great flavor involved and because the wings are very inexpensive.

30 center wing portions (see page 168)
⅛ cup light soy sauce
⅛ cup dry sherry
 1 clove garlic, crushed
 1 teaspoon grated fresh ginger
½ teaspoon sugar
 1 green onion, chopped

Marinate the wing portions in the remaining ingredients for 15 minutes. Steam in a low bowl for 45 minutes (if you need help with steaming, see page 301).

These make a fine main course or an easily prepared snack course for a party.

SERVES 4 OR 5.

Baked Chicken Wings
(China)

Prepare recipe for Steamed Chicken Wings above, using an additional teaspoon sugar. Bake at 375° for 35 to 40 minutes, or until the wings are browned and tender.

Chinese Drumsticks

How clever is the Chinese chef. With a little bit of knife work he is able to change the lowly chicken wing into a drumstick that is meaty and moist. It is worth your time to learn this quick change routine.

30 upper wing portions (page 168)
 2 tablespoons light soy sauce
 2 tablespoons dry sherry
¼ teaspoon sugar
 2 teaspoons grated fresh ginger
 2 teaspoons Chinese five spice powder *or* a
         mixture of cinnamon and anise
 4 tablespoons cornstarch
     Peanut oil for frying

With a very sharp paring knife, cut around the bone at the small end of each of the upper wing portions. Cut through the skin and muscle, and then pull the meat and skin down the bone toward the larger end. This will give you a ball of meat on the end of a stick, a clever little drumstick.

Mix all the other ingredients together, and marinate the wings for 15 minutes. Deep-fry in 375° peanut oil until the wings are golden brown and tender.

Serve at a party for a smashing snack or with a full Chinese meal at home.

SERVES 4 OR 5.

Wings in Spaghetti Sauce
(Italy)

This is a delicious way to use the center portions of the wing. Simply simmer the wing portions in your favorite spaghetti sauce for about 40 minutes, or until they are tender. Serve over pasta garnished with grated Italian cheese. Add a salad and a green vegetable, a bit of red wine, and you have a quick and delicious meal.

Wings Piquant

This dish is so simple it is absurd! Everyone will think you are a genius.

    24 wing pieces, either the center or upper arm
            (page 168)
     1 cup Basic Fennel Dressing (page 90)
     1 teaspoon oregano
     3 tablespoons fresh-grated Parmesan or Romano
            cheese
        Salt and pepper to taste

Marinate the wing pieces in the fennel dressing for ½ hour. Drain, and place on oiled baking sheet. Sprinkle with the oregano, cheese, salt, and pepper. Bake in a 375° oven for 35 to 45 minutes, or until wings are lightly browned and tender.

These make a great appetizer, a marvelous cold lunch, and an easy evening meal. Pasta goes well on the side, along with a tomato salad. Either red or white wine fits.

SERVES 3 OR 4.

Buffalo Chicken Wings

There are some foods in this world that have names that so intrigue that one has no idea what he or she is going to taste but cannot wait. Calvin Trillin, a hero of mine because he seems able to make a living by flying around the country and eating in strange spots, claims that the chicken wings served in Buffalo, New York, are a food product unto themselves. I have never been to Buffalo, but this recipe is authentic. The wings are deep-fried, then splashed with hot sauce and served with bleu cheese dressing and celery sticks . . . at least that is how they claim to eat them in Buffalo.

```
 1  tablespoon white wine vinegar
½  cup milk
 2  tablespoons fine-chopped yellow onion
 1  clove garlic, crushed
¼  cup parsley, minced
 1  cup mayonnaise
¼  cup bleu cheese, crumbled into fine pieces
 2  tablespoons lemon juice
¼  teaspoon salt
¼  teaspoon fresh-ground black pepper
    Pinch of cayenne pepper
¼  pound butter or margarine
 2  tablespoons bottled hot sauce* or more to taste
       if you can take it
50  pieces chicken wings, either center or upper
       portion (page 168)
    Peanut oil for deep frying
    Celery sticks for garnish
```

Mix the wine vinegar with the milk, and allow the milk to curdle. Add the yellow onion, garlic, parsley, mayonnaise, bleu cheese,

*Trappey's Red Devil or Tabasco would be fine.

lemon juice, salt, pepper, and cayenne. Mix well. Refrigerate before serving.

In a large skillet melt the butter or margarine over low heat, and stir in the hot sauce. Careful, this stuff may be too hot for your family. Try a bit that is mild first; then increase the amount of hot sauce to taste.

Deep-fry the wing pieces in small batches in peanut oil at 385° for about 10 minutes, or until browned and crisp. Drain on paper towels. (If you wish to avoid the fat in this dish, bake the wings in the oven at 400° for 25 minutes.)

When all the wing pieces have been deep-fried, reheat the skillet containing the hot sauce, and toss the wings about in the hot sauce. Serve with the dressing for a dip and the celery sticks on the side.

This is one of those marvelously messy meals. Serve with lots of beer, a gigantic green salad with Dill and Caper Dressing (page 96), and perhaps Onions Baked in Cinders (page 243).

SERVES 6 TO 8.

Looed Chicken Wings
(China)

I heard that remark! No, *looed* does not mean "lewd." *Looed* refers to a simmering process common in China. But you can have fun with some of your guests if you let them think you are going to serve lewd food.

> 2 cups water
> 2 cups dark soy sauce
> ½ cup dry sherry
> 5 slices fresh ginger, about the size of a quarter
> 2 star anise flowers*
> 1 tablespoon sugar
> 2 pounds chicken wings, cut (page 168)
>   Sesame oil

Bring to a boil the water, soy sauce, sherry, ginger, star anise flowers, and sugar. Simmer as many chicken wings as you wish in this fluid for about 20 minutes. Cool in the liquid.

*Available at Chinese markets.

Serve cold with a little sesame oil on top of the wings. Do not throw out the looing sauce because it can be used again and again; simply add a little more of the flavors you wish. Refrigerate!

SERVES 4 TO 6.

Game Hens with Lebanese Dressing

Stuffing a small bird with rice and pine nuts, sweet spices, and onions sounds like something from Omar Khayyam. You are close; you are very close.

> 1 yellow onion, peeled and chopped
> 2 tablespoons butter
> 1 cup rice
> 2 cups water
> ⅛ cup pine nuts
> ½ teaspoon cinnamon
> ½ teaspoon allspice
> Salt to taste
> 4 game hens

Sauté the yellow onion in the butter, and then add the rice. Sauté until barely golden brown. Add the water, pine nuts, cinnamon, allspice, and salt. Stuff the game hens with this cooked mixture, and bake at about 325° for 60 minutes. Serve split in half.

SERVES 4 TO 6.

Beef

How we Americans love beef! And we know that in the very near future we are going to have to cut down on our love of this food . . . for several reasons. The first is that we have been eating too much animal fat, a habit that is great fun but difficult on our health. Secondly, the cow is a most inefficient animal if you consider the amount of grain and fresh water that it takes to make a pound of beef. I expect that we will be spending more time in the future with piggies and chickens since they do a much better job in terms of cost and protein. Finally, we simply cannot afford to continue to use beef as the major food product. We shall learn the lesson that the Chinese and Europeans already understand: Beef is best used as a flavoring in a dish, not as the substance of the dish itself. So these dishes are offered with these concerns in mind, and even though they seem rather rich and heavy with meat, understand that they are to be eaten in the midst of the whole meal, rather than constitute the whole meal.

Boiled Beef Brisket with Green Sauce
(Italy)

There is an institution on Broadway in San Francisco called Little Joe's. The food is very good, the atmosphere late-1960s hippie, and the kitchen show is just terrific. The chef serves a dish very much like this one. This is as close as I can come, and I just love it.

1   **3- to 4-pound beef brisket**
    Salt and pepper to taste
1   **teaspoon whole thyme**
2   **cloves garlic, chopped**
1   **yellow onion, peeled and chopped**
3   **carrots, chopped**
4   **stalks celery, chopped**
½   **bunch parsley**

GREEN SAUCE
¼   **cup parsley**
¼   **cup chopped yellow onion**
6   **green onions, chopped**
1   **clove garlic, crushed**
    Salt and pepper
2   **tablespoons white wine vinegar**
2   **tablespoons olive oil**
¼   **teaspoon each oregano and rosemary**

Place the brisket in a tight-fitting pot, and add the salt, pepper, thyme, garlic, yellow onion, carrots, celery, and parsley. Cover with water, and bring to a boil. Turn down to a simmer, and cook for 2½ hours, covered, or until the meat is tender.

To make the green sauce, blanch the parsley, yellow onion, and green onions for just a moment in boiling water. Drain. Add the remaining sauce ingredients, and mix well.

Cut the brisket into thin slices, and serve with the green sauce. This is a lovely way to stretch out the roast by serving a rich sauce along with the meat. A green salad, some pasta, and a nice dry red wine complete the meal.

SERVES 6 TO 8.

Vegetable-Stuffed Round Steak
(Italy)

This is not a dish to be made when you are short of time, but if you are spending the day cooking, this would be a grand effort for your family or dinner party. The meat is not expensive, and this process makes the meat so rich that your guests will eat a sensible amount and they will savor that.

   2 **pounds round steak**
      Salt and pepper to taste
      Olive oil
   2 **cloves garlic, crushed**
   3 **eggs, hard-boiled and sliced**
   2 **carrots, grated into coarse pieces**
   ½ **cup thin-sliced zucchini**
      Fresh-grated Parmesan cheese to taste
   2 **cups tomato or spaghetti sauce**

Tenderize the meat with a wooden or flat metal meat pounder (I have even used a short piece of two-by-four). Pound the meat so that the steak is thinned a bit and certainly made much more tender.

Add the salt, pepper, 2 tablespoons olive oil, and the garlic to the meat, and rub it in as a paste.

Arrange the eggs, carrots, zucchini, and cheese down the center of the steak. Roll up the steak like a jelly roll, and tie it in several places.

Heat a large frying pan, and add a bit of olive oil. Brown the roll on all sides very quickly.

Place the roll in a covered baking dish (you may have to bend the roll into a U shape in order to get it into the pan). Add the tomato or spaghetti sauce, and cover. Bake in a 350° oven for 1 hour.

Place the sauce on a serving tray. Slice the meat across the roll, and arrange the slices on top of the sauce.

The sauce is just great on pasta. Start the meal with an anti-pasto; follow it with the pasta, then the meat and a salad.

SERVES 4.

Carpaccio
(Italy)

A high-class version, maybe the original version, of Steak Tartare. In this case the meat is sliced paper-thin and made very rich with olive oil and herbs. Try this at Avanzare Restaurant in Chicago. Just heaven!

>**Bottom round roast with little fat**
>**Salt and pepper**
>**Parmesan cheese**
>**Olive oil**
>**Fresh lemon juice**
>**Capers**

Almost freeze the meat so that it will be easy to slice thin . . . very, very thin. Place a few slices on each guest's plate, and then garnish with the remaining ingredients.

This is a classic antipasto in Italy; it also makes a great summer dinner with a large salad and ample crusty bread.

>**VARIATION**
>**Chopped yellow onion**
>**Parsley**
>**Olive oil**
>**Salt and pepper**
>**Fresh basil**
>**Capers**

Use the above to make a lovely garnish on the meat. This will be so beautiful that you will find yourself serving it at special parties throughout the year.

Braciole
(Italy)

I did this recipe on our very first show years ago in Tacoma. I had been given the recipe by my wife's aunt Suzy, in Brooklyn. I talked about Aunt Suzy and how she would stand over a frying pan of leftover spaghetti and stir and stir . . . with a long cigarette in her mouth. The ash would grow longer and longer, and then I would turn for a moment and . . . the ash was gone. It disappeared. She gave me her recipe, but I could never make the dish as well as she. I then realized that it must have been the cigarette ash. I laughed about it on the air because I never dreamed that the shows would ever hit New York. When the shows did reach Brooklyn, I expected a phone call from Aunt Suzy, a call filled with insulted Brooklyn anger. But the call never did come. However, she has sent me some more recipes.

    1 about 1½-pound flank steak
    2 cloves garlic
    1 tablespoon olive oil
       Salt and pepper to taste
    2 eggs, hard-boiled and sliced
    ½ cup chopped parsley
    ½ cup coarse-grated Swiss cheese
    3 teaspoons fresh-grated Parmesan cheese
       Peanut oil
    2 cups Tomato Sauce (page 263)

Place the flank steak on a board, and pound it with a wooden or flat metal meat pounder or two-by-four to tenderize. Crush the garlic in a garlic press, and place it on the meat. Add the olive oil, and rub the garlic and oil into the meat. Add salt and pepper. Arrange the eggs on the meat, and add the parsley. Add the Swiss cheese and the Parmesan cheese. Roll the whole thing up like a jelly roll (the slices must cut across the grain of the meat). Brown the roll in a little peanut oil, and place in an ovenproof dish. Add the tomato sauce, and bake, covered, at 325° for about 1½ hours. Slice, and serve with the sauce.

SERVES 4.

Tripe Florentine

Americans are reluctant to eat tripe, though I cannot understand why. We buy wieners—and who knows what they contain—but we avoid the elegant tripe. This dish will convince you that we have been foolish.

I have called the dish Florentine because I first tasted something like it while a student in 1960 and traveling by motorbike in Italy. I tasted everything I could, and this dish has remained a favorite. It is very rich.

2   **pounds tripe**
4   **tablespoons peanut oil**
2   **carrots, grated**
½   **cup chopped celery**
1   **yellow onion, peeled and chopped**
½   **cup parsley, chopped**
3   **cloves garlic, crushed**
1   **8-ounce can tomato sauce**
½   **cup Basic Brown Soup Stock (page 47)**
½   **cup dry red wine**
1   **teaspoon oregano**
1   **bay leaf, crushed**
½   **teaspoon basil**
    Salt and pepper to taste
2   **1-inch-long pieces lemon peel**
½   **cup fresh-grated Parmesan or Romano cheese**

Parboil the tripe for about 30 minutes. Drain and cool. Slice up the tripe into ½-inch-wide pieces. Sauté very quickly in a little of the oil in a large frying pan.

Sauté in a little of the oil the carrots, celery, yellow onion, parsley, and garlic. Add the canned tomato sauce. Add the soup stock and red wine. Add the oregano, bay leaf, basil, salt, pepper, and lemon peel. Simmer the sauce for a few minutes, and then add the tripe. Cook it on top of stove, covered, for 1½ hours, or until tender. Or bake it in a moderate oven. When it is ready to serve, add a little Parmesan or Romano cheese.

Serve with pasta.

SERVES 8.

Hot Beef Shreds
(China)

This is sometimes called Chungking beef shreds, and it refers to a region of China, not to a brand of canned food products. This is easy to prepare and is one of the best Chinese beef dishes I know.

      1 **about 1-pound beef flank steak**
      3 **tablespoons light soy sauce**
      2 **tablespoons dry sherry**
      ½ **teaspoon fresh-grated ginger**
      3 **carrots**
      5 **stalks celery**
      4 **tablespoons peanut oil**
      1 **clove garlic, mashed**
         Salt (optional)
      ½ **teaspoon Tabasco or Chinese red chili and garlic paste to taste**
      ¼ **cup beef broth**
      ½ **tablespoon cornstarch mixed with 2 tablespoons water**

Cut the flank steak, across the grain, into thin slices. Marinate in the soy sauce, sherry, and grated ginger. Cut the carrots and celery into thin slices. Set aside.

Fry or chow the drained beef in the peanut oil in a very hot pan or wok. Drain, and remove from the pan or wok. Sauté the carrots, celery, and garlic in a little peanut oil. Add the salt, if desired, MSG if desired, and a stiff shot of Tabasco or red chili and garlic paste. Add the cooked beef shreds. Add the beef broth and thickened cornstarch.

SERVES 4 TO 6 AS PART OF CHINESE MEAL.

Deep-Fried Liver

I know my mother will still not understand me, but the only way I can stand liver is cooked in the following way.

      Fresh liver
      Egg
      Farina
      Peanut oil for frying
      Mayonnaise assortment

Cut the liver into strips about ¼ inch wide. Dip them in egg whipped with a tiny bit of water, and then dredge them in farina. Deep-fry at 350° in the oil until barely brown. Set out mayonnaise, and dip the liver stick into any of your choice. Dilled, curried, or onion and parsleyed mayonnaises are only the beginning!

Youvarlakia—Greek Meatballs

When I prepared this dish on the Phil Donahue show, Mr. Donahue seemed surprised that I would prepare simple meatballs on his show, in front of 9½ million people. After he had tasted the dish, he understood. It is a very clever Greek invention.

Incidentally, the answer is yes. I did find Phil Donahue to be a very charming, gracious, and intelligent gentleman.

       1½ pounds hamburger
        1 cup rice
        1 tablespoon chopped yellow onion
        2 tablespoons chopped parsley
        ½ tablespoon dried dill
        1 egg
           Flour
        2 cups tomato juice
        4 cups water
        2 tablespoons butter

Mix the hamburger with the rice, yellow onion, parsley, dill, and egg. Mix and mold into small meatballs. Roll each in flour.

In a large frying pan place the tomato juice and water. Bring to a heavy simmer, and add the butter. Gently drop meatballs into this sauce, cover, and simmer for 45 minutes.

The rice will provide the starch, but the sauce is delicious on Red Beans with Peas and Pasta (page 132). A Hungarian Salad (page 91) would make this an international meal.

SERVES 6 TO 8.

Ming's Oyster Beef
(China)

The oyster sauce in this dish is really made from oysters, but it does not have any fishy flavor at all. It is very rich, so prepare this along with rice or noodles, or serve it in the midst of a much larger Chinese meal.

    1   **about 1-pound flank steak**
    2   **tablespoons light soy sauce**
    1   **tablespoon dry sherry**
    1   **teaspoon sugar**
    ¼   **teaspoon grated fresh ginger**
    3   **to 4 tablespoons Chinese oyster sauce***
    2   **tablespoons peanut oil**

Cut the flank steak across the grain into thin pieces. Marinate in the soy sauce, sherry, sugar, and ginger. Add the Chinese oyster sauce. Stir-fry the meat very quickly in hot pan and the oil. It will make its own gravy.

    Serve with rice.

SERVES 4 AS PART OF A CHINESE MEAL.

Oxtail Stew with Bread for Sopping
(England)

Oxtails have been given a bad name. I suppose it is because we don't want to think of eating animals' tails. Yet we will eat tons of ground-up hamburger. Where do the kids think hamburger comes from? Cook this dish, and enjoy it. Your English ancestors thought it grand. So do I.

*Available in Chinese markets or good delicatessens.

    4 pounds oxtails cut into 1-inch pieces
    3 tablespoons peanut oil
    4 carrots, chopped
    2 turnips, peeled and diced into big pieces
    4 stalks celery, chopped into large pieces
    2 yellow onions, peeled and cut into large pieces
    3 cups Basic Brown Soup Stock (page 47)
    1 cup red wine
    2 bay leaves, crushed
    1 teaspoon ground thyme
    ½ cup parsley
      Salt and pepper to taste
      Roux of ½ cup flour browned in ½ cup butter
        (optional)

Brown the oxtails in a hot pan with a little peanut oil. When they are a good dark brown, remove them from pan, and place in ovenproof casserole. In the used pan, sauté the carrots, turnips, celery, and yellow onions. When the mixture is a little brown, add to the oxtails with the soup stock, red wine, bay leaves, thyme, parsley, salt, and pepper. Simmer for 2½ hours, or until meat is very tender. You may thicken with a roux.

Serve with beer and bread to sop! Look in the index under "England" for proper menu suggestions to go with this very rich stew.

SERVES 6 TO 8.

■ HINT: On Deglazing a Pan

After browning meats or vegetables, add wine or broth to the pan while it is on high heat. The rich coloring that remains in the pan is gently scraped with a wooden spoon and stirred into the wine or broth. This is added to the sauce or gravy.

Pork

The pig has certainly been maligned. We are now learning that pigs are much smarter than dogs and can be trained to make great house pets. And given clean surroundings, the porker will be clean as well.

I love pork. It is easy to cook and inexpensive, and if you are on a low-salt/low-fat diet, the fat from pork can be easily removed from many good cuts of meat.

The wild pig was domesticated in China around 2900 B.C., and it has been feeding many cultures ever since. One of the reasons pigs became so popular is that they are efficient scavengers. They practically take care of themselves. They are also very efficient in converting grain or feed into meat. Swine are more efficient in this converting process than are cattle, lambs, and poultry. And the meat has high nutritional values and grand taste.

We should be careful about degrading the pig with our loose talk about eating habits and "looking like a swine." In fact, the pig is very close to us in many ways. Its skin is very much like ours, and we are now using such skin in burn cases on humans. The pig's digestive system is also similar to ours, and the animal is susceptible to many diseases that affect humans. We have used pig heart valves to replace worn-out human valves for years. All these gifts to us, and we still malign the pig. When you serve any of the following recipes, be sure to thank the old porker.

Northern Chinese Pork

There is nothing complicated about fine Chinese cooking. You will have immediate success with this dish, but please do not substitute dry ginger for the fresh ginger root. The fresh ginger is what does it!

 2 pork steaks
 2 tablespoons light soy sauce
 1 tablespoon dry sherry
 ½ teaspoon grated fresh ginger
 1 yellow onion
 2 stalks celery
 2 carrots
   Peanut oil
 1 clove garlic, chopped
   Salt (optional)
   Hot pepper sauce *or* Chinese red chili and garlic
     paste to taste
 1 tablespoon cornstarch dissolved in 6 tablespoons
     chicken broth

Debone the pork steaks, and cut up into small cubes. Marinate in the soy sauce, sherry, and ginger. In the meantime, peel and chop up the yellow onion, chop up the celery, and grate the carrots into coarse pieces.

Fry the drained pork in a little peanut oil and the garlic for about 5 or 6 minutes. Remove the meat from the pan. Add the vegetables and a little more peanut oil. Stir-fry until the vegetables are barely cooked and still crisp. Add the pork. Add a pinch of salt if desired and a bit of hot pepper sauce or red chili and garlic paste. Thicken with the dissolved cornstarch.

SERVES 4 AS PART OF A CHINESE MEAL.

Pork, Mexican Style

The first time I had this dish it was made with beef, but I really prefer the pork. This is very easy to do, and it will help you understand that there are great flavors outside the taco to be found in the Mexican kitchen.

2 **deboned pork steaks (about 1 pound meat)**
½ **yellow onion, peeled**
1 **green pepper, cleaned**
2 **tablespoons peanut oil**
2 **cloves garlic, sliced thin**
¼ **teaspoon ground cumin**
¼ **teaspoon oregano**
   Salt to taste
2 **tablespoons dry sherry**

Cut the pork steaks into thin slices. Slice up the yellow onion and green pepper. Sauté the pork quickly in oil and garlic. Add the onion and pepper, and continue to stir-fry. Add the cumin and oregano. Add salt. At the last minute add the sherry.

Serve with Potatoes, Old French Style (page 250) and Cold Vegetables in Mustard Dressing (page 225). Beer and bread!

SERVES 3 OR 4.

Pork Souvlakia
(Greece)

Pork is not as common as lamb in the Greek diet, but it is so good in this recipe that I have cheated again. But then, that is the point behind an enjoyable time in the kitchen. Few rules, few categories that cannot be violated.

1 **pound pork**
1 **yellow onion, peeled**
2 **green peppers, cleaned**
2 **tablespoons olive oil**
1 **tablespoon lemon juice**
½ **tablespoon light soy sauce**
½ **teaspoon oregano**
   Salt and pepper to taste

Cut the pork into ½-inch cubes. Cut the yellow onion and green peppers into 1-inch square pieces. Marinate the meat and vegetables in the olive oil, lemon juice, soy sauce, oregano, salt, and pepper for about 2 hours. Then alternate vegetables and meat on skewers. Broil until lightly browned, about 15 minutes.

Serve with Tzatziki (page 396), crusty bread, and perhaps an eggplant salad, Melitzanosalata (page 393). Dry red wine completes your Greek feast.

SERVES 3 OR 4.

Chinese Pork Kidney

The first time that I cooked pork kidney in the television studio the crew turned their backs on me. When the dish was finished, a fight broke out over who was to get the last tiny piece. So, if you have eaters in your home who lack imagination, try this dish on them. They will be amazed that they like it.

      1 pound pork kidneys, cleaned of fat
      ½ cup celery
      ½ cup carrots
      ½ cup yellow onions
      ½ cup zucchini
      1 about ⅓-pound pork steak
         Peanut oil
      2 cloves garlic, sliced thin
      ½ teaspoon fresh-grated ginger
      2 tablespoons dry sherry
      2 tablespoons light soy sauce
      ½ tablespoon cornstarch in 3 tablespoons water
         Brown sugar (optional)
         Hot pepper sauce (optional)

Cut the pork kidneys into very thin slices, and score them in a crisscross manner on one side. Slice up the celery, carrots, yellow onions, and zucchini to make ½ cup of each. Cut the pork steak into bite-size pieces.

Cook the pork steak in a hot pan or wok with peanut oil for a few minutes. Remove. Add the garlic and 2 tablespoons peanut oil to the pan. Add the celery, carrots, onions, and zucchini in that order, and cook for 2 minutes after each addition. Add the kidney and the pork, and stir-fry for 5 minutes more. Make a sauce of ginger, dry sherry, soy sauce, and a little cornstarch and water. You may wish to add a pinch of brown sugar or even some hot pepper sauce. Add the sauce, and cook until it thickens, about 2 minutes.

Serve this at a Chinese meal along with Cucumber Soup (page 367), Chinese Bean Curd with Oyster Sauce (page 363), and Shrimp with Gin (page 360). With rice, the dinner would be ample for 6 persons.

SERVES 3 OR 4.

Lamb

Lamb is a very efficient animal, easy to prepare and versatile. So why do Americans eat so little lamb? I suppose the reason has something to do with the odor of lamb on the meal line in high school or college. Do you remember how the lamb was cooked? It was cooked Old Testament style, burned on the altar with a pillar of smoke drifting up to the Holy One. Lamb should never be cooked well done. It should be a tiny bit pink on the inside. Then the flavor will not be gamey or strong but will be light and tender.

Lamb Shish Kebab
(Lebanon)

I have never had anyone come to my table and, after expressing obvious concern over the fact that lamb was on the table, not enjoy this dish. Do not overcook this, please.

   2 green peppers
   2 large yellow onions
   1 2-pound leg of lamb or shoulder of lamb, cut
       into 1½-inch cubes
  ½ cup olive oil
  ½ teaspoon oregano
  ½ teaspoon dried mint *or* 1 tablespoon of fresh
   2 cloves garlic, crushed
   1 tablespoon Chinese light soy sauce

Cut the green peppers first in halves and then in thirds the long way. Remove the seeds, and cut each piece across. You now have 12 squares of green pepper.

Peel the yellow onions, and cut in half across the middle. Cut each piece in quarters. Peel the layers so that you have 6 pieces about the same size as the green pepper squares.

Place the green peppers and onions in a large mixing bowl along with the lamb.

Make a sauce of the olive oil, oregano, mint (more if fresh mint), garlic, and soy sauce. Mix well, and pour over the meat and vegetables. Mix well again, and let sit for 3 hours.

Arrange on skewers in this order: onion, meat, green pepper, meat, onion, meat, green pepper, meat. End with an onion. Broil on a cookie sheet until lightly browned on all sides, no more than 15 minutes total cooking time. This is one of the best lamb dishes I have ever tasted!

SERVES 6 TO 8.

Kibbe
(Lebanon)

This is the national dish of Lebanon. It must be made carefully so that the flavor of the lamb is light . . . and then the dish can be eaten raw. Yes, I have eaten it raw many times, and I prefer it that way. If you insist on cooking this dish, do not cook it long. This is not an American meat loaf!

    4 **cups (about 2 pounds) very lean leg of lamb**
    1 **cup fine-grind bulgur wheat*, soaked in water**
          for 1 hour and then drained
    2 **teaspoons dried onion flakes**
    1 **teaspoon dried mint**
        Salt to taste
   ½ **teaspoon cinnamon**
   ½ **teaspoon allspice**
    2 **tablespoons olive oil (optional)**
        Large yellow onions, peeled and cut into wedges
          (optional)
        Pine nuts or almond slivers (optional)

All ingredients must be cold.

Grind the lamb with your coarsest meat grinder blade. Be sure you have removed all traces of fat or tendon. Add the drained bulgur wheat. Add the onion flakes, mint, salt, cinnamon, and allspice. Mix well with a wooden spoon, and then grind the whole again, using the fine blade this time. Be careful to keep all this cold.

This may be served in two ways. My favorite is raw, a classic dish in the Middle East.

Place a large amount of kibbe in the middle of a big plate, and score the top of the meat in a diamond pattern with a sharp paring knife. Pour a little olive oil over the top of the meat, and arrange petals, made from the wedges of large yellow onions, all around the meat. Eat the meat on a petal of onion. Delicious!

Or you may bake the kibbe in a cake pan. Score the top as above, and pour a little olive oil over the top so that you will not dry out the meat. You might sprinkle some pine nuts or almond slivers over the top. Bake at 375° for about 35 minutes, or until the meat is lightly browned. Cut into wedges, and serve.

Look in the index under "Lebanon," and choose other dishes to go with this classic.

SERVES 4 TO 6.

*Available in any Middle Eastern store and in most delicatessens.

Lamb and Artichoke Stew
(Greece)

I have just this minute realized that writing cookbooks is much harder for me than I would have ever imagined. It is hard not because I have to explain myself but because I have to think about these recipes, and it is not even *close* to lunchtime. This lamb and artichoke stew from Greece causes me particular pain. You must make this. You must.

>   4 tablespoons butter
>   2 pounds boneless lamb, cubed
>   3 yellow onions, peeled and chopped
>   2 cloves garlic, crushed
>   ½ cup parsley, chopped
>   Salt and pepper to taste
>   1 6-ounce can tomato paste
>   1 cup dry white wine
>   2 14-ounce cans artichokes in brine, drained
>   ½ teaspoon dried dill weed
>   3 tablespoons lemon juice

In very large frying pan melt the butter. Add the lamb, and sauté until lightly browned. Remove the meat. Sauté the yellow onions along with the garlic and parsley. Place the meat, onions, garlic, and parsley in a heavy kettle, and add salt, pepper, the tomato paste, and white wine. Simmer, covered, for about 1½ hours, or until lamb is tender. Add the artichokes, dill weed, and lemon juice. Simmer until all is tender, about 1½ hours.

Serve over pilaf. Along with the stew over the pilaf serve a nice fruit tray and a large salad. I would start the meal with a pâté or terrine.

SERVES 6 TO 8.

Pâtés,
Rillettes,
Terrines,
Sausages,
Quenelles,
and Other
Dumplings

Pâtés, Rillettes, and Terrines

We Americans don't really do much with pâtés, rillettes, and terrines. We do cook a mean meat loaf, the wandering child of a good pâté, but I dislike American meat loaf because it is too dry. When we cook these meat loaves in a mold, a terrine, they maintain their moisture and color and have a lovely shape.

A pâté is a meat loaf made of meat ground very fine, literally to a paste.

A rillette is a coarse meat loaf in which the meat is cooked for a very long time until it falls apart.

A terrine is simply a molding device, and you can find it in many shapes. A bread pan works fine, though you may wish to invest in a more substantial piece of equipment or in porcelain or iron with a lovely glaze.

When a pâté is molded in a terrine, it becomes a pâté terrine; the same is true of a rillette. And some dishes are simply called terrines because they are molded meat loaves and the texture is that of ground meat, halfway between a coarse rillette and a fine-ground pâté.

In any case, it is great fun to prepare any of the following, and it is always good to know that you have a treasure in the refrigerator . . . just waiting for some special person to drop by.

You can also mold or cook many of these dishes in little individual ramekins or little casseroles. In that way each can have his or her own little terrine or rillette. It does add to the fun.

Rillettes de Porc—Potted Pork Loaf
(France)

A basic principle behind *The Frugal Gourmet* is that you always have a treasure in the refrigerator in case some charming person should stop by. This one takes some time, and I suppose it will not last long in your house anyway, but give it a try. It is a completely different way of eating pork.

> 2½ pounds pork butt, cut into 1½-inch cubes
> ½ cup water
> Salt and pepper to taste
> 1 teaspoon dried whole sage
> Bouquet garni*
> 1 teaspoon marjoram
> 3 large cloves garlic, crushed

The day before, place the pork, water, salt, pepper, sage, and bouquet garni in a heavy kettle, and simmer, covered, for 4½ hours. Check from time to time to be sure that it does not dry out, and add a bit of water if necessary.

When the pork is cooked, drain the kettle in a colander, reserving the fat, and remove the bouquet garni. Break up the pieces of meat with a fork. In a bowl mix the meat with the marjoram and garlic.

Mix all well, and place in a greased mold. Press down well into the mold, and refrigerate, covered, overnight. You may wish to top the rillettes with some of the drained fat. This will help preserve it, but it also adds to the fat content of the dish.

Serve the rillettes cold in slices, along with a nice green salad

*Wrap several sprigs of fresh parsley, along with the tops of 3 or 4 stalks of celery, 2 bay leaves, and 1 teaspoon whole thyme in a piece of cheesecloth a bit bigger than a handkerchief. Pull together the four corners, and tie with a piece of string. In this way you can use the flavors of the herbs without letting them get loose in the pot.

and some very fresh French or Italian bread. Dijon mustard and
tiny pickles are traditional in France. A good red wine is perfect
with this dish.

SERVES 8 TO 10 AS A FIRST COURSE.

Beef, Pork, and Liver Terrine

This recipe will certainly make my point about the American
meat loaf's being too dry. Once you have become accustomed to
making a molded terrine, you will probably want to try your meat
loaf recipes in such a terrine. And I bet they will work well.

> 6 slices bacon
> 1 pound ground lean beef
> 1 pound coarse-ground pork
> ½ to ¾ pound beef liver, ground very coarse or
>   chopped
> 4 cloves garlic, crushed
> 2 eggs, at room temperature
> 2 tablespoons brandy or dry sherry
> 2 teaspoons salt
> 1 teaspoon whole thyme
> ½ teaspoon marjoram
> ½ teaspoon allspice
> ½ teaspoon pepper
> 1 bay leaf

The day before, first, be sure to be ready with a mold or terrine (a
bread pan or a 2-quart terrine is fine). Cut a piece of plywood so
that it just fits inside the top of the terrine or pan. It will need to
go down into the pan far enough to press the meat.

Blanch the bacon by placing it in boiling water for just a
couple of minutes. Remove, and drain. Place 3 slices bacon on
the bottom of the mold.

Mix together all the other ingredients except for the bay leaf
and the remaining bacon slices. Place the mixture in the mold or
terrine, and top with the remaining bacon and, finally, the bay
leaf. Cover with aluminum foil, and place in a pan of water that
will come about halfway up the side of the pan.

Bake, covered, in the water bath, at 350° for 2 hours. Remove
from the oven, and pour the water from the pan. Put the mold

back into the pan, and place the wooden form on the top of the loaf. Leave the aluminum in place, but loosen the sides of the foil. Place a weight on the top of the wood to press the loaf as it cools. Cans work well. Allow the mold to cool for an hour, and then place the whole works in the refrigerator overnight.

To serve, remove from the mold, and slice. Serve on bed of lettuce along with a light wine and a bit of fruit.

SERVES 10 TO 12 AS A FIRST COURSE.

Beef and Pork Terrine with Ham

When you refrigerate a terrine, remember that you want to leave the fat and gelatin on the loaf until you are ready to serve it. It keeps much longer that way, and it remains moist and attractive.

      1 small yellow onion, peeled and diced fine
      3 tablespoons brandy or dry sherry
     ½ teaspoon whole thyme
     ½ teaspoon allspice
    1½ pounds pork, ground coarse
      1 pound ground lean beef
      3 tablespoons parsley, chopped
      2 eggs, at room temperature
     ¼ cup cream plus ¼ cup milk *or* ½ cup Half-and-
        Half
      2 teaspoons salt
     ¼ teaspoon black pepper
     10 slices bacon
     ¼ pound smoked ham, cut into thin strips
      2 bay leaves (optional)

The day before, choose a 2-quart mold or large bread pan, and prepare wooden pressing form, as on page 206.

Mix together well all the ingredients, except for the bacon, ham, and bay leaves.

Blanch the bacon in boiling water for 2 minutes. Remove, and drain.

Place half the bacon slices on the bottom of the mold or pan. Put half the mixture into the mold, and smooth it flat. Lay the ham slices lengthwise, and cover with the remaining meat mixture. Top with the remaining bacon slices and bay leaves if desired. Cover the top with aluminum foil, and bake, press, and refrigerate overnight according to directions given for the Beef, Pork, and Liver Terrine (page 206).

To serve, remove from the mold, and slice at table.

Serve as a first course with a lettuce garnish and perhaps pickles and wedges of hard-boiled eggs. A dry white wine would certainly not be rejected!

Variation: You can have great fun using vegetables for the center color in this dish. I have used frozen green beans, defrosted and blanched, and blanched carrot sticks with great success. Zucchini strips work well, too.

SERVES 10 TO 12 AS A FIRST COURSE.

Veal and Pork Pâté
(France)

I know that hamburger is not veal. Veal is very young beef, and much more delicate in flavor. The cost of veal is very high, however, and hamburger—good, lean hamburger—will work very well in this dish.

This dish is a lovely addition to your French dinners, particularly if you have a very fancy pâté mold. However, you may also use a bread pan, so let's get started!

> 1 **pound ground veal or 1 pound leanest hamburger**
> 1 **pound ground pork**
> 2 **eggs, at room temperature**
> 2 **cloves garlic, crushed**
>   **Salt and pepper to taste**
> 1 **teaspoon basil**
>   **Pinch each of rosemary and nutmeg**
> 8 **slices bacon, blanched in boiling water for 2 minutes**
>   **Brandy or dry sherry**
> 1 **cup chopped parsley**
> 8 **green onions, chopped**
> ½ **cup cooked ham, cut into strips**
> 1 **bay leaf**

The day before, mix the veal or hamburger with the pork. Add the eggs, garlic, salt, pepper, and basil. Add the rosemary and nutmeg. Line a pâté mold or bread pan with bacon slices. Mix ½ cup of brandy or dry sherry with the meat mixture, and place it in the mold until it is half full. Cover the top with the parsley, green onion, and ham. Add the rest of the meat mixture until the mold is full. Cover the top with the remaining bacon, and add the bay leaf. Pour a little more (maybe ¼ cup) brandy or sherry over the top, and you are ready to bake.

Place the mold in a pan of water. Water should reach up one-third of the side of the mold. Cover with aluminum foil and a lid, if you are using one, and place the whole in a 325° oven for about 1½ hours. You check for "doneness" by looking to see if the juices are clear rather than pink.

Remove from the oven, and remove the lid. Place a piece of wood on the top of the meat. The wood should be cut to fit the mold exactly, allowing for a little space so that the wood may press the meat down. Place a brick or cans on the board, and allow the meat to cool. When it is cool, place it in a refrigerator, still with the brick or cans, and chill. It is best the next day.

To serve, remove from the mold, and slice. Serve on beds of lettuce with a nice green salad and plenty of Chablis. If you have a fancy mold, serve it right from the mold at the table!

SERVES 8 AS AN APPETIZER.

Sausages

Italian Sausage

I got this recipe from an Italian sausagemaker in Brooklyn. After much pleading, he finally agreed to give me the recipe. "Five pounds of salt," he began, and then went on to give me the recipe for 250 pounds of meat! Just lucky for you that I cut it down a bit.

2 pounds coarse-ground lean pork
1 tablespoon coarse-ground fennel
2 bay leaves, crushed
1 tablespoon dried parsley
3 cloves garlic, crushed
⅛ teaspoon hot dried red pepper flakes
1 teaspoon salt
¼ teaspoon pepper
4 tablespoons water

Mix all the ingredients carefully, let stand for 1 hour, and mix again.

Stuff into casings, or fry plain.

MAKES 2 POUNDS.

Orange Sausage
(Greece)

Sausage with fresh orange peel in it may sound strange, but you will love this one. I like to make meatballs of this and then brown them and simmer them in a light tomato sauce.

>   1   clove garlic, crushed
>   Grated peel from ½ orange
> 1½   teaspoons salt
>   1   teaspoon cinnamon
>   1   teaspoon allspice
>   1   teaspoon pepper
>   ½   cup white wine
>   2   pounds coarse-ground beef
>   1   pound coarse-ground pork

Mix all the ingredients except the meats in a food blender. Then add to meat.

Stuff into casings, or fry plain.

MAKES 3 POUNDS.

Bratwurst
(Germany)

When I make bratwurst for my sons, they eat it until I expect the boys to look like fat bratwursts. After being cooked, these are also great for the lunch bag set.

    1 **pound coarse-ground pork**
    1 **pound coarse-ground veal or beef**
    2 **teaspoons ground celery seed**
    2 **teaspoons ground caraway seed**
    1 **tablespoon powdered milk**
    1 **egg**
    2 **teaspoons onion powder**
       Salt and pepper to taste
    ¼ **teaspoon fresh-grated lemon peel**
    1 **tablespoon dried parsley**
    3 **tablespoons water**

Combine all ingredients. Let sit for 1 hour, and mix again.
   Stuff into casings, or fry plain (best in casings).

MAKES 2 POUNDS.

Chorizo
(Mexico)

A favorite Mexican meal at our house is chorizo con huevos, or
sausage with eggs. This meat dish is also a basic necessity to a
good paella. Easy and spicy.

    1 **pound coarse-ground lean pork**
    1 **teaspoon salt**
    2 **tablespoons chili powder**
    ¼ **teaspoon cloves**
    ½ **teaspoon cinnamon**
    1 **tablespoon paprika**
    1 **clove garlic, crushed**
    1 **teaspoon oregano**
    2 **tablespoons cider vinegar**
    2 **tablespoons water**

Combine all ingredients. Stuff into casings, or fry plain (best in
casings).

MAKES 1 POUND.

Quenelles and Other Dumplings

The French have given us a lovely meat or fish dumpling called a quenelle (pronounced ke-nell). Originally I suppose these dumplings were made with scraps in an effort to avoid waste yet still create something palatable. In our time we can use inexpensive fish and chicken and enjoy a dish that is very fancy and quite rich. I contend that when something is rich in flavor, you are not likely to stuff yourself on that single item. That concept is a major component in frugal cooking.

Whitefish Quenelles
(France)

No, this is not a French gefilte fish. But very close. Very close indeed.

> 1   **pound skinless and boneless whitefish* fillets**
> ¼   **pound shrimp, peeled**
> 2   **egg whites**
> ¼   **cup whipping cream**
> 1   **teaspoon salt**
>   **Pepper to taste**
> 2   **quarts Chicken Soup Stock (page 53) or chicken bouillon**

Grind the fish and shrimp to a fine paste in a food processor. Scrape down the sides so that no lumps remain. Add the egg whites, cream, salt, and pepper, and process until light and fluffy.

Bring the chicken broth or bouillon to a simmer in a deep

---

*Any kind of whitefish will do. You might also try a mixture of whitefish and salmon.

frying pan with a lid. Using a large kitchen spoon, form 1/12 of the batter into an oval pillow. With a rubber spatula, gently scrape off the formed quenelle and slide it into the broth. Cover and poach lightly for 8 to 10 minutes.

Serve with a white sauce if you wish. Traditionally quenelles are served as a first course. However, with a salad, Baked Pasta with Sautéed Vegetables (page 145) and Fried Cucumbers (page 228), you have a complete meal.

MAKES 12.

Chicken Quenelles
(France)

If you are careful handling these little pillows of chicken, you will have a meal that will cause your guests to cheer. Don't pack them when you mold them; just roll them lightly into shape.

> 8 slices white bread
> 1¼ pounds skinless and boneless chicken meat
> ½ cup whipping cream
> 3 egg whites
> 1 teaspoon salt
>   Pinch of nutmeg
> ¼ teaspoon white pepper
> 2 tablespoons parsley, chopped
> 2 quarts Chicken Soup Stock (page 53)
>   Flour

Remove the crusts from the bread. Grind up the bread in a food processor until you have light crumbs. Remove the crumbs from the processor.

Place the chicken in the processor bowl, and grind to a paste. Scrape down the sides of the bowl to avoid any lumps. Add the cream, egg whites, salt, nutmeg, and pepper; process until very smooth. Add the bread crumbs, and process until mixed well. Add the parsley, and process for an instant, so that it is just mixed in. Refrigerate the mixture for 4 hours or so.

Bring the soup stock to a simmer in a deep frying pan with a lid. Wet your hands, and roll, do not pack, about 3 tablespoons of the mixture into a very fat cigar shape, about 3½ inches long. Prepare the whole batch, and then roll each in flour. Place the quenelles in the simmering broth, and poach, with the lid on, for 8 to 10 minutes.

Serve with a white sauce or a light gravy, or with Baked Barley Casserole (page 138), Pea Salad with Bacon (page 99), and fresh melon.

MAKES 10 TO 12.

Pork and Liver Dumplings

The French use only white meats for quenelles. However, in Germany red meats and liver make great dumplings. The following recipe uses the red meats but in a French style. It is very delicious.

    8 slices white bread
    1 pound boneless and fairly lean pork, chopped
           into small pieces
   ¼ pound beef liver
    2 egg whites
    1 teaspoon salt
   ¼ teaspoon pepper
   ¼ cup whipping cream
   ¼ cup parsley, chopped
    2 quarts Chicken Soup Stock (page 53)
       Flour

Remove the crusts from the bread, and place the slices in a food processor. Grind until you have fresh crumbs, and remove from the bowl. Place the pork in the machine, and process to a fine paste. Add the liver, and continue to process until all is fine. Scrape down the sides of the bowl so that you have no lumps.

Add the egg whites, salt, pepper, and cream; process until smooth. Then add the bread crumbs; process for just a moment, and then add the parsley; process just long enough to mix it in.

Refrigerate the mixture for at least 4 hours so that it will be easy to work with.

Bring the chicken soup stock to a simmer in a deep frying pan with a lid or in a large saucepan. Roll the dumplings into little tube shapes, using about 3 tablespoons mixture for each. When all are formed, roll each in flour, and then gently place them in the simmering broth. Cover, and simmer for 15 minutes.

Serve with a very light gravy or with butter and chopped parsley. These are great served with Boiled Red Cabbage (page 229) and a platter of Bubble and Squeak (page 247).

MAKES 10 TO 12.

Danish Meatballs
with Caper Sauce

This dish is terribly easy, inexpensive, and delicious enough to serve at a dinner party!

MEATBALLS
- 1 **hard roll, soaked in water for 15 minutes**
- 1 **pound lean ground beef**
- 1 **strip bacon, diced fine**
- 4 **flat anchovies, chopped fine**
- 1 **small yellow onion, peeled and chopped (about ¼ cup)**
- 1 **egg**
  Pepper to taste
- 2 **tablespoons white wine**
- ¼ **cup chopped parsley**

BROTH
- 6 **cups water**
- 1 **bay leaf**
- 1 **small yellow onion, peeled and chopped**
- 6 **peppercorns**
- 1 **teaspoon salt**

CAPER SAUCE
Roux of 1½ tablespoons each flour and butter
2 cups broth from the pot
1 tablespoon capers
   Juice of ½ lemon
1 tablespoon Dijon-style mustard*
1 egg yolk
   Salt and pepper to taste

Drain the soaked hard roll, and squeeze out the water. Blend with the remaining meatball ingredients. Mix well. Mold the mixture into 10 meatballs.

Bring all the broth ingredients to a heavy simmer, add the meatballs, and simmer them, covered, for 20 minutes.

While the meatballs are cooking, prepare the roux. Melt the butter and the flour together in a very small frying pan, and cook until the mixture turns a very light brown. Do not burn.

When the meatballs are finished, remove the kettle from the heat. Take 2 cups of the broth from the kettle, and place in a small saucepan. Bring to a simmer, and add the capers, lemon juice, and mustard. Thicken with the roux. Place the egg yolk in a small bowl, and beat with a fork. Slowly stir a bit of the sauce into the egg yolk. Gradually add the rest of the sauce. In this way you avoid cooking the egg yolk, and it will become a very rich thickener. Add salt and pepper.

Serve the sauce over the meatballs. Boiled potatoes are the traditional accompaniment. Beer is the proper beverage, and try Green Beans and Lettuce (page 224) for the vegetable.

SERVES 4 OR 5.

*Grey Poupon is fine.

Vegetables

Assorted Vegetables

Carrots in Beer and Dill

Most of us are not very creative with winter vegetables. This recipe will help your children enjoy fresh carrots, a vegetable we are beginning to understand is one of the healthiest foods we can eat.

    4 large carrots, peeled
    1 tablespoon butter
    1 cup beer
    ¼ teaspoon salt
    1 teaspoon sugar
    1 teaspoon dill weed, dried

Cut the carrots into small sticks and sauté in butter, uncovered, over medium heat until they are barely browned. Add the beer and dill and cover. Cook slowly until the carrots are tender, stirring often, for about 15 minutes. Add the salt and sugar and continue to cook, uncovered, for about 3 minutes more.

SERVES 4.

Green Beans with Oregano
(Italy)

Try this with another blend of herbs from your kitchen. Green beans just love to be pan-fried along with some light herbs.

    1   **clove garlic, sliced very thin**
    2   **tablespoons olive oil**
    1   **10-ounce package frozen green beans, Italian**
          cut
      Salt and pepper to taste
    ¼   **teaspoon oregano**
    1   **tablespoon lemon juice**

Sauté the garlic in the oil until lightly browned. Add the green beans, salt, pepper, and oregano, and cook, covered, until tender. Add the lemon juice, toss, and serve.

SERVES 4.

Italian Vegetable Sauté

This is a great way to serve vegetables, and they are not soggy or overdone. Many of the family-style Italian restaurants in San Francisco prepare something very close to this dish. The advantage here is simple. Everything is partially cooked ahead of time and then sautéed at the last minute. Great for your family or company.

    4   **medium carrots, peeled and sliced**
    1   **head cauliflower, divided into flowerets**
    3   **small zucchini, sliced**
    2   **cloves garlic, sliced thin**
    3   **tablespoons olive oil**
    2   **yellow onions, peeled and sliced**
      Salt and pepper to taste
    ¼   **cup beef stock**
    2   **tablespoons fresh-grated Parmesan or Romano**
          cheese

In a pot of boiling water blanch the carrots—i.e., boil them for about 5 or 6 minutes, or until they are tender; remove, and cool. Add the cauliflower to the same boiling water and cook until barely tender; remove, and cool. Add the zucchini to the pot, but do not cook long at all.

When you are ready to serve dinner, in a large frying pan or a wok sauté the garlic in the olive oil. Add the carrots, cauliflower, zucchini, and onions. Toss for a few minutes, and then add the salt, pepper, and beef stock. Cover the pan, and cook just long enough to heat everything through. Stir gently often. Sprinkle the cheese on top, and serve.

SERVES 6 TO 8.

Sautéed Squash

You can also add parsley and carrots to this dish; cook the carrots separately. Once I added a whipped egg at the very last minute.

All possibilities will go well for you as long as you remember the cardinal rule concerning the cooking of light summer squashes: *Don't.* Don't cook it to death. Rather simply get it hot and serve it.

    3 small zucchini
    1 medium yellow summer squash
    2 tablespoons peanut oil
    2 cloves garlic, sliced thin
    1 yellow onion, peeled and sliced thin
    2 ounces dried mushrooms, soaked in warm
        water, drained, and chopped (page 231) *or*
        ½ pound mushrooms, sliced
      Salt and pepper to taste
    3 tablespoons whipping cream
    3 tablespoons white wine
    2 tablespoons fresh-grated Parmesan or Romano
        cheese

Cut the squashes into matchsticks, or use a very coarse grater. Heat the oil in a large frying pan or wok, and sauté the garlic and onion until barely tender.

Add the squashes, mushrooms, salt, and pepper, and sauté for a few minutes until the vegetables are hot. Add the cream and white wine. Cook for a moment, and place in a serving bowl. Top with the cheese.

SERVES 4 TO 6.

Spinach and Artichoke Casserole

No, my wife is not happy with the fact that I love to cook. Whenever she discovers a really good dish, she claims that she gets two or three dinner parties out of the dish, and then I do it on television. This one is such a dish.

- 1 9-ounce package frozen artichoke hearts, defrosted, *or* 1 14-ounce can artichoke hearts
- 3 10-ounce packages frozen chopped spinach, defrosted
- ½ pound cream cheese
- 2 tablespoons mayonnaise
- 4 tablespoons butter or olive oil
- 6 tablespoons milk
  Pepper to taste
- ⅓ cup fresh-grated Parmesan or Romano cheese

If frozen artichokes are used, cook according to instructions. Do not overcook. Drain the artichokes, and place them on bottom of a 3-quart casserole. Squeeze as much moisture as possible from the spinach, and layer it on top of the artichokes. In an electric mixer blend the cream cheese, mayonnaise, and butter or oil until light and fluffy. Gradually beat in the milk, and spread this mixture over the top of the spinach. Sprinkle with pepper and the cheese.

Bake, uncovered, at 375° for 40 minutes, or until the top is lightly browned.

You can refrigerate this dish after putting it together and before baking it, but if it is chilled, slightly increase the baking time.

SERVES 10 TO 12.

Zucchini with Fresh Rosemary
(Italy)

This dish is delicious, but it is best with fresh rosemary. You can substitute dried whole rosemary, and you will still have a delicious dish—but I want you to put a few rosemary shrubs in your garden. They will thrive in most of the country, and you will never be without this lovely Italian herb.

    1 **clove garlic, sliced thin**
    2 **tablespoons olive oil**
    4 **zucchini, sliced**
    1 **teaspoon fresh rosemary *or* ½ teaspoon dried**
        whole rosemary
      Salt and pepper to taste

Sauté the garlic in the oil, and add the zucchini. Shake the pan to coat the squash with the oil. Add the rosemary, salt, and pepper. Cover, and simmer gently until barely tender, about 6 minutes.

SERVES 4 TO 6.

Green Beans and Lettuce
(France)

Both the Europeans and the Chinese enjoy cooked lettuce, but we Americans just have not gotten into it. We should because this combination is unusually good. Do not overcook the lettuce.

> Roux of ½ tablespoon butter and ½ tablespoon flour
> 1 10-ounce package frozen green beans, French or julienne cut
> ½ cup chicken broth
> 1 medium yellow onion, peeled and sliced
> ¼ teaspoon sugar
> Salt and pepper to taste
> Pinch each of dried dill weed and thyme
> 1 medium head iceberg lettuce

Prepare the roux by stirring the butter and flour together over medium heat until the flour begins to turn very light brown. Set aside.

Place the beans in a 3-quart saucepan along with the chicken broth and onion. Simmer until the beans are tender, and then add the sugar, salt, pepper, dill, and thyme. Simmer for 1 minute. Cut the lettuce into slices across the grain, and place in the pot. Cook for 3 minutes, and thicken with the roux.

SERVES 4 OR 5.

■ Hint:

To keep fresh vegetables green when you blanch or cook them, use a bit of peanut oil in the water. The ratio of 1 tablespoon oil to 2 or 3 quarts water preserves the bright green color.

Cold Vegetables in Mustard Dressing

This is a quick one, and you can leave it in your refrigerator for a couple of days. It will still be delicious. Don't worry about serving a cold vegetable dish at a nice dinner. Why not serve vegetables cold?

> 2 **tablespoons wine vinegar**
> 1 **tablespoon Dijon-style mustard***
>   **Salt and pepper to taste**
> 1 **egg, at room temperature**
> 1 **tablespoon lemon juice**
> 8 **tablespoons olive oil**
> 6 **carrots, peeled and sliced**
> 3 **medium zucchini, sliced**

Place the vinegar, mustard, salt, pepper, egg, and lemon juice in a food blender, and mix for 30 seconds. Slowly add the olive oil. Refrigerate. (You will not need all this for the vegetables, so you will have some left for a salad or two.)

Blanch the carrots for 10 minutes in boiling water; then add the squash. Cook for another 5 minutes, drain, and refrigerate.

When the vegetables are cold, toss them with a bit of the dressing, and serve as a vegetable side dish.

SERVES 4 TO 6.

Baked Cauliflower

An easy way to help your children love this much-maligned vegetable.

*Grey Poupon is fine.

1 **head cauliflower**
2 **eggs, beaten**
   Salt and pepper to taste
2 **tablespoons fresh-grated Parmesan or Romano**
      cheese

In a stainless steel vegetable steamer* steam the cauliflower for about 15 minutes, or until tender. When the vegetable is tender, remove it from the steamer, and place in a casserole, with a cover, just large enough to hold the head. Pour the egg over the top of the cauliflower, add salt and pepper, and top with the cheese.

Bake, covered, at 375° for 10 minutes, or until the cheese has melted and the egg is cooked.

SERVES 4 TO 6.

Zucchini Pilaf

There is no reason not to have vegetables in rice for a bit of additional color at the evening meal. This one is rather Italian, and I am willing to bet that you can think up better combinations than I.

     2 **zucchini, cut up**
     2 **tablespoons olive oil**
     2 **cloves garlic, chopped fine**
     1 **cup long-grain rice**
     2 **tablespoons butter**
  1½ **cups Chicken Soup Stock (page 53)**
    ½ **cup dry white wine**
        Salt to taste
        Fresh-grated Parmesan or Romano cheese

Sauté the zucchini in the oil and garlic. Remove from the pan. Add the rice, and brown it in the butter. Place the rice in a

*Available in any department or gourmet store.

saucepan, and add the soup stock and white wine. Bring to a boil
without lid. Add salt. Place the zucchini on the top of the rice.
Do not stir. Cover, and simmer until rice is tender, about 20
minutes.

Add the cheese when serving.

SERVES 4 TO 6.

Mixed Sautéed Vegetables

I prefer to do this kind of cooking in a wok because the Chinese
pan gets very hot quickly and allows room to throw things around
a bit. Any variation can be used in such a dish. The point here is
barely to cook the vegetables and to offer a nice variety all in one
dish.

> 2 cloves garlic, sliced thin
> 2 tablespoons olive oil
> 2 yellow onions, peeled and cut into large pieces
> 2 green peppers, cut into large pieces
> ¼ pound mushrooms, cut into large pieces
> 1 15-ounce can artichoke hearts, cut into large
>   pieces
> 1 tablespoon butter
>   Salt and pepper to taste
> 2 tablespoons dry sherry

Brown the garlic in the oil in a large frying pan. Sauté the yellow
onions, green peppers, mushrooms, and artichokes until tender
but still firm, about 8 minutes. Add the butter, salt, pepper, and
sherry. Serve right away!

SERVES 4.

Pease Porridge
(England)

This is a dish from England. Tough food for the winter, but with
a little butter you can make a lovely dish for an early American
dinner.

    **2 cups dried green split peas, rinsed and picked
        over**
**2½ cups water
    Salt to taste
    Butter
    Pepper**

Place the split peas and the water in a pan with a lid. Add a little salt, and bring to a boil, stirring. Simmer, covered, until the whole thing turns to mush, about 1 hour (you may have to add a little water). Be careful not to burn this. Stir often. When a nice mushy consistency has been reached, add a little butter, salt, and pepper, if needed.

    Serve as a side vegetable.

SERVES 6 TO 8.

Fried Cucumbers
(Germany)

A German dish that will surprise you. We do not think of cooking cucumbers and use them only in salad. Taste this, and see what you have been missing.

    **Cucumbers, unpeeled and sliced
    Butter
    Salt and pepper to taste**

Fry the cucumber in butter until barely tender. Add salt and pepper.

Boiled Red Cabbage
(England)

Shades of Charles Dickens! This dish will take on a very mellow sweet flavor, and the children may begin to call it Candy Cabbage. Mine did!

> 3 **heads red cabbage**
> 2 **cups Chicken Soup Stock (page 53)**
> ½ **cup white vinegar**
> 2 **bay leaves, crushed**
> ½ **cup brown sugar**
> ½ **stick (⅛ pound) butter**
>   **Salt and pepper to taste**

Chop up the red cabbage, being careful to remove the cores. Place in a kettle, and add the remaining ingredients. Simmer this for 1 hour or longer, or until the cabbage is sweet and tender.

SERVES 6 TO 8.

The Mushroom

The mushroom is a clear and obvious sign to me that the Creator has a totally unreasonable affection for us. Further, He will go to outlandish extremes to prove this affection. From rotting leaves and horse dung comes the mushroom, one of the most glorious foods in the world.

We have been eating mushrooms for thousands of years, though in the ancient days in Egypt you had to be a pharaoh or a member of royalty in order to be invited to taste the delicate morsel. This love of mushrooms so celebrated by the nobility of the past probably accounts for the high number of deaths attributed to poisonous fungi in that particular social level. The Roman emperors Tiberius and Claudius both may have died from a feast on the woodsy, flavored treasure, as did Alexander I of Russia, Pope Clement VII, and France's Charles V. The Enlightened One, Gautama Buddha, died in the middle of a feast of mushrooms offered in love by one of his followers, Cunda, the goldsmith. On his deathbed the Buddha thanked Cunda for the gift of the meal. Finally, that greatest of the royalty in the minds of children, Babar, king of the elephants, watched his father die after eating some delicious, but poisonous, mushrooms.

I am listing all these deaths so that you will not think that I am advocating your marching into the wild woods in search of the elusive morel. One should hunt mushrooms only after exacting training and experience; there remain many deadly varieties that offer only sickness and no joy whatsoever.

The best plan is to purchase your mushrooms from a good market or a skilled hunter. In this country the only fresh mushrooms you generally see on the market are cultivated white meadow mushrooms. As early as 200 B.C., the Greeks cultivated them, and the Europeans finally got started by Louis XIV during the 1700s.

Although the mushroom has been credited with everything from "trips" into religious insight to aphrodisiacal abilities, it is actually a very fine food product. It is high in protein, vitamins, and minerals, and there are only 66 calories in an entire pound of mushrooms.

■ HINT: Cleaning a Mushroom

The quickest way to clean a mushroom is to wipe it with a damp cloth. I see no point in scrubbing them with those silly little brushes now on the market. The soil in which mushrooms are grown is sterilized properly so you need not act like one of my cooking students who was so upset when I told her that mushrooms are grown in horse dung that she washed hers in Mr. Clean.

If you must wash them, just rinse them quickly, and then drain and dry them before cooking them. I have good luck simply brushing them clean with a small paintbrush.

Rules for Cooking Mushrooms
Do not wash unless you have to.
Do not peel.
Do not soak.
Do not overcook.

Types of mushrooms available:
White Meadow Mushroom: fresh in all supermarkets.

Dried European Mushroom: cepé, boletus, or porcini. These are delicious, but if they come from Europe, they will be terribly expensive. Find an Italian market that brings them in from South America, and you will pay only somewhere between $10 and $14 a pound. The real Italian dried mushroom will cost you a fortune! You may also find some that are domestic. In any case, keep them in a tightly sealed jar at the back of your refrigerator, where they will keep for a year.

Chanterelle: the most elegant of the wild mushrooms. Can be purchased dried or canned, rarely fresh because no one is willing to give them up!

Morel: dark-capped beauty. Canned or dried.

Japanese Enoki-dake: fresh, tiny, slender-stalked. Expensive but very "in" with the nouvelle cuisine crowd as a garnish.

Chinese Black: dried. Soak in tepid water for 1 hour before use. Not expensive if you buy them in a Chinese market.

Japanese Shiitaki: very similar to Chinese black. Dried; some supermarkets carry them fresh. Expensive.

Chinese Straw Mushroom: so tender sometimes called a jelly mushroom. Very fragile. You will see them only canned.

Cloud's Ears: Chinese black fungus. Look like wood chips when purchased, but when soaked, they become delicious and tender. They can also be purchased in white and are called silver ears. A less expensive and thicker version of the tree fungus is also black and called Juda's ears. All must be soaked before being cooked.

■ HINT: Mushroom Powder (France)

Chop up ¼ pound dried mushrooms, and then grind them to a flourlike powder in your food blender or electric coffee grinder (I find that the coffee grinder works best for this). Don't even try a food processor because the mushrooms will get stuck on the edges of the blade. Do them in small batches.

Keep the mushroom powder in a tightly capped jar in the refrigerator. When preparing a gravy or sauce, soup or stew that lacks flavor, sprinkle a bit of this marvelous powder into the pot.

Mushrooms à la Provençale
(France)

I divide the peoples of the world into two groups: those who love mushrooms and those who do not. Mushroom lovers will read this recipe and begin to shake. It is very good.

    2 cloves garlic, crushed
    ½ small yellow onion, peeled and chopped
    4 tablespoons butter or olive oil
    1 pound white mushrooms, sliced
      Salt and pepper to taste
    ¼ cup fresh-ground bread crumbs
    ¼ cup parsley, chopped

Sauté the garlic and yellow onion in the butter or oil until soft.
Add the mushrooms, and sauté over high heat until all vegetables
are hot and tender; do not overcook. Add the salt, pepper, bread
crumbs, and parsley. Toss, and serve.

SERVES 4 TO 6 AS A SIDE DISH.

Cream of Mushroom Soup

In Chicago every Polish restaurant has a mushroom soup that you
cannot believe. The secret is the use of both dried and fresh
mushrooms. Read the instructions about finding these marvelous
dried mushrooms, and you will have a grand time cooking.

CHICKEN BROTH
    3 pounds chicken backs and necks
    2 quarts water
    4 stalks of celery, chopped
    6 carrots, chopped
    1 yellow onion, peeled and chopped

    1 ounce dried European mushrooms
 1½ cups water
    1 pound white mushrooms, sliced
    2 tablespoons butter or peanut oil
      Roux of 4 tablespoons flour and 4 tablespoons
        oil or butter
    3 cups cream *or* milk *or* Half-and-Half
    2 teaspoons chervil
    ½ cup dry sherry
      Salt and pepper to taste
      Sugar (optional)

Bring all the broth ingredients to a simmer, and then cook for 2 hours. Add water during the cooking time in order to keep it up to proper level. Drain, and refrigerate. Remove the fat.

Soak the dried mushrooms in 1½ cups water for 1 hour. Drain, and add the water to the chicken broth. Chop the mushrooms fairly fine, and sauté for 5 minutes in a little oil.

Sauté the white mushrooms in 2 tablespoons butter or oil. When they are tender but not discolored (do not overcook), remove them from the heat.

Bring the broth to a boil. Add the dried mushrooms. Prepare the roux by lightly pouring the flour in the butter or oil. Remove the stockpot from the burner, and stir in the roux. Return the stockpot to the heat, and stir until slightly thickened. Add the white mushrooms, and simmer for 10 minutes. Add the cream or milk or Half-and-Half, chervil, sherry, salt, pepper, and sugar if you wish.

Serve hot or ice-cold (I prefer this dish very hot).

SERVES 10 TO 12.

Two-Mushroom Sauté

I just love mushrooms on the side, and these two belong together. You might even chill the remains of this dish and use them in a salad.

    ½ ounce dried European mushrooms
   1½ cups tepid water
    ½ pound white mushrooms, sliced
    2 green onions, chopped
    2 tablespoons butter or olive oil
       Salt and pepper to taste
    ¼ cup sweet vermouth
    1 tablespoon lemon juice

Soak the dried mushrooms in the water for 1 hour. Drain, and chop. Squeeze out most of the water.

Sauté both mushrooms, along with the green onions, in the butter or oil until barely tender; do not overcook. Add the salt, pepper, vermouth, and lemon juice. Toss until everything is hot. Serve hot.

SERVES 3 OR 4 AS A SIDE DISH.

Mushrooms Steamed in Custard

    ¼ **pound white mushrooms, sliced**
    Butter
    Steamed Custard (page 302)

Sauté the mushrooms in butter until barely tender. Blend in with the steamed custard mixture, omitting the ham and onions, and steam as directed.

SERVES 2.

Marinated Mushrooms

    ½ **pound mushrooms**
    Basic Fennel Dressing (page 90)

Clean the mushrooms, rinse if necessary, and pat dry with paper towels. Marinate overnight in the fennel dressing.

SERVES 6 TO 8 AS HORS D'OEUVRE.

Straw Mushrooms and Baby Corn
(China)

A very elegant and rare dish from Peking. The straw mushroom cannot be found fresh, only in cans. It is so delicate that I have never seen it fresh. This dish is so unusual that you will not feel bad about the mushrooms being canned.

    1 **clove garlic, crushed**
    ½ **teaspoon fresh-grated ginger**
    1 **tablespoon peanut oil**
    1 **15-ounce can baby corn, drained**
    2 **tablespoons oyster sauce**
    4 **tablespoons chicken broth**
    ⅛ **teaspoon sugar**
    1 **15-ounce can straw mushrooms, drained**

In a hot frying pan or wok, sauté the garlic and ginger in the oil. Add the corn, and sauté until hot. Add the oyster sauce, chicken broth, and sugar. Stir, and toss. When the mixture is hot, add the mushrooms, and stir gently, over high heat, until all is hot.

Serve with rice or noodles.

SERVES 3 OR 4.

Mushroom Quiche

Mushroom quiche is a favorite of mine. You might also try this with a bit of dried dill weed added.

- ½ **pound white mushrooms, sliced**
- 2 **tablespoons butter**
- 3 **green onions, chopped**
  Salt and pepper to taste

Sauté the mushrooms in the butter, along with the green onions. When vegetables are barely tender, add the salt and pepper, and proceed with a basic quiche recipe and filling (page 117).

SERVES 6 TO 8.

Shrimp and Fungus
(China)

We know that the color of food changes our opinion of the food. For instance, Alfred Hitchcock once served a buffet in which every food was blue or dyed blue. I think the names of dishes do the same thing. If we were to call this dish something else, perhaps you would concentrate on it. But Shrimp and Fungus? Yes, all mushrooms are fungi. So enjoy. This is a fine dish. And very rich.

2 ounces dried cloud's ears fungus
2 cups tepid water
½ pound large shrimp, shelled
1 tablespoon light soy sauce
½ teaspoon fresh-grated ginger
1 tablespoon dry sherry
1 clove garlic, crushed
½ tablespoon peanut oil
2 tablespoons chicken broth
2 tablespoons oyster sauce
½ tablespoon cornstarch mixed with ½ tablespoon
      cold water
   Pinch of sugar

Soak the fungus in the water for ½ hour. Drain.

Clean the shrimp, and marinate them in the soy sauce, ginger, and sherry for about 15 minutes.

Sauté the garlic in the peanut oil in a hot wok or frying pan just for a moment. Drain the shrimp, and sauté them with the garlic until they change color and are white and reddish, rather than gray. Add the fungus, and cook for a few minutes, or until everything is hot. Mix together the chicken broth, oyster sauce, cornstarch and water mixture, and sugar. Add to the pan. Sauté until the sauce thickens.

Serve with rice or noodles.

SERVES 4 AS PART OF CHINESE DINNER.

The Onion

The history of the onion goes back so far that we simply have lost track of this marvelous lily bulb. Yes, all onions are lilies. The onion as we know it probably came originally from Asia or Palestine and was already common in ancient Egypt, where it was worshiped as a minor god. (No wonder. Can you imagine our life without onions?)

Onions You Will Most Often See in the Market:

Yellow Onion: most common and most versatile.

White Bermuda Onion: great for salads; eat raw.

Spanish Onion: same use as the yellow onion.

Purple Salad Onion: raw on salads.

Tiny White Onion or Boiling Onion: peel and boil; serve with a white or cream sauce.

Walla Walla Sweet: a specialized onion from Washington State that is very sweet and lovely for salads.

Vidalia: a prizewinning onion from Georgia that is to be used as the Walla Walla (both onions are very fragile and are seen on the market only during a very short growing season).

Stuffed Onion Leaves
(Armenia)

This dish takes a bit of time for preparation, but it is certainly not complicated, and the results are spectacular.

4 or 5 very large yellow onions
1 pound ground lean lamb or beef
1 teaspoon ground cinnamon
1 teaspoon ground allspice
  Fresh-ground pepper and salt to taste
½ cup long-grain rice, soaked in water for ½ hour,
  then drained
3 ripe tomatoes, diced
  Olive oil
⅓ cup beef stock

Onion Leaves

Place the whole unpeeled onions (the larger the better) in a pot, and cover with water. Bring the water to a boil; then turn down to a simmer. Cover, and simmer the onions for 20 minutes. Remove, drain, and cool the onions so that you can handle them.

Filling*

Mix together the lamb or beef. Add the cinnamon, allspice, pepper, salt, and rice. Mix well, and then add the tomatoes. Gently mix again, being careful not to squeeze the juice out of the tomatoes.

*For an interesting variation you might also add some dried dill weed and *some* cardamom to the filling. This would make the dish very Moroccan.

Grand Construction

Cut the top and the bottom from the cooked unpeeled onions. Slice into the onion by making a cut down the side of the onion that goes to the center of the onion. Remove the outer skin, and then, very carefully, remove the large outer leaves of the onion. (Save the center of the onion, the core, for some other dish.) You will get about five or six leaves from each large onion.

Place a bit of the filling in the middle of each onion leaf, and roll it up like a fat sausage. The skins will practically roll themselves, so let the onion do the work.

When all are rolled, select a large frying pan with a tight-fitting lid (a heavy kettle will do also; you need something large enough to hold all the onion rolls in one layer). When the pan is hot, add a bit of olive oil and then the stuffed onions, all in one layer. Cook for a few minutes on medium heat until they begin barely to brown on the bottom. Add the beef stock, and cover. Simmer for 40 minutes, and enjoy.

Serve with a light salad and a side of green vegetable. A dry white wine is perfect.

SERVES 6 TO 8.

Onions Marinated with Feta
(Greece)

This is a simple dish, but the flavor is delightful. I use a sweet onion such as Walla Walla or Vidalia, although a white Bermuda will do well. A purple onion gives this "white on white" dish a little more color.

    2   to 3 sweet onions, peeled and sliced paper-thin
    ¼   pound feta cheese, crumbled
        Parsley or green pepper, chopped (optional)
    ¼   cup olive oil
    2   tablespoons white wine vinegar
    2   tablespoons lemon juice
    ½   teaspoon dried oregano
        Salt and pepper to taste
        Sugar to taste (optional)

Place the onion slices and feta cheese in a bowl, along with the parsley or green pepper if desired. Mix together the oil, vinegar, lemon juice, oregano, salt, and pepper. Add to onion and cheese, and allow to marinate for 2 or 3 hours before serving. You may need a pinch of sugar if the dressing is too tart for your taste.

This is a great side dish for practically any meal.

SERVES 5 TO 6 PERSONS.

Jewish Stuffed Onions
(Israel)

I could not help overhearing one of our cameramen comment, "Good Lord, today he is stuffing onions." I am not easily hurt, and I sent the recipe home for his girl friend. He asked for it!

8 large onions, peeled
½ pound beef or lamb, ground (I prefer lamb)
¼ teaspoon allspice, ground
¼ teaspoon dill weed, dried
2 tablespoons lemon juice
2 tablespoons fresh parsley, chopped
　Salt and pepper to taste
1 raw egg
2 tablespoons all-purpose flour
3 tablespoons olive oil
　Juice of additional fresh lemon

Cut the onions in half, cutting across the onion, not from bottom to top, and scoop out the cores. Chop 3 tablespoons of the cores and add to the meat, allspice, dill weed, lemon juice, parsley, salt, pepper, and egg. Fill the onions with this mixture, leaving a bit of the meat overflowing from the top of the onion to form a crown. Dust the meat tops with flour and fry them, meat side down, in the oil, just until brown. Put the onion cores in another saucepan and add the juice of the lemon and just enough water to cover this onion bed, which will act as a steamer. Put the filled onions, meat side up, over this bed. Simmer, covered, for about 1 hour or until the onions are soft, adding water from time to time if the onion-core bed should become too dry.

Complete the meal with Carrot Ring (page 404), Cucumber Salad (page 405), and Blintzes (page 407) for dessert.

SERVES 12.

Onions Sautéed with Peppers
(Italy)

Talk about rich food! This dish may be a little much for you if you serve it in place of a vegetable. Better to serve it along with other vegetables. It will be a hit.

> 3 to 4 yellow onions, peeled and sliced
> 2 cloves garlic, crushed
> 3 tablespoons olive oil
> 2 green peppers, sliced
> 2 red bell peppers, sliced
> 2 tablespoons tomato paste
>   Salt and pepper to taste
> 3 tablespoons red wine
> 1 teaspoon oregano
>   Dash of Tabasco (optional)
>   Fresh-grated Parmesan or Romano cheese

Sauté the onions and the garlic in the oil just until tender. Add the peppers, and sauté for a few minutes more. Stir in all remaining ingredients except for the cheese. Place in a small, deep baking dish or casserole, and top with the cheese. Bake at 375° for 45 minutes.

SERVES 6 AS A SIDE DISH.

■ HINT:

To peel small onions for boiling or sautéing, simply place them in boiling water and let them simmer for a few minutes. Drain and cool them. The onions can be peeled in a few minutes.

Onions Baked in Cinders
(France)

We know the onion is very old, and we can only guess who first thought up this method of baking the onions in the cinders of the campfire—peel and all. It was not a chef de haute cuisine. It was probably a thief in the night.

> 12 **medium yellow onions**
> 6 **tablespoons olive oil**
> 2 **tablespoons wine vinegar**
> 3 **cloves garlic, peeled and crushed**
>   **Chopped parsley**
>   **Salt and fresh-ground black pepper to taste**

Wrap the unpeeled onions individually in aluminum foil. Push into the coals of the fire or barbecue, and leave for 30 to 40 minutes. Or place in a 375° oven for 1 hour.

Make a dressing of the remaining ingredients.

Unwrap the onions carefully, remove the skins, and serve hot, with a little of the dressing poured over each one.

SERVES 12.

Baked Whole Onions
(England)

These were served at open theaters during the sixteenth and seventeenth centuries. We have them each Christmas along with the roasted goose.

> **Several medium yellow onions**
> **Chicken broth**
> **Melted butter**
> **Paprika**
> **Bread crumbs**

Peel the onions, and simmer them in chicken broth to cover for 30 minutes. Remove, and place in a buttered baking pan. Mix melted butter with a little paprika, and brush the onions with this mixture. Sprinkle the tops of the onions with bread crumbs, and add butter and paprika. Bake at 375° for about 20 minutes, or until lightly browned.

■ HINT: To Clean a Yellow Onion in a Hurry

First cut the bottom end off the onion (you will be much less likely to cry). Then cut off the top end. Cut a slash in the side of the onion, horizontally, and remove the first outer peel of the onion, including the skin. Save the peel for your soup stock; it will give the stock nice color and flavor.

The Potato

There are some things in the world that we take so much for granted that we do not understand the impact that they have made upon our culture. I am thinking of the printing press, which changed the whole concept of living in private spaces since one needed a place in which to read. Or the refrigerator, which meant that one did not have to shop every day . . . and life gradually became even more private. And the birth control pill, which changed the path and course of American banking since young people were able to plan the birthing of their children and therefore the purchasing of their housing.

The potato has had an equally profound influence upon the Western world.

It is one of those American foods that came to us by a very strange route. The conquistadors from Spain found the potato common food among the Incas in South America during the 1500s. The Spanish thought the small, peanut-shaped potato looked like truffles and called it *tartuffo*. The Germans call it *Kartoffel* and the Russians call it *Kartofel*. Actually, the conquistadors were not terribly fond of these tiny brown creatures. They preferred the sweet potato that they found in the markets of the South American cities; in Ecuador this root was called a *batata*, and the white potato got its Spanish name, *patata*, from *batata*.

From Spain the new food product moved into France in 1540. The French, however, were not eager to see it as a food product. It was probably poison, according to the thinkers of the day, and they recommended it be used only as an ornamental plant, what with the nice leaves and all. It was called *pomme de terre*, or apple of the earth. This should not sound strange; many fruits and vegetables, including the eggplant and the tomato, were called apples during the Middle Ages. It probably accounts for the fact that fruit on the tree in the Garden of Eden, which is never fully explained, was called an apple during the Middle Ages.

245

In 1785 Antoine Augustin Parmentier, a French botanist who listed the potato along with such useless plants as the acorn and the lily, decided that the tuber could be eaten in times other than those of drastic famine. He went so far as to present a bouquet of potato flowers to Louis XVI with the admonition "Sire, from now on famine is impossible!"

The remark concerning a potato's preventing famine was well founded. The root was fed only to prisoners and the destitute in Parmentier's time, and while he himself was in prison the constant diet of potato caused him to reconsider its value. His research later proved that enough potatoes to feed a family can be grown on a quarter to a sixth of the ground that it would take to produce the amount of grain to do the same feeding job. The potato was launched!

The bulb was brought to the American colonies during the early 1700s, and it proved to be a lifesaver. It also proved to be a problem. People began to depend upon the potato for daily food, and the drought and the famine of the 1840s, which hit both this country and the British Isles, caused many Irish families, similarly inclined to depend upon the potato, to come to this country in a search for food. Today we grow 160 varieties of the vegetable in this country alone, and most of them come from California. Washington State and Idaho produce potatoes of very high quality, and in our time even gourmets are wont to eat a fine baked potato with dinner, sometimes nothing else! We now eat 100 pounds of potatoes per year per person in this country, and more than half that amount comes in the form of processed potatoes.

I am a purist when it comes to a potato. I want to make it from scratch, and I mean to enjoy it. You will enjoy these recipes as well.

Marilyn's Baked Potato with Bay Leaf

Marilyn was my producer at KING-TV, NBC, in Seattle for two years. No matter what I had thought up for a cooking demonstration, dear Marilyn had another recipe. She is a fine cook and a gracious and flamboyant woman.

If you avoid the salt in this dish, it will be great for low-salt/low-fat dieters. You won't even miss it.

> 1 **baking potato**
> 1 **bay leaf**
>   **Salt and pepper to taste**
>   **Butter (optional)**

Split the raw potato down the middle, and insert a whole bay leaf. Add salt, pepper, and a dot of butter if desired, and wrap in aluminum foil. Bake at 425° for about 40 minutes, or until tender.

SERVES 1.

Bubble and Squeak
(England)

This is an old dish from Wales and Ireland, and in its original form it is not very exciting. The original recipe called for potatoes and cabbage cooked in a pan. I have added some special ingredients that make this old British dish a real treat.

> 3 **unpeeled potatoes, boiled**
> 4 **cups cabbage, chopped and blanched**
> ½ **medium yellow onion, peeled and chopped**
> 1 **zucchini, grated**
> 3 **slices bacon, chopped and browned (save the
>   fat)**
> ¼ **cup chopped ham**
>   **Fresh-ground black pepper to taste**

Mash the unpeeled potatoes with your hands (we don't want to mash these too much, just smash them up). Add the rest of the ingredients except for the reserved bacon fat, and toss gently to mix.

Heat a frying pan (preferably one with a SilverStone lining). Place the bacon fat in the pan, and press the potato mixture in on top. Brown over medium-low to medium heat until golden brown on the bottom. This will probably take about ½ hour. Invert onto a plate, and serve.

Delicious with a beer and a nice green salad.

SERVES 4 TO 6.

Potato Bird's Nests

This very dramatic dish is really simple, but you need a pair of metal strainers for the frying process. Ask for a potato bird-nest fryer in any gourmet shop.

6 potatoes
2 pints peanut oil

Peel the potatoes, and keep in salted water so that they will not discolor. Grate them into coarse pieces, and press dry.

In a saucepan heat the oil to 380°. Dip the frying basket once into the pan to oil it. Take the baskets apart, and fill the bottom basket with the grated potato, forming a basket of potato within the wire basket. Replace the smaller basket within the larger, and clamp shut. Deep-fry until golden brown, about 3 minutes.

To remove, gently take out the smaller basket. Knock out the potato basket by gently tapping the wire frame, upside down, on the counter. The potato basket will fall out. Drain on paper towels.

Fill these potato baskets with anything from leftover stew to cold chicken salad. An old French classic consists of creamed peas and tiny onions in a bird's nest. The crisp and delicious basket will make the plate.

MAKES 8.

Piped Potato Border

Prepare mashed potatoes in your usual way. Be sure the potatoes have been well drained before they are mashed and have not been overcooked because they will be too wet. After the mashing, place the potatoes in an electric mixer, and whip in 1 egg for each 2 large potatoes.

Fill a large piping bag with the potato mixture, and pipe a large and attractive border around a large metal or ovenproof plate. Broil until the border barely begins to brown. Fill the center of the plate with vegetables, meats, or heavy stews.

Potato Cakes Filled
with Vegetables
(France)

We Americans are funny, aren't we? We will work long and hard to cook a piece of meat in a particular way but spend little time on the vegetables. My sister-in-law Carolyn thinks a really fancy dinner consists of opening *two different* packages of frozen prepared vegetables in those thick sauces.

This dish will take some time, but the crowd will pay less attention to the meat course.

> 2 **pounds (about 6 medium) potatoes**
> 6 **tablespoons butter**
> 2 **whole eggs**
>   **Salt and pepper to taste**
> ⅛ **teaspoon nutmeg**
> 1 **cup Mirepoix of Vegetables (page 278)**
> 1 **egg, beaten**

Peel and cut the potatoes into quarters. Boil in salted water until tender. Drain, and place the pan in a hot oven for a few moments to remove excess moisture. Mash the potatoes well. Then return the pan to the stove, and stir about a few moments in order to get rid of more moisture. Let potatoes cool a bit.

Place potatoes in an electric mixer, and blend in the butter, whole eggs, salt, pepper, and nutmeg. Shape into 16 balls, and allow to cool.

When the balls are cool, flatten each into a thick, little round patty. Place 8 on a greased baking sheet, and put 2 tablespoons of the mirepoix in the center of each. Place the second patty on top of the first, and press together. Brush with the beaten egg, and bake in a 375° oven for about 15 to 20 minutes, or until golden and hot.

SERVES 8.

Potatoes, Old French Style

This is a very simple but elegant dish from nineteenth-century France.

> 2 **pounds boiling potatoes**
> 1 **medium yellow onion, peeled and chopped**
> 2 **tablespoons flour**
> 4 **tablespoons olive oil**
> 2 **tablespoons parsley, chopped**
> ¼ **teaspoon ground nutmeg**
> **Salt and pepper to taste**
> **Grated rind and juice of 1 lemon**

Peel and cut the potatoes into quarters. Parboil in salted boiling water for 3 minutes, and then drain. Mix all the remaining ingredients, except for the lemon juice, in a large salad bowl. Place in a buttered baking dish, and drizzle a little more oil on the top if you wish. Bake in 450° oven for 20 to 25 minutes, or until nicely browned and tender. Pour the lemon juice over the top just before serving.

Keep this dish very hot until you serve it.

SERVES 6 TO 8.

Potato Salad with Pesto
(Italy)*

This one is simple and most unusual. Boil new or red potatoes with the skins on, cool them, then chop them into salad-size chunks. Toss with chopped green onions and pesto sauce, which you can make yourself or purchase commercially.

Greek Potato Salad

A gift to me from the wife of our Greek Orthodox priest in Tacoma. This one is a little different from regular potato salad. Since it has no mayonnaise, it can be considered low-fat if you cut down on the amount of olive oil.

> 2 **pounds unpeeled new potatoes, cooked and**
>   **cooled**
> 2 **medium yellow onions, peeled and sliced very**
>   **thin**
> ½ **cup parsley, chopped**
> ½ **cup olive oil**
> ¼ **cup white wine vinegar**
> 2 **teaspoons whole oregano, crumbled in your**
>   **hand**
>   **Salt and pepper to taste**

Cut up potatoes, and toss with all the remaining ingredients.

I prefer this chilled and served the next day, though it can be served hot.

SERVES 6 TO 8.

*Another great dish from the Little City Antipasto Restaurant in San Francisco.

The Tomato

I cannot imagine what our American culture would do without tomatoes. Pizza, catsup, tomato soup, spaghetti sauce—all very "American foods"—would not be.

The history of this lovely goes back to the Americas, not to Europe. The *tomatl* was being cultivated in ancient times by the Nahuatls of Mexico, and when Cortés rumbled through that great nation, gathering treasures with which to fascinate the European, he knew only that the red fruit would cause some interest at home. The fruit traveled throughout Western Europe in a very short time and was discussed by Italian herbalists as early as 1554, though the discussion centered on the fact that the tomato was surely poisonous and a narcotic.

The "American" fruit was brought to this country by the early colonists and enjoyed great popularity with the likes of Tom Jefferson, who not only grew the fruit at Monticello but classified and listed several varieties.

When you wander through a supermarket, it is hard to believe that some Americans as recently as 1900 considered the tomato poisonous. It has also been labeled an aphrodisiac, a medicine, a vegetable when it is actually a fruit, and a low form of produce that will never amount to much.

The contemporary market carries many varieties, and the uses for this once exotic fruit are almost endless.

Broiled French Tomatoes

This simple dish will add color and flavor to almost any dinner. Just remember that your children will simply leave the table if you overcook these. They should be hot but firm.

4 ripe tomatoes, cut in half
   Salt and pepper to taste
2 cloves garlic, crushed
2 tablespoons olive oil
½ cup bread crumbs
   Dried basil
   Fresh-grated Parmesan or Romano cheese

Slice the tomatoes in half, cutting across the grain. Arrange on a baking sheet. Add salt and pepper.

Mix the garlic, oil, and bread crumbs together, and spread a bit on the open face of each tomato half. Sprinkle a bit of basil on each, and top with about 1 teaspoon cheese for each tomato.

Broil until the cheese melts a bit and turns a lovely golden brown. Remove from the oven, and heat the oven to 375°. Heat the tomatoes for about 15 minutes before serving. Do not overcook, or they will be mushy.

SERVES 8.

Broiled Italian Tomatoes

Prepare the recipe for Broiled French Tomatoes above, omitting the bread crumbs and adding a bit of oregano along with the basil.

Tomato Sauté

This is an attractive and tasty dish that will add color to any plate. Be careful not to overcook the tomatoes.

2 cloves garlic, crushed
1 yellow onion, peeled and chopped
3 stalks celery, chopped
3 tablespoons olive oil
6 tomatoes, cut into large dice
   Salt and pepper to taste
2 tablespoons butter

Sauté the garlic, yellow onion, and celery in the oil. When the vegetables are tender but still firm, add the tomatoes (if you have cut the tomatoes into large dice using a very sharp knife, you should not have a wet mess on your hands). Add a bit of salt and pepper, and just heat the tomatoes. Garnish with butter, and serve hot.

SERVES 8 AS A VEGETABLE DISH.

Tomato Soup

This is so common in our culture, but few of us have ever eaten tomato soup that was fresh. Most of us simply remember the canned soup lunches that we used to have in grade school. Please try this one.

> 6 ripe tomatoes, chopped
> 2 tablespoons butter or oil
> 3 cups Chicken Soup Stock (page 53)
> 1 cup milk or cream
>   Salt and pepper to taste
>   Butter
>   Celery leaves for garnish

Sauté the tomatoes in the butter or oil until they are tender. Mix the tomatoes with the soup stock, and simmer for 20 minutes. Run the mixture through a food blender. Put back into the saucepan, and add the milk or cream and a pat of butter. Heat, and serve with celery leaf garnish.

SERVES 4 TO 6.

■ HINT: To Peel a Tomato—*two quick methods*

Hold the tomato on the end of a fork, and turn the fork over a gas burner until the skin begins to darken and blister. The skin will come right off.

Or place the ripe tomatoes in boiling water, and remove from the heat. Let them sit for 1 minute, and the skin will come off with little effort. Be sure to plunge the tomatoes into cold water when you remove them from the heat. You do not want to cook them, just to peel them.

Tomato and Vodka Appetizer

The flavor of this combination is recognizable. Virginia Miller, the wife of my doctor, is a serious entertainer, and she serves these on a warm summer evening. Really a hit.

    1 box ripe cherry tomatoes
    ¼ cup very cold vodka
    2 tablespoons kosher salt

Blanch the tomatoes, cool in cold water, and peel. Arrange in a bowl with a toothpick in each. Instruct guests to dip the tomato into the vodka and then into a tiny bit of kosher salt. And they have a Bloody Mary on a stick!

Stuffed Tomatoes, Middle Eastern Style
(Lebanon)

The Middle Eastern chefs are so clever with vegetables and spices. We rarely think of spicing up vegetables with cinnamon and allspice. In this dish you will find a refreshing surprise.

    ½ cup long-grain rice
    ½ pound hamburger
    1 yellow onion, peeled and chopped
    6 tomatoes
    ½ teaspoon cinnamon
    ½ teaspoon allspice
      Salt and pepper to taste

Cook the rice, and set aside.
    Brown the hamburger along with the onion. Allow to cool.
    Core the tomatoes so that they can be stuffed. Use a very sharp knife, and cut a circle about 2 inches in diameter around the

stem point. With a spoon remove the center pulp (save pulp for soup).

Mix the hamburger and onions with the cinnamon, allspice, salt, pepper, and rice. Fill each of the tomato cups with the filling, leaving a bit on the top. Do not pack down. Bake at 350° for 15 to 20 minutes.

SERVES 6.

Sauces

Béchamel Sauce—
White Sauce
(Greece, France)

Though this basic white sauce has a French name, it was invented
by the Greeks. It appeared in Greek cuisine 150 years before it
was seen in France. The Greeks were never given credit for this
sauce or for many other dishes.

> 2 cups milk
> 3 tablespoons yellow onion, chopped
> 1 bay leaf
>   Cayenne pepper to taste
> ½ stick (⅛ pound) butter
> 3 tablespoons flour
>   Salt to taste

Bring the milk to a simmer. Add the yellow onion, bay leaf, and
cayenne pepper. Simmer for a few minutes, and strain the milk
stock. Return to the stove. Melt the butter, and stir in the flour.
Remove the milk from its burner and stir in the flour-butter mixture. Continue to simmer, stirring until thick, about 10 minutes.
Add salt.

This fine white sauce is good for creamed meat dishes, fish,
and I put it over chicken before baking it.

MAKES 2½ CUPS.

Mornay Sauce
(France)

Once you have a béchamel prepared, you can do many other things with this basic sauce, such as the following cheese sauce.

    ¼ cup fresh-grated Parmesan or Romano cheese
    1 cup Béchamel Sauce (above)
      Dash of Worcestershire sauce to taste
    1 tablespoon dry sherry
      Salt and pepper to taste

Stir the Parmesan or Romano into the béchamel sauce. Add a little Worcestershire and dry sherry, and additional salt and pepper if needed.

Great on poached fish or shrimp (cover shrimp, and bake until sauce begins to brown; you might want to top with a little more cheese).

MAKES 1 CUP.

Hollandaise Sauce
(France)

The great and rich egg lemon sauce of France! The old method of preparation was time-consuming and not always foolproof. This method, using a food blender, works very well and is totally simple.

    4 egg yolks, at room temperature
    ½ teaspoon salt
    ½ teaspoon dry mustard
    1 tablespoon lemon juice
      Shot of Tabasco
    ¼ pound butter, melted

Into a blender place the yolks, salt, mustard, lemon juice, and Tabasco. Blend for 3 seconds. Then, while blender is going, pour in the butter, which should be hot. (The temperature of the butter is the secret: Make it very hot without burning it, and the hollandaise will thicken immediately.)

Serve on vegetables, poached eggs, or meats.

MAKES 1 CUP.

Béarnaise Sauce
(France)

Here we are actually preparing a reduced béarnaise that we will then stir into the hollandaise. You can make this days ahead and refrigerate until you need it.

> ½ teaspoon coarse-cracked black pepper
> ½ tablespoon whole tarragon leaves
> 4 tablespoons white wine vinegar
> ¼ cup chopped shallots or yellow onion
> ½ cup beef stock
> ½ cup dry red wine

In a small frying pan simmer the black pepper, tarragon, and vinegar until the vinegar is almost gone. Add some shallots or yellow onion, and simmer for a moment. Add the beef stock and wine. Reduce the liquid to half.

This is reduced béarnaise. Keep in closed container in your refrigerator. When you want to make béarnaise sauce, simply add a little of this reduction to hollandaise.

Béarnaise! Fine on beef steaks or hamburger.

Glaçage
(France)

This is simply a hollandaise sauce to which you have added some unsweetened whipped cream. Try this on vegetables or omelets. Lovely.

Bordelaise Sauce
(France)

You may add garlic to this sauce, but in France it is traditionally made without it.

>   1 **cup red wine**
>   1 **cup Basic Brown Soup Stock (page 47)**
>   ¼ **pound mushrooms, sliced**
>   3 **tablespoons chopped shallots or yellow onion**
>   **Garlic, crushed (optional)**
>   1 **tablespoon butter or marrow fat**
>   2 **tablespoons parsley, chopped**
>   **Salt and pepper to taste**
>   1 **tablespoon cornstarch mixed with 2 tablespoons**
>   **water**

Place the wine and soup stock together in a small saucepan and reduce the liquid to half. Sauté the mushrooms and shallots or onion and optional garlic in the butter or fat until tender; add to the reduced wine and stock mixture. Add the parsley, salt, and pepper, and simmer for a few minutes. Thicken with the cornstarch and water mixture.

Delicious on meats of any kind.

MAKES 1½ CUPS.

Velouté Sauce
(France)

This very simple sauce is used in the preparation of other, more complex sauces.

>   **Chicken Soup Stock (page 53)**
>   **Roux of half flour browned in half butter**

Thicken the soup stock with the roux. Then simmer it for 1 hour.

This rich sauce may then be flavored with a host of other ingredients. Try adding some lemon and dill, and use with vegetables.

Tomato Sauce

Keep some of this on hand at all times. It will keep for several days, and it is most useful in the frugal kitchen.

    3 tablespoons olive or peanut oil
    2 carrots, chopped
    2 stalks celery, chopped
    1 yellow onion, chopped
    ½ green pepper, chopped
    2 cloves garlic, crushed
    3 cups canned tomato sauce
    ¾ cup Basic Brown Soup Stock (page 47)
    ¾ cup red wine
    1 teaspoon each of rosemary, basil, and oregano
    ½ tablespoon chopped lemon peel
       Salt and pepper to taste

Sauté the carrots, celery, onion, green pepper, and garlic in the oil until lightly colored.

Add remaining ingredients. Simmer all together, covered, for 1 hour.

Use for pasta, shrimp dishes, omelets, meats, soups, etc.

MAKES 5 CUPS.

Quick Cheese Sauce

This is so simple that I hesitate to give it to you. However, if you don't need it don't read it. You may also thicken this with a roux.

    Sharp cheddar cheese
    Hot milk
    Worcestershire sauce
    Salt to taste
    Dry sherry

Melt cheddar cheese in a little hot milk on the stove. Add a little Worcestershire, salt, and a tad of dry sherry.

Fine over eggs and muffins for breakfast.

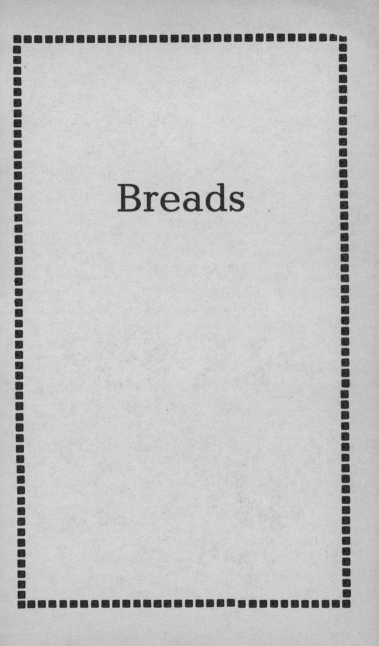

Breads

The history of bread goes back to the Jews wandering to Egypt in order to search out grain for a starving people.

With them they had their desert sourdough or wild yeast, and with this yeast they changed the eating habits of the world. Prior to their arrival, the Egyptians had baked bread, but it was hard and had the consistency of a tender brick. In order to be eaten, it was first soaked in water, which turned it to a mush. The water was drained off and allowed to ferment. Thus the invention of beer. When the Jews fled Egypt, they left behind their yeast because there would not be time to allow the dough to rise if they were to be running across the desert. Thus raised bread, as we know it.

Classic French Bread

Classic French bread, something that we rarely see in our country, is not to be confused with the soft-center, thin-crusted lightweight "French bread" that we buy at the supermarket. Bread that is loved by the Parisians is much heavier and made with a very hard wheat flour. So, in order to get that kind of bread, you must weigh your ingredients, and you need to seek out hard wheat flour. The best that I know of comes from Montana. Even the French love hard Montana wheat flour. It produces a crust that you will not believe. If you cannot find a hard wheat flour, use a good unbleached white. If you can find a hard wheat flour, blend it half and half with the unbleached white.

2   packages dry yeast
2½ cups tepid water
2   pounds and 3 ounces hard wheat flour mixed
      with unbleached white flour, or just
      unbleached white flour—mix them ½ and ½
1   teaspoon salt dissolved in 1 teaspoon water
      Cornmeal (optional)

Dissolve the yeast in the water. (Tepid: not hot, not cool, but barely warm.) Let stand for 5 minutes. Stir to dissolve.

Using a small paper sack on your scale, weigh out a total of 2 pounds and 3 ounces of flour. (If you can't get hard wheat flour, use a good unbleached white.)

Make a sponge of the water and yeast, together with 4 cups of the weighed-out flour. Whip for 10 minutes with an electric mixer. It will pull away from the side of the mixing bowl.

Add the salted water. Add the remaining flour and knead for 5 minutes in a good machine, or 15 minutes by hand.

Place on Formica counter, or on a piece of plastic wrap, and cover with a large metal bowl. Let rise for 2 hours. Punch down, and let rise for another 1½ hours.

Punch down again, and mold into 3 or 4 loaves. Let the loaves rise. I use an extra oven with a pan of hot water in the bottom. This allows for steam heat, perfect for raising dough. Place the loaves on a greased baking sheet before letting them rise; you may wish to place cornmeal on the greased baking sheet.

Preheat the oven to 450°. When the loaves have risen to double in original bulk, place them in the upper one-third of the oven. IMPORTANT: Place a pan of hot water on the bottom shelf. This will assure you of a great crust.

Bake in the oven for about 25 minutes, or until the bread is nicely browned and the loaves sound hollow when you thump their bottoms with your finger.

If you wish an old-world look to your bread, simply dust the loaves with flour before the final rising. You can use an egg and water glaze, but I am convinced that you will get a much better crust if you simply use flour.

This bread is so rich that you need not put butter on it. The French rarely eat butter on bread. And if you wish to eliminate both salt and butter, simply cut down on the amount of the salt in the recipe. It is tasty without.

MAKES 3 OR 4 LOAVES.

Italian Focaccia—Onion Bread

This is a classic bit of Italian cuisine that is common in some of the great Italian restaurants and sandwich bars in San Francisco. It is much like a soft pizza, and it is great to eat just as it comes from the pan; or sliced through the middle, it provides a sandwich cover that you will not believe!

> 2 **packages dry yeast, dissolved in 1 cup lukewarm**
>   **water**
> 3 **cups unbleached flour**
>   **Olive oil**
> 1 **teaspoon sugar**
> 1 **teaspoon salt**
> 3 **tablespoons tomato paste**
> 1 **yellow onion, peeled and chopped**
> 6 **green onions, chopped**
> 1 **clove garlic, crushed**
>   **Fresh-cracked pepper**

Place the water and yeast in a mixing bowl. Add half the flour, ¼ cup olive oil, the sugar, and salt, and mix with an electric mixer until smooth. Add the remaining flour, and blend in by hand. Place the dough on floured board, and knead for 5 minutes. Place the dough on a Formica countertop or on plastic wrap, and cover with a large metal bowl. Allow to rise about 1 hour, or until doubled in bulk.

When it is doubled, punch the dough down, and knead it for 1 or 2 minutes. Roll the dough out to fit a greased 9- by 13-inch shallow pan, and place the dough in the pan. Let the dough rise until not quite doubled in bulk, and then punch holes all over it, using a fork. Brush the top of the dough with some olive oil and then the tomato paste. Mix together the yellow onion, green onions, and garlic; use to sprinkle top of dough. Sprinkle with the pepper. Preheat the oven and bake at 375° for about 25 minutes, or until lightly browned.

This bread is great on a buffet. Or slice in half and use for Italian sandwiches. I like a little Italian salami, some yellow onion, and a few green olives. Drizzle a little Italian salad dressing on the sandwich, and enjoy with a heavy red wine.

MAKES 1 LOAF.

Lebanese Bread

When I was a child, my Lebanese uncle's mother died. Since he was the oldest son in the family, he was given the responsibility of making the family bread for the rest of the brothers, sisters, and even cousins. The passing of the bread paddles was a most important event. This is as close to his recipe as I can come, and once you have learned to make this, you will never buy pocket bread or pita from a bakery again.

> 2 cakes yeast
> 2 cups lukewarm water
> 8 cups unbleached white flour
> 2 cups whole wheat flour
> ½ tablespoon salt

Dissolve the yeast in the water. Place the flours in a large bowl. Mix in the salt. Pour in the yeast and water mixture, and add enough water to make a very stiff dough. Knead until smooth. Cover, and let rise until doubled. Punch down, and mold dough into small pieces about 3 inches in diameter. Be sure to seal the dough by rolling it around in your hands until it is smooth. Place on a tray; cover with plastic wrap; allow to rise for 1 hour.

Preheat your oven. It must be at 525° minimum. Fun to have a glass door so you can see. Roll out balls of dough on floured board, one at a time, into pancakelike circles 8 to 9 inches in diameter. Place on a small wooden board and slide onto upside-down cookie sheet in oven. While one loaf is baking, roll out the next. The loaf takes only a few minutes to bake. Very light brown spots will form on the loaf after it has puffed up like a ball. Remove it from the oven, and place on a terry-cloth towel. Cover the bread with another towel, and stack the loaves one on top of the other as they come from the oven. Keep covered until cool.

MAKES 12 TO 15 LOAVES.

Low-Salt/
Low-Fat
Cooking

My recent experience with heart surgery has caused me to become aware of a whole new problem in American cuisine. And with every problem comes the possibility of some creative solutions.

Following open heart surgery for the replacement of a faulty valve (no, it was the result not of my diet but of the rheumatic fever I had as a child), I was subjected to the most tasteless food that anyone could imagine. Heart patients are fed food without any salt or fat whatsoever, and the result is not exciting. I realized that a famous surgeon, Dr. Lester Sauvage in Seattle, saved my life . . . and then four dieticians tried to kill me!

The problem stems from our overconsumption of salt and animal fat. Both work to cause great stress on many of our bodily organs, but the heart seems to receive the worst of the blows.

Salt is so common in our diet that we generally are not aware of it at all. We use it in cooking; we use it at the table; we expect it in all prepared or fast foods, and as a result, we consume about six times more salt per year than our bodies can even handle, let alone need. Salt goes immediately to the blood system, which is actually just a system of salt water that carries about little platelets or corpuscles. When we ingest too much salt, the saline, or salt, content of our bloodstreams is increased, and our bodies pump in more water to dilute the salt content. Thus, our blood systems must carry additional water, and the tubes and arteries and blood vessels can carry only so much. We increase the fluid in our veins and thus increase the pressure in the system . . . and our hearts have to work beyond their capacity to move all that extra fluid. Very often our hearts simply cannot take it, and they blow! The result is heart attack or heart failure. Salt also causes our arteries to constrict, thus complicating the whole problem. Even our kidneys are put under pressure to remove all that extra salt and water from our systems, and often they wear out before or along with our hearts.

Animal fat contains cholesterol. While all fats, animal and vegetable alike, can cause cholesterol to form in our systems, animal fat is the most dangerous. The fat molecules build up on the insides of our arteries, thus making the arteries or channels smaller in diameter. Now couple that problem with the salt problem discussed above, and you will see why the great American lunch of the hamburger, french fries, and a milk shake is going to put us all out of commission.

I offer a few solutions for cutting down on salt and animal fat:

1. Cut down on the salt that you use in the kitchen. It is probably not possible to eliminate it entirely, nor is this necessary. Simply attempt to cut down.
2. Remove the salt shaker from the dining room table.
3. In flavoring foods, use flavors instead of salt. I suggest the use of white wine, garlic, herbs and spices, and lemon juice in your food.
4. Avoid salt substitutes that simply replace sodium chloride with potassium chloride. Using one chemical to replace another is probably not the route that we need to take. Try to eliminate as many additives as possible, and cook using a bit of flair with the herbs and spices shelf.
5. Cut down on your intake of animal fat. Use meat for flavoring rather than as the basis of the entire meal. Trim all beef and pork carefully so that you can enjoy your meals without all the fat.

These suggestions are not difficult to follow. Use the principles to cause some changes in the eating habits of yourself and those you love. Each of the recipes in this section is tasty and easy to prepare. Try them as a discipline at first and then for the sake of good eating the second time around.

Many of the recipes in this book can be adapted to low-salt/ low-fat diets with very little difficulty. Please see the following in addition to the recipes in this section:

▓ HINT:

It is very easy to remove the skin from a chicken. Most of the fat resides in the skin, and while it is delicious, we should really cut down. Simply pull the skin off the thighs before using them, or if you are using a whole chicken, remove the wings, then cut the bird down the breastplate, lay it out flat with the back up, and pull off the skin.

Chicken with Apricot Glaze

        4 cloves garlic
        ½ cup dry white wine
        2 pounds chicken pieces, skin removed
        1 12-ounce can apricots, drained and pits
           removed
        ½ teaspoon dried dill weed
        ½ teaspoon dried tarragon

Crush the garlic into the wine, and marinate the chicken pieces
for about 15 minutes. In the meantime, place the apricots in a
food blender, and turn it to a paste or sauce. Add the dill and
tarragon to the paste.

Place the chicken pieces on a lightly oiled baking dish along
with the marinade. Brush the chicken liberally with the apricot
paste. Bake at 375°, uncovered, for about 45 minutes.

Serve with a green salad with Cottage Cheese and Dill Dressing (page 95), use low-calorie mayonnaise and low-fat cottage
cheese).

SERVES 6.

Poached Fish with Cucumber
and Dill Sauce

This lovely sauce is, in its original form, sour cream and heavy
mayonnaise. The method below will give you a great sauce that
is not a substitute, but a fine sauce in its own right.

        1 cup mock sour cream*
        ¼ cup low-fat "imitation" mayonnaise
        1 teaspoon dried dill weed
        1 cup coarse-grated peeled cucumber
           Lemon juice to taste
           Fresh-ground black pepper to taste

Mix all well and chill. Serve over poached fish or meat dishes.

*Put low-salt/low-fat cottage cheese into a food blender. Blend ½ pound with 1½ table-
spoons low-fat milk until it is smooth, like sour cream.

POACHED FISH

- 2 **pounds sole or flounder fillets**
- 3 **to 4 cups Chicken Soup Stock (page 53)**
- 3 **tablespoons white wine**
- 2 **tablespoons lemon juice**
- 2 **tablespoons white vinegar**

Roll the fillets like a small jelly roll. Put into your frying pan the following: 1 inch of soup stock, wine, the lemon juice, and vinegar (to help keep the fish firm).

Bring the stock to a boil, turn to a light simmer, add the fish rolls, and cover. Poach lightly for 5 to 10 minutes.

Begin the meal with Lentil Soup (page 53), prepared without salt (use lemon juice instead). A green salad and a dry white wine complete the meal.

SERVES 6.

Mustard and Caper Sauce

You will find yourself putting this sauce on many dishes. It is certainly easy, and it will be a great help to the low-salt/low-fat eaters in your house. There is no reason to stop enjoying food just because you are trying to cut down on salt and fat!

- ½ **cup mock sour cream (see footnote, page 276)**
- 1 **tablespoon Dijon-style mustard***
- ½ **teaspoon capers, chopped**
- 2 **tablespoons lemon juice**

Mix together all ingredients. Refrigerate.

Serve over chicken without the skin, fish, or leftover lean red meat. This also makes a great salad dressing.

MAKES ⅔ CUP.

*Grey Poupon is fine, or you may use a low-salt mustard if you wish.

■ HINT:

If you wish to cut down on the salt and butterfat content of your family's diet, simply take the butter dish and the salt shaker off the dining table. Use good breads that will not need butter for flavor, and herbs and spices in your cooking instead of so much salt.

Butter and Lecithin Mixture

I really do not care for the flavor of margarine, and I am not convinced that hydrogenated vegetable oil is that much better for your system than butter. Butter, however, lacks the necessary lecithin to aid your system in breaking down the butterfat, so this recipe is an attempt to add the lecithin. Additional peanut oil will lower the level of animal fat in this fresh-tasting spread. No, you will not taste the lecithin.

However, for the sake of your health and the health of those you love, cut down on butter and fat in every form.

    1 pound butter
    1 cup peanut oil
    4 tablespoons powdered lecithin (from health food
          stores or pharmacies)

Allow the butter to soften enough to blend. Blend all three ingredients together with an electric mixer until smooth. Place in covered container, and refrigerate. It will set up again just like regular butter and can be used the very same way you would use butter. And it is lower in animal fat content than regular butter.

Mirepoix of Vegetables

This blend of vegetables and herbs will be of great help to you if you intend to cut down on salt and fat. Use it to increase flavor in everything from soups to gravies to stews. Normally, when something seems to lack flavor, our first inclination is to throw in more salt. Try using herbs and spices, lemon juice, white wine, or garlic instead. And you may use this vegetable blend for flavoring as well as for a topping for meats or fish.

>   2 cloves garlic, crushed
>   1 cup diced celery
>   1 cup diced carrot
>   2 cups chopped yellow onion
>   1 teaspoon peanut oil
>   2 teaspoons Herb Blend (below)
>   2 ounces dry sherry

Sauté the garlic, celery, carrot, and onion in the oil for a few minutes. Add the Herb Blend, and sauté until the vegetables are not quite tender. Deglaze the pan by adding the sherry and stirring it about with a wooden spoon until the brown glaze formed on the bottom of the pan is liquefied. Cool, and refrigerate.

MAKES 3 CUPS.

Herb Blend

>   1 teaspoon fresh-cracked pepper
>   3 bay leaves
>   ½ teaspoon whole oregano
>   ¼ teaspoon marjoram, whole leaves, dried, work
>   best
>   ¼ teaspoon savory, whole leaves, dried, work best
>   ¼ teaspoon basil, whole leaves, dried, work best
>   ¼ teaspoon thyme, whole leaves, dried, work best
>   ¼ teaspoon rosemary, whole leaves, dried, work
>   best

Crush all the ingredients together with your fingers, and store in a tightly capped jar. No need to refrigerate. Use in any way you like for a little extra flavor in your cooking.

MAKES 3 TABLESPOONS.

Chicken in Lemon

Marinate chicken pieces in a few tablespoons of lemon juice, a little whole thyme, and some fresh-cracked pepper, for 15 minutes. Broil until tender. Delicious and low in calories, and no salt at all. You might also consider removing the skin, which contains most of the fat in the bird.

Low-Salt/Low-Fat Chicken Italian

This dish will give you all the flavor of a good chicken dish without the salt and very little fat. Remove the skin of the chicken since that is where most of the fat in the bird resides. I know, you love the skin. Please cut down on the skin in any case.

- 1 **3- to 3½-pound whole frying chicken, skinned (see Hint, page 275)**
- 2 **tablespoons olive oil**
- 2 **tablespoons lemon juice**
- 2 **cloves garlic, crushed**
- ¼ **tablespoon oregano**
- 2 **tablespoons dry white wine**
   Pepper to taste

Cut the chicken in half.

Blend marinade of all the remaining ingredients. Soak chicken for 10 minutes. Bake in greased pan at 375° for 45 minutes to 1 hour, or until browned and tender.

Begin with Pasta Primavera (page 143): simply omit the salt, and cut down on the oil. Add Herbed Cheese Spread (page 287) on toast squares, a dry red wine, and you have a lovely meal. You might enjoy a green salad as well.

SERVES 4.

Yogurt and Yogurt Cheese

Yogurt and Cheese—Make Your Own

Cheeses and yogurt, the original cheese, are easy to make and much cheaper than those you buy from the market. Besides, you can control the salt and fat content.

Yogurt is probably the oldest cheese that we know. Originally it was discovered by nomads in the desert when natural yeasts that were present in the air landed in their milk products and preserved them. The yeasts or yogurts were saved and used to thicken and preserve more batches of milk. Milk was also stored in bags made of the stomach of an animal, thus providing a natural rennet that would turn the milk to a curd.

We can find terrific yogurt starters in most delicatessens and all health food stores. You may have to try more than one until you find one that is to your liking, perhaps not as sweet as the commercial yogurt. The starter will live for years if you care for it and continue to make fresh batches.

Yogurt

The rules here are simple. Just remember that you can kill the yogurt by getting it too hot. On the other hand, the yogurt will not grow if you do not keep it warm enough. So use the old heating pad method.

EQUIPMENT
6- to 8-quart stainless steel or enamel kettle
    Cheese or yeast thermometer (needs to go from
        about 100° to 220° Fahrenheit)
    Heat diffuser or flame tamer*
4   quarts fresh milk
4   1-quart widemouthed canning jars with lids,
        sterilized
    Heating pad

Heat the milk to 180° Fahrenheit in a stainless steel or enamel kettle. You may use skim, low-fat, or whole milk. Remember that flavor is not terribly affected by butterfat. I prefer using low-fat milk for yogurt so that the final product can be used in low-fat/low-salt dishes.

Cool the milk to 115°. Add starter or yogurt from your last batch. You generally need about ½ cup of a previous yogurt to 1 quart of new milk. Blend it in carefully so that the yogurt will be smooth. Place the mixture in a sterile jar, and cap with lid.

In another kettle (any kind will do), place water that is 115°, right on the button! Put the jars of new yogurt into the water, which should come up about three-fourths of the way to the lid of the jar. Cover the kettle, and place it on a heating pad set for medium heat. Eight hours later you will have fine yogurt. Refrigerate before using.

The above method works for any amount. I usually make a gallon at a time, so that I have enough yogurt around for the following recipes.

Yogurt Cheese
(Lebanon)

A cheese that is simple to make, delicious in flavor, and very low in fat. It is also cheaper than cream cheese. This is a grand addi-

---

*Available at department or gourmet stores.

tion to your frugal kitchen. You will find yourself using this in salad dressings, snacks, sandwiches, etc.

Place a piece of cheesecloth or muslin, 1½ feet by 1½ feet, in a large colander. Pour in 2 quarts chilled yogurt, bring up the corners of the cloth, and tie them together. Hang this bag in the kitchen with a bowl beneath, for 2 days. At the end of that time you will have a product that is very close to cream cheese in texture, but not in butterfat content. Cream cheese is 32 percent butterfat, and yogurt cheese contains a tenth that amount. So enjoy.

Use in recipes in this section, or spread on toast for breakfast. You can use this in any recipe that calls for cream cheese.

MAKES 1½ CUPS.

Yogurt Balls in Oil
(Lebanon)

You must make this dish and then serve the balls in a bowl at your next party or at dinner with your family. The cheese is spread on a small cracker and served with a good dry sherry. When I taste this dish, my memory retreats to my childhood and to the meals that my cousin's Lebanese grandmother would serve. I eat it now and recall her smile and her affection. Her name was Selma Abdo, and that woman cooked out of sheer love for the family.

This is a classic example of frugality in the Old World. In Lebanon when the yogurt cheese becomes too sharp from age, it is rolled into little balls the size of a chocolate. It is then placed in olive oil to cover along with a bit of garlic and oregano. It is left for a few days in this oil, which preserves it.

Yogurt and Eggs
(Armenia)

The whole of the Middle East uses yogurt in many forms. This dish is a favorite in our household.

1 clove garlic, crushed
1 medium yellow onion, peeled and chopped
2 tablespoons olive oil
1 cup yogurt
6 to 8 eggs
  Pepper to taste

Sauté the garlic and onions in 1 tablespoon olive oil until the onion is clear. Add the yogurt to the pan, stir, and remove from the heat. In another frying pan heat the remaining olive oil and add the eggs. Pour the yogurt and onion mixture over the top of the eggs. Add pepper. Cover, and cook the eggs to taste.

SERVES 3 OR 4.

Yogurt Sauce

No food can be too sour for my wife, Patty. However, the boys are in a different camp. They suggest just a pinch of sugar to this to cut down on the tartness.

2 tablespoons flour
2 tablespoons water
½ cup yogurt
½ cup white wine
½ cup chicken broth

Mix the flour and the water, and blend with the remaining ingredients. Simmer for 15 minutes over medium heat, stirring constantly as the sauce thickens.

Serve over meats and vegetables.

MAKES 1½ CUPS.

Yogurt with Chocolate

I originally developed this recipe two years ago when I realized after heart surgery that I was going to have to cut down on my beloved chocolates. This recipe has no salt and very little fat, so those on low-salt/low-fat diets can enjoy this dish and know that they are still maintaining their diets.

Mix powdered cocoa with yogurt cheese and sugar to taste. Add vanilla. You might even try a bit of dry instant coffee. Mold into balls, and chill. Eat chocolate without guilt!

Herbed Cheese Spread

You can replace those fancy little imported herbed cheese mixtures with this one. If this cheese is too tart for you, add a tiny bit of sugar. This is great for cocktail parties.

> 2 **cups Yogurt Cheese (page 284)**
> 2 **cloves garlic, crushed**
> 2 **tablespoons chopped parsley**
> 1 **teaspoon oregano**
> ¼ **teaspoon fresh-ground black pepper**
> ¼ **teaspoon whole thyme**
> ¼ **teaspoon basil**
> **Salt to taste (use very little, if any)**

Blend all together, and refrigerate. Mold into a ball, or place in small ramekins and serve with dark crackers.

You may vary the amounts of herbs to your own taste.

MAKES 2 CUPS.

Cooking
in Paper

This "new" method of cooking is actually very old. The Chinese, French, and Greeks have been cooking in paper for many generations, so you should get in on the fun. The advantages are mainly two: The paper helps maintain natural juice retention, and you have few pots and pans to clean up.

The paper used in this method is simply called cooking parchment. You can purchase it in rolls in many supermarkets and in all gourmet shops. You need not buy anything expensive that claims it is a special paper for vegetables, etc. A roll of simple cooking parchment will do fine.

Whenever paper is mentioned in this section, it refers to cooking parchment. *Do not use wax paper or cellophane.*

Whole Chicken in a Bag

I love to do this kind of thing with small birds or even small roasts. There are no pans to wash, the dish is easily prepared, and it is great fun to open the package at the table. There, that does it for frugal!

    2 tablespoons olive oil
    2 cloves garlic, crushed
    1 teaspoon whole thyme
      Juice of ½ lemon
      Salt and pepper to taste
      Cooking parchment paper
    1 3-pound chicken
      Paper bag, lunch sack size
      Aluminum foil

Prepare a dressing of the oil, garlic, thyme, and lemon juice. Rub the bird with this dressing, and add a bit of salt and pepper. Tear off an 18-inch-long piece of parchment paper, and carefully wrap up the chicken. Place the bundle in a paper bag, and then wrap in aluminum foil. Place the bundle on a rack in the oven. Bake at 375° for 1 hour and 15 minutes.

Spinach and Artichoke Casserole (page 222), Swiss Cheese and Bacon Crepes (page 114), and a green salad dressed with Dill and Caper Dressing (page 96): not a light menu, but it will be a popular one!

SERVES 3 OR 4.

Whitefish in Paper
(France)

This takes a bit of time to prepare, but the results are so delicious and the presentation is so dramatic that you must try it. The natural moisture of the fish is kept within the beautiful heart-shaped packet.

    3 pounds whitefish fillets
      Olive or peanut oil
      Cooking parchment paper
      Mirepoix of Vegetables (page 278)
      Butter

Cut the fish into 8 serving pieces. Barely brown the pieces very quickly on both sides in a bit of olive or peanut oil; do not cook long.

Tear off one 18-inch-long sheet of parchment paper for each of the 8 servings. Fold the paper in half so that the packet is now 9

inches wide. Cut a heart from the paper, using the full width and length of the paper.

Open the paper, and place one serving of fish on one side of the heart, close to the fold. Top the fish with a few tablespoons of the mirepoix. Lightly butter the other side of the heart, and fold over; crimp the edges, except for the point, by rolling and folding and twisting the edges (this is easy to do, and you will catch on right away). Puff up the envelope by blowing into the open point, and then seal the point.

Place each of the packages on an oiled baking sheet, and bake at 400° for 7 to 10 minutes, or until the top of the paper is lightly browned. Place each packet on a serving plate, and let your guests open their treasures.

This dish can be prepared ahead of time and baked at the last minute. However, do not refrigerate the packages. Make them close to your guests' arrival time.

Begin the meal with Spaghetti with Two Mushrooms (page 145). Serve a Cucumber Salad (page 405) along with the fish in paper. Rolls and white wine would complete the meal. You might make your own French rolls.

SERVES 8.

Lamb Chops with Leeks, Lemon, and Dill

This will absolutely make your next dinner party, provided you do not overcook the lamb. This is to be a delicate and moist dish, not the old overcooked lamb routine.

This dish is so delicious that you need to plan an outrageous menu. Try anything and everything because this dish is actually very versatile. That's frugal cooking!

- 6 **cooking parchment paper hearts (above)**
- 6 **lamb chops or thick lamb steaks**
- 2 **tablespoons olive oil**
  Salt and pepper to taste
- 4 **leeks**
- 2 **cloves garlic, crushed**
- ¼ **cup whipping cream**
- 1 **teaspoon dried dill weed**
- 1 **lemon, sliced very thin**
  Butter

Brown the lamb very quickly in 1 tablespoon of the oil. Use high heat, and turn when nicely browned. Salt and pepper the lamb and set it aside.

Clean the leeks by cutting them into 2-inch lengths and then cutting them in half lengthwise. Do not use the tough part of the top of the leek; stop just where the leek begins to change from white to green. Wash the leaves in water, and drain.

Sauté the leaves in the remaining oil, along with the garlic, just until they are tender but not browned. Add the cream and dill. Remove from the heat.

Place each chop or steak on one half of the heart as on page 293. Top each with a bit of the leek and cream sauce and then with a thin slice or two of lemon. Butter the other side of the paper, and seal as on page 293.

Bake on greased baking sheet at 400° for about 10 minutes, or until the paper is lightly browned. Serve as on page 294.

SERVES 6.

Scallops with Vegetables

If you like scallops, and I love them, this dish will become a favorite. Scallops are expensive, so they should be treated with some class. But then, I suppose that every creature that gives its life for our table should be treated with class.

> 1 pound scallops
>   Butter
> 4 cooking parchment paper hearts (page 293)
> 1 clove garlic, crushed
> 1 tomato, chopped
> 1 small yellow onion, peeled and chopped
> 2 tablespoons parsley, chopped
> ⅛ teaspoon dried rosemary
>   Salt and pepper to taste
> 2 tablespoons olive oil

Sauté the scallops in 3 tablespoons butter; do not overcook; use high heat, and cook for only a moment. Divide the scallops among the 4 heart packages. Sauté the garlic, tomato, yellow onion, and parsley, with the rosemary, salt, and pepper, in the olive oil until they are not quite tender. Place over the scallops. Seal and bake as on page 293. Don't forget to butter only one side of the heart package (page 293).

Since scallops are expensive, you need to add some heavy dishes to the menu. Try Ratatouille (page 386) for a vegetable and an Asparagus Quiche (page 119). White wine, very dry, is the choice.

SERVES 4.

Fish with Garlic and Green Pepper

Everyone is tired of plain old pan-fried fish. This will give you a new excuse for serving fish to your family or guests.

Cooking parchment paper
⅓ **pound fish fillet**
 1 **tablespoon peanut oil or butter**
 3 **slices green pepper**
 2 **cloves garlic, finely chopped**
Salt and pepper to taste

Tear off a piece of parchment paper that is about 18 inches long. Fold in half, and cut into a heart shape, using the full size of the paper.

Lightly sauté the fish fillet in the butter or oil. Place it on one side of the heart-shaped paper, and lightly butter the opposite side of the heart. Top the fish with the garlic and green pepper. Add salt and pepper, and fold the paper heart around the fish by folding one flap over on the other and then bending and folding the paper so as to seal the outer edge of the heart. Place on a baking sheet, and bake at 375° for 15 to 20 minutes, or until the paper is lightly browned. Serve in the paper.

SERVES 1.

Chinese Chicken in Paper

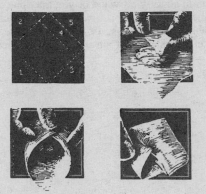

This is a very tasty morsel. It is great as an hors d'oeuvre, but it can also fit into a full Chinese meal in which you would serve several courses. Teach the kids how to fold the paper. They will have a great time.

- 2 **boneless chicken breasts, cut into 1-inch by ½-inch pieces**
- 3 **tablespoons dark soy sauce**
- 2 **tablespoons dry sherry**
- 1 **teaspoon fresh-grated ginger**
- 2 **cloves garlic, crushed**
- 2 **teaspoons brown sugar**
- 3 **green onions, chopped**
   Cooking parchment paper
   Peanut oil for deep frying or topping

Mix all the ingredients except for the paper, of course, and the peanut oil together in a mixing bowl, and allow to marinate for 15 minutes.

Cut 20 squares of cooking parchment, each 4½ inches square. Fold each sheet first, according to the diagram above. Do not put the chicken in the paper until you have first folded the paper. What you are making is a tiny envelope in which you will seal the chicken. If you can fold a diaper, you can do this dish!

Wrap each piece of chicken, along with a bit of green onion, according to the diagram. The little tail remaining is tucked into the envelope so that the package is sealed completely. These may be deep-fried until slightly browned or you may place them on an oiled baking sheet, and brush each with a bit of peanut oil. Bake at 400° for about 15 minutes, or until the paper is slightly browned (I prefer this method since it is not as greasy as deep frying).

MAKES 20.

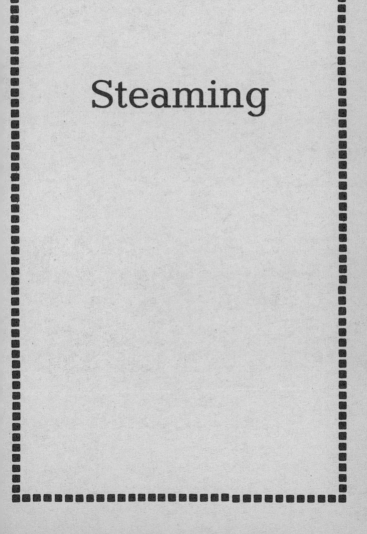

Steaming

Ancient Method
of Steaming

There are many methods of steaming and many foods that respond beautifully to this sensible and efficient method of quick cooking.

Devices

Stainless Steel Basket Steamer: This is best for vegetables and is available in any department or hardware store.

Chinese Bamboo Steamer: This uses several layers and will not allow water to drip on your food. This is my favorite steaming gadget.

Aluminum Chinese Steamer: This is like the above, but moisture will condense on your food.

Red Clay Steamer from Hunan, China: This looks like an angel food pan with a lid; sits atop a pot of boiling water. Expensive, but it is attractive, and it works very well. Serve from the cooker.

My Cheap Steamer: Remove the bottom and the top from a small tuna fish can, and place middle section in the bottom of a deep kettle. Add a couple of inches of water to the bottom of the kettle, and place the heatproof bowl of food to be cooked on the top of the tuna can. Place a towel over the top of the kettle to catch dripping or condensing water; place the lid on the pot, and bring the ends of the towel up onto the top of the pot. Hold in place with an upside-down cup.

Chicken with Onions and Green Peas
(China)

One of the marvelous things that steaming will do is to free you for the last few minutes before dinner is served. Instead of standing at the stove until it is time to sit down, you can prepare most of these dishes ahead of time and then pop them in the steamer in time for dinner.

>   2 tablespoons light soy sauce
>   1 tablespoon dry sherry
>   1 teaspoon fresh-grated ginger
>   ½ teaspoon brown sugar
>   1 fryer, cut into large bite-size pieces
>   2 tablespoons peanut oil
>   1 large yellow onion, peeled and chopped
>   1 10-ounce package frozen peas

Combine the soy sauce, sherry, ginger, and sugar. Use to marinate the chicken pieces for about 15 minutes. Sauté or chow the chicken with the oil in a wok or frying pan until it is browned but not cooked through. Remove from the pan, and lightly brown the onion pieces. Return the chicken to the pan, and add the frozen peas. Toss for a moment so that all the products mix well, and then place in a bowl that will fit your steamer. Steam for 35 minutes, or until the chicken is tender.

SERVES 8 AS PART OF A CHINESE DINNER OF SEVERAL COURSES.

SERVES 4 OR 5 AS A MAIN COURSE.

Custard with Ham and Onions

One cup of water and two eggs? I can just hear your disbelief. What you are doing is preparing a very light and tender custard. The water must first be boiled and then cooled so that it is flat, or has no free oxygen. Otherwise the free air in the water will expand during cooking, and you have a soufflé effect.

1 **cup water, boiled and cooled**
2 **eggs, whipped**
1 **teaspoon sesame oil**
3 **green onions, chopped**
4 **ounces ham, chopped**
  Pepper to taste

Mix together all the ingredients, and place in a small bowl or soufflé dish. Steam for 15 minutes.

SERVES 1 OR 2 FOR SNACK OR BREAKFAST.

Steamed Eggs for Breakfast

Much easier than poaching, but you must learn to judge the time carefully because these eggs will cook quickly. Since steam heat is very even, you can put as many into a steamer at once as you wish. This is a great idea for a breakfast party in which you have many people.

Butter each Chinese teacup, and place egg in the cup. Place in steamer along with others, and steam until done to your taste. To serve, run table knife around the inside of the cup, and invert the egg onto toast or muffin.

Steamed Vegetables, Mixed

You can try any vegetables you wish. The point here is to stop boiling vegetables in gallons of water and simply to steam them, without any water. Very rich flavor.

    Very thin carrot sticks
    Very thin zucchini sticks
    Melted butter

Blend vegetables with a bit of melted butter, and steam until tender. Should take no more than 14 minutes.

Pork Shu Mei—Steamed Meatballs
(China)

These little treasures are a part of a fancy meal in China during the early part of the day. They are delicious and can be served at any time. Simply great for parties.

    ¾ pound ground lean pork
    ½ tablespoon cornstarch
    ½ tablespoon dry sherry
    1 tablespoon light soy sauce
    1 teaspoon grated fresh ginger
    1 clove garlic, crushed
    2 green onions, chopped
    1 teaspoon brown sugar
    1 teaspoon sesame oil
    1 package won ton wrappers*

Mix together all the ingredients except the wrappers. Stir the mixture by hand until you can feel it begin to bind together. This takes a minute or so of hard mixing.

Place a fat tablespoon of the mixture in the middle of a wrapper. Fold the four sides up around the meat so that you have a little cup or open bag. Squeeze the meat gently so that a little

*Available at supermarkets.

begins to come out the top of the little bag, and then push that meat back into the bag. Seal the edges of the wrapper by running your thumb around the top of the opening. Press the bottom flat so that the bag sits up in place in a steamer. Be sure to oil the racks of the steamer with a bit of peanut oil so that the shu mei will not stick. Steam for 15 to 20 minutes.

MAKES 25 TO 30.

Fish Steamed with Lemon

People who dislike the fishy flavor of fish will enjoy this dish because the cooked lemon cleanses the flavor. Very easy and very delicious.

This method of cooking fish works for just about any kind of fillet that you wish to use.

> 1 **pound fresh fish fillets**
> 2 **tablespoons or less light soy sauce**
>   **Fresh-cracked black pepper**
>   **Thin lemon slices**

Place the fish in a steaming bowl, and add the soy sauce along with a bit of black pepper. Top with several slices, very thin slices, of lemon. Steam for about 20 minutes.

SERVES 4 TO 6

Steamed Chicken with Lemon
(China)

You may use any kind of steamer you wish for this one, but be sure to put the chicken in a bowl. You cannot simply place the chicken on a rack.

      1   3-pound chicken, cut up
      2   tablespoons light soy sauce
      2   tablespoons dry sherry
      1   teaspoon grated fresh ginger
      ½   tablespoon mashed dow see*
      1   teaspoon brown sugar
      2   teaspoons cornstarch
      1   lemon, sliced

Mix together all the ingredients except the lemon. Place in a bowl or Hunan steamer. Place the lemon slices on top of the chicken. Steam for about 45 minutes to 1 hour, or until the chicken is very tender.

SERVES 4.

Steamed Meatballs
(China)

You will find your children asking for this one often. And since it takes so little time to prepare and will get your kids out of the hamburger patty rut, you can oblige them.

      1   pound lean hamburger
      1   tablespoon light soy sauce
      1   tablespoon dry sherry
      1   teaspoon grated fresh ginger
      1   clove garlic, crushed
      1   egg
      1   teaspoon cornstarch

*Fermented black beans, available in any Oriental market. Store in closed jar in refrigerator.

Mix together all ingredients. Form into small meatballs, place in a glass pie plate, and steam for about 35 minutes.

I use a bit of mustard green in the serving bowl for color and flavor.

SERVES 2 OR 3.

Smoke
Cookery
(Barbecue)

Barbecue, Southern Style

The term *barbecue* originally referred to an animal roasted whole. In our time it has come to mean many things, but the instructions listed below are designed to offer you a southern smoked barbecue with little effort . . . and we use a garbage can for the smoker.

Using the following diagram, construct the smoker.

1. Cut a square hole in the lid of a can, beginning along the edge. Fold the seams back and then over again so that another piece of metal can be inserted for a movable vent. Cut the vent piece, and slide into place.

2. Cut another vent at the bottom of the can. Bend back the flaps, and form another pair of seams as above. Make the hole about 10 inches high and 10 inches wide. Cut another piece of metal to use for the vent door. Use thin sheets of aluminum for each of the vent doors.

3. Cut a circle of sheet aluminum large enough to hang inside the can about two-thirds of the way down, with 2 inches of space around the circle. Hang the circle on an angle down two-thirds of the way. Use coat hanger wire for the suspension wires.

4. Place two heavy rods down 10 inches from the top. Punch holes in the side of the can so that the rods will support a round grill rack. These can be purchased at a hardware store. Insert the rack.

5. Punch a hole in the side of the can 8 inches down from the top, and insert a meat thermometer.

6. Purchase a small hot plate with a porcelain element holder. Place it in the bottom of the smoker. Place a pie tin filled with wet hickory or alder chips on top of the burner. Run the cord for the burner out the bottom vent of the smoker. Turn on the burner, close the vents, and you are ready to go. You may wish to purchase a burner with a thermostat attached; in that way you can control the temperature easily.

The temperature should always be about 130° to 150° Fahrenheit. Control the temperature by the use of the vents and the burner thermostat.

Watch the pan of wood chips so that you may replenish them. When the temperature gets too high, it generally means that your wood chip supply is gone or is down to ashes.

You can also do this trick with a small charcoal fire in the bottom of the smoker. However, you will burn out the bottom and the temperature is generally much too hot. I find it easier to use the old hot plate method.

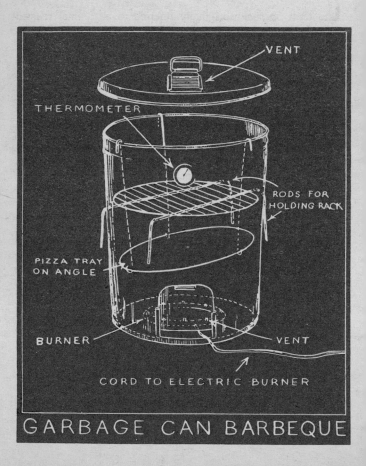

GARBAGE CAN BARBEQUE

Smoked Barbecue Chicken

Chicken smoked in my smoker will be very moist, and the color will remain bright. The flavor is as good as any you can find in barbecue restaurants, and much better than most.

Place whole cleaned chickens in the smoker, and smoke for 3 to 4 hours. Remove, and bake in oven at 375° for 1 hour. Put barbecue sauce on just before serving.

Serve with a Black-Eyed Pea Salad (page 133), rolls, beer, and more beer.

Smoked Barbecue Spareribs

I think barbecued pork spareribs are one of the greatest dishes ever. I just love them, and even with my low-fat/low-salt diet I have to give in once a month and enjoy.

Place 2 2-pound sides of pork spareribs in the smoker, and smoke it for 3 to 4 hours. Remove, and bake in oven at 350° for 1 hour and 15 minutes, or until golden and toasted. Watch this closely because the ribs may be done before expected, depending on the temperature at which they were smoked. Apply barbecue sauce just before serving.

SERVES 4.

Smoked Barbecue Beef Brisket

This dish is just delicious, and it is worth the effort to prepare a proper smoker. A covered American barbecue device will simply not do the job because the charcoal fire is always too hot.

Place a 4-pound brisket of beef in water to cover. Place the lid on pot, and simmer it for 2½ hours, or until tender. Drain the meat, and place it in the smoker for 4 hours. Slice, and serve with barbecue sauce.

Potato Cakes Filled with Vegetables (page 249), along with a Spinach Salad (page 92), would make an attractive plate.

SERVES 8 TO 10.

Southern Barbecue Sauce

Why is the sauce added after the cooking? Serious barbecue experts from the South tell me that you cannot add the sauce until the meat is away from the fire or oven, lest you burn the sugar in the sauce and change the flavor of the meat. If you are one of those who like the flavor of crunchy, toasted sugar sauce, add the sauce to the meat during the last 15 minutes of the roasting.

    1 teaspoon salt
    ½ cup granulated sugar
    ¼ cup brown sugar
    3 cups Basic Brown Soup Stock (page 47)
    ½ cup prepared mustard
    ¼ cup white vinegar
    ⅛ cup liquid smoke
    ½ cup Worcestershire sauce
    1 cup tomato paste
    ½ teaspoon crushed red pepper flakes
    1 tablespoon chili powder

Combine all the ingredients, and simmer in a heavy kettle for 2 hours, uncovered. Be careful with this because it will burn. Stir often, and watch that the liquid content does not evaporate. You may need to add a bit of water.

You may use stainless steel for this, but be sure to place a heat diffuser under the pan so that the sauce will not burn.

MAKES 1 QUART.

Chinese Oven-Barbecued Spareribs

This one you can do in your regular oven. It will be far superior to the dish that you find in most Chinese-American restaurants. Make plenty of these, and you will be loved by all!

2 cloves garlic, crushed
3 tablespoons dark soy sauce
2 tablespoons dry sherry
1 teaspoon grated fresh ginger
½ tablespoon brown sugar
½ tablespoon sesame oil
½ teaspoon five spice powder* *or* ⅓ teaspoon each
     of cinnamon, ginger, ground fennel, anise,
     and clove
1 tablespoon hoisin sauce
   Shot of Tabasco or to taste
1 tablespoon catsup, tomato sauce, or tomato
     paste
2 to 3 pounds pork spareribs

Mix well all the ingredients except the ribs. Use to marinate the pork spareribs for 2 hours in the refrigerator.

Place on a roasting rack in a 350° oven for 1 hour. Turn temperature up to 400°, and roast for an additional 15 minutes, or until browned and deliciously tender. It is a good idea to place a baking pan containing about 1 inch water in the oven beneath these ribs as they cook; it will prevent the sauce from dripping on the floor of the oven and causing smoke.

SERVES 4.

Low-Salt/Low-Fat Barbecue Sauce

All of us should watch our salt and fat intake, but for some it is more important than for others. If you are restricted to low salt and low fat, try this sauce on chicken (without the skin), fish, and any meat from which you have trimmed the fat very carefully first.

*Found in Oriental markets.

1 12-ounce can no-salt-added tomato paste
½ cup dry white wine (helps replace the experience
      of salt)
1 tablespoon dry mustard
2 tablespoons red wine vinegar
1 tablespoon Worcestershire sauce
   Dash of Tabasco to taste
¼ cup brown sugar
1 tablespoon mild chili powder
2 tablespoons chopped yellow onion
   Juice of ½ lemon
1½ cups water
2 teaspoons liquid smoke

Blend all ingredients well, and simmer for 25 minutes. Careful, this is a ploppy sauce, and it will bubble and splash on your shirt or dress. Keep refrigerated for up to 1½ weeks.

MAKES ABOUT 1 QUART.

Garlic

Garlic is one of the most common foodstuffs that we know of, anywhere in the world. It is seen as both a food and a medicine and is surely one of the most popular flavoring agents anywhere.

We cannot trace garlic historically since it seems to have been around prior to recorded history. We do know that garlic was very common in ancient Egypt and that the Egyptians ate a large form of garlic very close to what we call elephant garlic . . . and I mean they ate it, by the whole bud. When the great pyramids were being constructed, garlic was issued daily to the slaves in order to keep up their strength. When the cost overruns for the pyramids began to bother the pharaoh, he decided to cut down on the costs by taking away the garlic ration for the slaves. They struck! It was the first labor strike in history, and it was over garlic.

In ancient Greece garlic was seen as a symbol of strength and courage, and Roman soldiers used to rub it on the soles of their feet in order to assure swiftness in battle.

Long reputed to be a great source of health, garlic has in our time come to be seen as an aid to a healthy heart. The herb contains kyolic, a natural blood thinner, so when we eat lots of garlic, we are doing our hearts a favor. Maybe we are doing all of us a favor since we are now eating three times as much garlic each year as we did ten years ago.

Buying and Storing Garlic

I do not ever purchase garlic in any form except that which the Creator intended. All salts and pastes and powders and juices taste nothing like the real thing.

Try to purchase a long string of garlic, generally available in autumn. Hang it in the corner of your kitchen, and use it for the year. If you must purchase garlic in the supermarket, be careful to find full heads because most of this product has spent a good deal of time in cold storage and has probably dried out.

I have heard of people trying to preserve garlic in all kinds of strange ways, but I contend that all you need do is leave the garlic out on the counter in a small basket. The rest of the supply hangs on the wall. Never put garlic in the refrigerator; the peel will become moist, and the head will dry out. And never store the garlic in sherry. The result is simply an embalming of the garlic, and we don't need that.

■ HINT: Cleaning Garlic

There should be no pain involved in such a process. Many people use instant garlic products, claiming that fresh garlic takes too long to clean. Not so!

With the palm of your hand crush the entire head so that the cloves fall apart. Select a clove, and bang it with the bottom of a drinking glass or crack it with the flat side of a large knife. Place your knife over the clove, and hit the knife gently with your hand. The cracked clove will render itself skinless without effort.

Baked Garlic

I know this sounds a bit strange to you, but once you have tried it, you will offer it to your family and friends on a regular basis. No, it is not strong at all.

Place whole heads of garlic in a small baking dish, and bake them at 325° for 1 hour.

To serve, have each guest pull off a clove of garlic and squeeze out the roasted garlic paste. Squeeze it onto a cracker for a hors d'oeuvre. Serve it alongside any meat or vegetable dish in the main course.

Russian Garlic Salad

One of my dearest friends, Dr. William Campbell, a man with a most brilliant mind and blatant charm, is a garlic freak. He called me recently upon his return from a scientific meeting in Georgia, Russia, to tell me about the following salad. I could not believe it, and I still cannot. But he loves the stuff, and now and then we prepare it for each other.

    30 cloves garlic, cleaned and peeled
    ½ cup olive oil
    ¼ cup lemon juice
     4 tablespoons white wine vinegar
        Salt and pepper to taste
    ½ teaspoon oregano (optional)

Blanch the whole cloves of garlic in boiling water for 5 minutes; remove, and plunge into cold water. Drain, and mix with the remaining ingredients. Allow to marinate for 5 days in the refrigerator before serving.

The salad is served as it is, in small bowls alongside the main plate. Or you may chop this up and add it to a layered green salad.

MAKES 3 SMALL SALADS.

Aïoli Sauce—Garlic Mayonnaise
(Italy)

A lovely excuse to eat garlic, and easy to make.

    5 cloves garlic
    1 egg, at room temperature
    1 cup olive oil, at room temperature
    1 tablespoon lemon juice

Crush the garlic in a food blender. Add the egg, and blend for 15 seconds. Very slowly add the oil through the top of the blender so that an emulsion can take place. Stir in the lemon juice by hand.

This aïoli sauce makes a heavenly salad with cold unpeeled cooked new potatoes. Use it, too, on cold meats and heavy green vegetables such as broccoli.

MAKES 1½ CUPS.

■ HINT:

To get the smell of garlic off your hands, simply rub your hands in used coffee grounds. End of odor. In Italy it is common to eat a whole coffee bean after a big meal so that your lover will not be bothered by garlic.

Garlic Pasta

Quick and easy, you should always have the ingredients about for this one. Your lover will love it!

    8 cloves garlic
    3 tablespoons olive oil
    ½ cup whipping cream
      Salt and pepper to taste
    ½ pound pasta, cooked (weight before cooking)
      Fresh-grated Parmesan or Romano cheese to
        taste
      Parsley for garnish

Cut the garlic into thin slices, and sauté in the olive oil until not quite browned. Add the cream, tiny bit of salt, and ample pepper. Simmer for a moment to reduce the cream, and then toss with the hot pasta, just removed from the water. Add lots of cheese and a parsley garnish.

SERVES 4.

Bagna Cauda
(Italy)

This is a hot dip, or literally hot bath, common in the hills of Italy. It is loaded with salt and fat, so it is one of those dishes that you prepare "once in a while," but you must be careful because you could very well become addicted.

> ½ cup olive oil
> 1 stick (¼ pound) butter
> 3 to 5 cloves garlic, chopped fine
> 6 anchovy fillets, chopped or mashed
>   Pepper

Heat the oil and butter together in an earthenware pot over hot water or in a double boiler. In another pan cook the garlic in a bit of the oil until it is soft. Add the anchovy fillets, and cook until the fish dissolves into a paste, about 5 minutes. Add all to the pan of hot oil and butter.

The bagna cauda is kept hot in the middle of the table. Guests dip celery, cooked and cooled artichokes, endive, cucumbers, green onions, and Italian bread into this lovely mixture.

SERVES 8.

Early American Cuisine

We Americans have a depressing image of our own food history. This image is probably due to the stories about the first hard winters endured by the English colonists, but following those first few years things were very good for us. As a matter of fact, we have always eaten rather well.

Things were tough in the beginning, but it was certainly not the fault of the new land. Wild game, including the turkey, was abundant, and squashes, pumpkins, cranberries, and nuts were common. But the new people were tradesmen, not hunters or farmers. We lasted only through the patience of the first American citizen, the one wrongly called the Indian. He gave us the gift of corn, and we lived on corn for more generations than we can now remember. We made johnnycakes, hoecakes, Indian pudding, corn bread, succotash, cornmeal mush, hasty pudding, so called because it took only 6 hours to cook, and finally, just plain corn.

We were criticized by the English, as well we should have been. To the eyes of the European we were gross and uneducated eaters, a definition that seemed to charm old Ben Franklin. And Frances Trollope, who came from England in 1827 to assess American domestic habits, claimed that we "eat with greatest possible rapidity and in total silence . . . and consume much too much whiskey." It seems that some things remain constant.

We did eat a great deal of fat and salt, a taste that seems to be with us to this day. In the early days of the colonies a mother often fed children on little more than beans and salt pork, and we can only imagine her anguish when she "scraped the bottom of the salt pork barrel." What was she to feed her family?

We need to remember that kind of history and certainly that kind of woman. But we need also to remember that our food has a grand background. We are new in the business of cuisine, not ancient like the Chinese and not flamboyant like the French. The first American cookbook was not even published until 1796. It was called *American Cookery* by Amelia Simmons, and it was the first book in history to offer recipes for the use of our beloved cornmeal. Now that is an American cookbook!

The following recipes come from cookbooks that are in the rare book collection of the New York Public Library. These volumes give us some idea of the nature of the food during the formation of the colonies, and from the recipes we can agree that there were some fine feasts going on outside the residence of that highly respected American cook Thomas Jefferson. The recipes give us no exact amounts, so you and I must guess at what the gracious cook intended. If you wish to remove my quantities and create your own, do so, by all means.

Matalote

(The Virginia Housewife, 1824, the first cookbook to be published in the South)

        2 **pounds whitefish fillets**
        2 **yellow onions, peeled and chopped**
        ½ **cup parsley, chopped**
        ½ **cup mushrooms, sliced**
        1 **teaspoon whole thyme**
           Pepper and salt to taste
           Spice*
           Red wine "to wet it completely"
    1½ **tablespoons flour**
    1½ **tablespoons butter**

Cut the fish into serving pieces, and place them in a heavy pot with a tight lid. Add the onions, parsley, mushrooms, thyme, pepper, salt, and spice, and almost cover with the wine. (Red wine makes a very strange-looking dish, though the flavor is fine. You may wish to use a white wine.)

Bring to a heavy simmer, and cook, covered, for 15 to 25 minutes, or just until the fish begins to flake. Remove the fish pieces to a heated platter, and reduce the sauce. Blend the flour and butter over medium heat until a very light brown roux. Use to thicken the sauce.

---

*We cannot be sure what was meant by *spice*, but it was probably a bit of mace and nutmeg.

This dish was served over pieces of bread that had first been fried in butter.

SERVES 6.

Chicken Pudding
(The Virginia Housewife, 1824)

This dish is actually a chicken in Yorkshire pudding. It is delicious and dramatic.

       1 **3-pound chicken, cut up**
          Thyme
          Parsley
          Pepper and salt to taste
       3 **eggs**
       ½ **cup milk**
       1 **cup flour**
       3 **tablespoons butter, melted and cooled**

Simmer the chicken pieces in very little water along with some thyme, parsley, pepper, and salt. When the chicken is not quite tender, remove it from the broth, and place it in a baking dish. Mix the eggs and milk together, and gradually stir in the flour. Add the butter and a bit of salt and pepper. Pour this batter over the chicken pieces.

Bake at 400° for 15 minutes, and then turn the oven down to 350°. Bake for another 10 minutes, or until lightly browned and puffy.

SERVES 4 TO 6.

Pickled Oysters
(The Complete Cook, London, 1658)

This dish is very English indeed. It is typical of the recipes that came over on the early ships from England, and I expect that if you owned a cookbook, you were a fairly wealthy person.

In the old days in England these oysters were supposedly kept in small copper barrels and eaten after six days. I cannot imagine such a thing!

- 1 **pint small oysters, cleaned, with their liquor or juice**
- **Pinch of mace**
- 8 **black peppercorns**
- ¼ **teaspoon salt**
- ¼ **cup white wine vinegar**

Place all the ingredients in a stainless steel pan, and simmer for about 6 minutes, or just until tender.

Chill, and serve over lettuce as a first course.

SERVES 4 TO 6 AS AN APPETIZER.

Celery Sauce
(The Frugal Housewife, Philadelphia, 1802)

A sauce "for boiled fowl, Turkeys and all."

- **Celery, chopped**
- **Mace, nutmeg, salt, and pepper to taste**
- **Flour**
- **Butter**

Simmer the celery in very little water until tender. Add mace, nutmeg, salt, and pepper. Thicken with a roux of equal parts butter and flour, blended together over medium heat until the flour barely begins to brown. "Then boil it up and pour it in the dish."

Boston Baked Beans
(Durgin Park, Boston)

Baked beans belong to the American culture, and properly prepared, as they are at the old Durgin Park Restaurant in Boston, they are stupendous. The idea of a canned bean product's even being called baked beans makes me ill. Use this recipe, and you will have great success.

2 pounds white beans
1 teaspoon baking soda
1 large yellow onion, peeled
1 pound bacon or fatback, chopped
8 tablespoons sugar
⅔ cup molasses
2 teaspoons dry mustard
4 teaspoons salt
½ teaspoon pepper

Soak the beans in water to cover overnight.

Cook beans in ample water with the baking soda. Simmer for 10 minutes. Drain, and rinse.

Place the onion in the bottom of a 3-quart ovenproof casserole. Add half the bacon or fatback.* Add the beans. Top with the remaining bacon or fatback.

Mix together the sugar, molasses, mustard, salt, and pepper. Pour this over the beans, and add enough water barely to cover. Do not stir. Bake, covered, at 300° for 6 hours. After a couple of hours, stir and check beans. You may have to add a bit of water now and then. Don't make the beans too wet.

SERVES 6 TO 8.

*I prefer bacon.

Pepper Pot Soup
(New England)

This is what kept the boys alive at Valley Forge—and George ate it with them! The cook had nothing but tripe and vegetables, so he came up with this great dish. Please try this one. It is great! I have adapted it to your kitchen, of course, but it is a strictly American dish.

    4 or 5 slices bacon, chopped
    ½ cup chopped onion
    ½ cup chopped celery
    2 green peppers, seeded and chopped
    2 quarts Basic Brown Soup Stock (page 47)
    ⅛ teaspoon marjoram
    ⅛ teaspoon ground cloves
    1 potato, peeled and chopped
    1 pound blanched tripe, cut into ½-inch squares
    1 bay leaf
      Ground black pepper to taste

Fry the bacon. Add the onion, celery, and green peppers to the pan. Sauté all lightly. Add all to a soup kettle along with the soup stock. Add the marjoram and cloves. You might also supply some authenticity by adding a potato to the pot.

Fry the blanched tripe until lightly browned, about 15 minutes.

Add to the soup pot along with a bay leaf, and bring to a boil. Simmer gently for about 3 hours, until the tripe is well cooked, or you may have to add water.

In the colonies so much pepper was added to the soup that it was "pepper pot, smokin' hot." You add as much ground black pepper as you think you can take!

SERVES 8 TO 10.

Misaquatash
(American Indian)

This is the original dish from which we get the term *succotash*. The Indians, the gracious original Americans, were kind enough to teach us how it was done.

- **1   16-ounce can kidney beans, drained**
- **1   10-ounce package frozen corn**
   Butter
   Salt and pepper to taste

Cook the kidney beans and corn together. Originally bear grease was added to this dish, but I suggest a little butter, salt, and pepper.

SERVES 6.

Indian Pudding
(Durgin Park, Boston)

Corn puddings kept our forefathers alive during their first days in this country. The corn, and, therefore, our lives, were a gift from the gracious Indians. Without them the settlers surely would have died.

This dish takes a long time to prepare, but it is worth it!

- **1   cup yellow cornmeal**
- **½   cup black molasses**
- **¼   cup sugar**
- **¼   cup butter**
- **¼   teaspoon salt**
- **¼   teaspoon baking soda**
- **2   eggs**
- **6   cups hot milk**
   Vanilla ice cream

Mix the cornmeal with the molasses, sugar, butter, salt, baking soda, and eggs. Add 3 cups of hot milk, stirring carefully. Place in a 2-quart bean pot or other covered pot, and bake in a 400° oven until all comes to a boil. Then stir in another 3 cups of hot milk, and bake at 275° for 4 to 6 hours, or until all is absorbed. Stir every half hour.

Serve hot in little bowls with a bit of vanilla ice cream on top.

This dish was also called hasty pudding. Now you know why.

SERVES 8 TO 10.

New Orleans

I have never in my life had so much fun eating in a single city as in New Orleans, which is, without a doubt, the best restaurant city in the United States: red beans and rice at Buster Holmes; barbecued shrimp at Pascal Manale's; gumbo at K. Paul's; dinners at Galatoires and Chez Hélène's; lunch in Louis Armstrong Park, eating alligator sausage and crawfish pie with Chef Paul Prudhomme.

The following recipes are close to the flavors that I experienced in New Orleans. The food is terribly rich, and you must either go on a binge and then diet for several days or eat this sort of creativity very sparingly.

Barbecued Shrimp

This is one of the most spicy and delicious shrimp dishes that I have ever eaten, and it is close to that served in New Orleans. You must try this.

   3 slices bacon, chopped
   ½ pound margarine
   2 tablespoons Dijon-style mustard*
1½ teaspoons chili powder
   ¼ teaspoon basil
   ¼ teaspoon thyme
   1 teaspoon fresh-ground coarse black pepper
   ½ teaspoon oregano
   2 cloves garlic, crushed
   2 tablespoons Rex crab boil or similar brand†
   ½ teaspoon Tabasco
1½ pounds large shrimp, with shells

Preheat oven to 375°.

In a small frying pan, fry bacon until clear. Add the margarine and all other ingredients except the shrimp. Simmer for 5 minutes.

Place the shrimp in an open baking dish, and pour sauce over the top. Stir once to coat all of the shrimp. Bake in an uncovered dish for 20 minutes, stirring twice during the baking process.

Serve hot and at once! You may peel these shrimp before eating, but not before cooking. I eat them shell and all, leaving only a pile of tails on my plate. Many people in New Orleans do the same. Have a towel ready for each guest, for this most delicious dish is very messy.

SERVES 6.

Gumbo Filé

This classic soup takes some time to prepare, and it is not cheap. But once you have tasted this culinary treasure, you will understand why all the restaurants of New Orleans serve it . . . and in each place it is different. You can witness the battle of the gumbo, a battle waged between restaurants just as seriously as any battle in our time.

---

*Grey Poupon is fine.
†Available in most fish markets and many supermarkets.

         3 cups fine-chopped onions
     1½ cups fine-chopped celery
         1 cup fine-chopped green peppers
         3 cloves garlic
            Peanut oil
         2 pounds fresh okra, chopped into ¼-inch
              pieces, or 1½ pounds if frozen
         2 tablespoons flour
         1 16-ounce can tomatoes, drained
       ½ cup diced ham
         1 teaspoon thyme
         1 teaspoon basil
         3 bay leaves
         1 tablespoon filé powder*
         4 quarts fish stock†
         1 quart Basic Brown Soup Stock (page 47)
            Shrimp, oysters, or crab
       ½ cup parsley, chopped
            Pepper and salt to taste
            Dash of Worcestershire sauce
            Dash of Tabasco
         3 cups cooked white rice

Sauté the onions, celery, green pepper, and garlic in a bit of the oil.

Sauté the okra separately in a bit of oil in a SilverStone skillet (so the okra does not stick) over medium flame for about 25 minutes (or less with frozen), or until the okra is soft and the ropy texture is gone.

In another frying pan cook 1 tablespoon peanut oil and the flour until the flour begins to brown a bit into a roux. Add the tomato pulp, and cook to a paste. Add the ham, thyme, basil, bay leaves, and filé. Cook for 5 minutes more. Add the vegetables to the combined fish and brown soup stock. Heat the stock, and slowly add the tomato and roux mixture, stirring all the time, until the mixture thickens. Simmer for 1 hour.

When close to serving time add the shrimp, oysters, or crab, parsley and cook for only 15 minutes. Season with pepper, salt if

*Available in spice shops, fish markets, and delicatessens.
†Prepare by cooking fish scraps in water along with a few carrots; 1 yellow onion, peeled and chopped; and 1 cup chopped celery. Simmer for about 1 hour.

you need it, and a dash each of Worcestershire and Tabasco.
Serve in bowls with ¼ cup cooked rice.

SERVES 8 TO 12.

Red Beans and Rice

This dish originally came from the slave quarters in the South.
Many children grew up with their memories of the table involv-
ing this dish at almost every meal. It remains a classic dish coming from poverty and is still eaten in good times because we need
to remember. You may have some trouble getting your family to
understand that this dish provides you with an almost complete
meal in terms of nutrition, but it is worth the effort.

       ½ pound small red beans
       ½ pound ham hocks or smoked ham
       1 large yellow onion, peeled and chopped
       3 stalks celery, chopped
       1 tablespoon parsley, chopped
       ½ green pepper, chopped
       1 or 2 bay leaves
       2 large cloves garlic, crushed
       ⅛ pound margarine
          Pepper to taste
       1 tablespoon Worcestershire sauce
          Tabasco to taste
          Salt to taste
       3 cups cooked white rice

Soak the beans overnight in ample water. The next day drain the
water from the beans, and place in a heavy kettle. Add the ham,
onion, celery, parsley, bay leaves, and garlic, and add water to
the pot barely to cover the contents. Bring to a boil, and then turn
to a simmer. Simmer, uncovered, for 2 hours, being careful that
the beans do not stick or become too dry. You may have to add a
little water.

After the initial two hours of cooking, add the margarine,
pepper, Worcestershire, and Tabasco to the pot. Continue cooking for 1 more hour, this time with a lid on the pot and the heat
quite low.

Correct the seasonings. You may wish to add a bit of salt, but do not add salt until this point because salt cooks out of the ham hocks or ham and seasons the dish well.

Serve over white rice with a nice green salad and a good white wine or beer.

SERVES 4 TO 6.

Jambalaya

Everyone I have talked with from the South tells me, "This dish is not the way my mother made it!" Ten people in town give you ten variations on this classic. This is close to what I tasted at several of the restaurants or park stalls in New Orleans. The black women at the Methodist Church have this dish down pat, but mine isn't bad. As a matter of fact, I think I like it better than theirs. It is a combination of several variations, and it is a whole meal in itself. Salad, some wine, some barbecued shrimp, and a pot of Gumbo Filé (page 338) to start. Well, that's a complete meal in New Orleans.

    2 ham hocks
    4 carrots, chopped
    1 yellow onion, peeled and chopped
    3 stalks celery, chopped
    1 3-pound chicken, cleaned
    2 bay leaves
    2 tablespoons peanut oil
    1 cup chopped yellow onion
    1 green pepper, chopped
    1 cup celery, chopped
    5 green onions, chopped
    1 28-ounce can tomatoes (reserve
         liquid), chopped
    4 tablespoons tomato paste
    ¼ cup chopped parsley
    3 cloves garlic, crushed
    1 teaspoon whole thyme
    1 teaspoon basil
       Salt and pepper to taste
    ⅛ cup Worcestershire sauce
    1 pound hot smoked link sausage
    2 cups Uncle Ben's converted rice

Place the ham, carrots, the 1 yellow onion, and celery in a pot, and cover with water. Cook for 2 hours, and then add the chicken and 1 bay leaf. Cover, and simmer for about 1 hour, or until the chicken is tender. Allow the pot to cool a bit. Bone the chicken, and chop the meat. Bone the ham hocks, remove the skin, chop the meat. Reserve the stock (need 3 cups), and the two meats.

In a Dutch oven heat the oil. Add the cup chopped yellow onion and pepper, and sauté until tender. Add the celery, green onions, and tomatoes, and cook until soft. Add the ham hock pieces and tomato paste, and sauté the mixture until it begins to brown. Add the parsley, garlic, 1 bay leaf, basil, salt, pepper, Worcestershire sauce, the reserved tomato liquid, and 2 cups reserved stock. Cook this gravy for 1 hour.

Cut the sausages into bite-size slices, and brown them in another pan; discard any grease, and place the sausage slices in the gravy. Rinse out the frying pan with 1 cup reserved stock, and pour into the gravy. Place the rice in the gravy, along with the boned chicken, and cover. Bring to a boil; then reduce heat, and cook for about 25 minutes, or until the rice is tender. Keep careful check so that the pot does not dry out; you may have to add a little water in order to finish cooking the rice.

SERVES 10 TO 12.

Oysters Bienville

Bienville, the Frenchman who founded New Orleans in 1718, must have been a great lover of food. To this day there is a grand oyster dish which carries his name. The French, the Spanish, the Cajuns or Acadians, the southern blacks, and the English settlers all were in on the development of this New Orleans cuisine. I consider the city and its food a national treasure. Just this one dish alone should make the whole town qualify for such an honor.

> 3 dozen oysters on half shell
> ½ stick (⅛ pound) butter
> 1 yellow onion, chopped
> 1 bunch green onions, chopped
> 1 cup mushrooms, chopped
> 3 ounces shrimp, cooked and chopped
> 3 ounces ground smoked ham
> 2 tablespoons parsley, chopped
> 2 cloves garlic, crushed
> 2 tablespoons brandy
> ¼ cup fine-chopped yellow onion
> ½ cup chicken stock
> 2 cups cream or milk
> 2 tablespoons butter
> 2 tablespoons flour
> ½ cup white wine
>   Salt and pepper to taste
> ½ cup bread crumbs (optional)
> 4 pounds rock salt

To prepare oysters, remove from shells, and reserve. Wash shells, and dry. Melt the ½ stick butter in saucepan. Add the 1 yellow onion, green onions, and mushrooms, and sauté. Add the shrimp, ham, parsley, garlic, and brandy. Simmer for 2 to 3 minutes.

Simmer the onion in the chicken stock until reduced to ½ cup. Combine with the cream or milk, and simmer for a few minutes.

In another pan melt the butter, add the flour, and cook over low heat for about 2 minutes or until the roux is browned. Add the white wine to the cream sauce, and heat. Stir in the roux, and cook until thick, stirring all the time. Add salt and pepper, the mushroom mixture, and cook for another few minutes to blend the flavors.

Place the oysters on shells. Spoon the white sauce over oysters. Place oysters on preheated pans of rock salt or on a baking pan. Bake at 475° for 15 minutes. You may wish to sprinkle with bread crumbs before baking; they add color and flavor.

SERVES 8 TO 10.

The
International
Community

Africa

Dishes of Africa

When you consider the size of Africa, and the number of nations involved there, you realize the term *African* food is probably no more helpful than the term *Chinese* food or *American* food. The categories are too broad since there are too many food styles involved to lump under one heading.

The following dishes are typical only of the regions from which they come. In order to gain a proper understanding of the nature of the foods of the enormous continent, we must remember that many of the dishes grew out of poverty. Many came about because the high temperature of the climate necessitated the use of heavy spices for preservation. Spices were also common so that one could keep one's system flowing with cooling perspiration during a hot summer day.

You can offer each of the dishes in this section for a complete meal.

Sweet Potatoes with Coconut Milk
(Kenya)

The children will be fascinated by coconut sweet potatoes. Although the sweet potato originally came from America, it has been a lifesaver to those in the Dark Continent.

3 to 4 sweet potatoes, peeled and cubed
1 15-ounce can coconut milk*
1 teaspoon ground cardamom
1 tablespoon brown sugar

In a heavy pot with a lid, blend all the ingredients. Simmer, covered, until the potatoes are tender, about 30 minutes.

SERVES 6 AS A VEGETABLE.

Biafran Stew

Biafra as a nation exists only in the memory of those who recall the late 1960s. One of my students from my days as a college chaplain was from Biafra. He gave me this recipe shortly after the war in which all his people were wiped out. He had 217 cousins, and he corresponded with 70 of them . . . in earlier times. When you cook this delicious dish please think of the people of Biafra and of my friend George Obiozer . . . and of the stupidity of wars of starvation.

1 1½-pound chuck steak, deboned,
    trimmed, and cubed
1 2½-pound chicken, cut up
1 28-ounce can whole tomatoes
1 green pepper, cut into 12 chunks
1 yellow onion, peeled and chopped
1 teaspoon Tabasco or to taste
  Salt and pepper to taste

Brown the chuck steak. Place all the ingredients in a large kettle with a lid, and simmer, covered, for about 1½ hours, or until the chicken and beef are tender.
    Serve with Couscous (below).

SERVES 6 TO 8.

*Available in Oriental markets.

Couscous
(Nigeria)

Couscous is a processed wheat product, and George Obiozer suggested that I use farina cereal because it is close to the type he knew as a child. I have added another form of processed wheat, bulgur, which provides a bit of nutlike flavor to the dish.

    ¼ cup bulgur wheat
    ¼ teaspoon salt
    3 cups water
    ½ cup farina cereal

Place the bulgur, salt, and water in a kettle with a tight-fitting lid. Simmer, covered, for 15 minutes. Add the farina slowly, stirring constantly. Continue to stir, and cook for about 10 minutes, or until thick.

Serve, as you would potatoes, along with Biafran Stew (page 348). The dish is eaten with the fingers, and it is great fun for everyone involved.

SERVES 6 TO 8.

Baked Curried Fish
(Kenya)

The marvelous thing about this kind of food is that it is eaten with the fingers and from a common pot. Sharing a common pot is a lesson in our dependency upon one another, something that tribal peoples have always understood. In our day many tribes with traditional customs of sharing and living refuse to adapt to more modern ways since they know that they will have to give up too much only to gain anxiety and loneliness.

So enjoy an African dinner, and remember that we all were tribal people, all nomads, at an earlier time in our history.

    3 yellow onions, peeled and sliced
    2 tablespoons peanut oil

SAUCE
    ½ cup white vinegar
    ½ teaspoon cardamom
    2 teaspoons turmeric
    2 teaspoons chili powder
    ½ teaspoon cumin
    3 cloves garlic, crushed
    ½ teaspoon salt
    1 1-ounce can tomato paste
    1 cup water

    2 pounds whitefish fillets

Sauté the onions in the oil until clear. Set aside.

Prepare the sauce by simmering all the ingredients for 20 minutes.

Place the fish in a greased baking dish. Cover first with the sautéed onions and then with the sauce. Bake at 350° for 45 minutes to 1 hour.

You might wish to serve this with steamed wheat tortillas, something that is very close to a bread common in many countries in Africa.

SERVES 4 OR 5.

China

Hunan Treasures

The province of Hunan is one of the great farming regions of China. The summers are hot, and the winters are very cold, so one has an image of hearty farmers who love good food, enough food and joy to return them to the fields. They spend a great deal of time thinking about their next meal and are some of the wisest and most spirited cooks in the whole of that great nation. We sometimes find it hard to understand why their food is so spicy hot, but please remember that hot peppers make you sweat on a hot summer day, thus cooling you, and that they keep you warm during a cold winter. So in climates where the temperatures are extreme, spices and peppers are used to keep you happy and comfortable. In mild climates, such as our own, the food is much more boring, to go along with the weather.

The Chinese dinner does not have a single dish that is the center of the meal. Rather, many dishes are served, in small amounts, of course. It is not uncommon to serve fish, pork, duck, and chicken, along with vegetables and noodles, all at the same meal. The index will be helpful to you as you choose a full menu.

Hunan Onion Cake

Wheat and wheat noodles are common in Hunan, thus the following dish. Rice is much more typical of the south of China. The
pancakelike dinner delight can be made from scratch, but I really
think you get better results using prepared wheat tortillas.

        1 egg
        1 tablespoon water
        1 teaspoon sesame oil
        1 package wheat tortillas
        1 bunch green onions, chopped fine
           Peanut oil

Mix the egg with the water and sesame oil. Mix well. Brush one
side of a flour tortilla with the mixture, and sprinkle some green
onions on top. Brush another wheat tortilla with the egg mixture,
and press together the two tortillas, basted sides facing. Cover
with a plate or some other weight for about 15 minutes, or until
the edges are sealed. You may stack up many of these as long as
you separate each pair with a sheet of wax paper.

Place enough peanut oil in a frying pan to give you about
1-inch depth. Heat the oil to 370°. Fry each cake until puffy and
light golden brown on one side, and then turn the cake over,
cooking about 2 minutes altogether. Drain on paper towels, and
then cut into pie-shaped wedges for serving.

MAKES 5.

Bean Curd in Hot Meat Sauce

This recipe is very close to what is served by my friend Henry
Chung of the Hunan Restaurant in San Francisco. He was really
the first to make Hunan cooking popular in this country. He is a
fine chef and a charming gentleman. He claims that this dish is
very popular with the farmers since it is spicy and will certainly
fill one's belly in a most marvelous way. My son Channing will
do almost anything for this dish.

1 cake fresh firm or Chinese-style bean curd
1 cup coarse-ground pork
2 tablespoons white wine
    Cornstarch
4 tablespoons peanut oil
1 tablespoon hot bean sauce (*or* mein see and
        mixed with red chili and garlic paste)
½ tablespoon minced fresh ginger
2 cloves garlic, crushed
2 tablespoons light or dark soy sauce
1 cup frozen green peas
2 teaspoons hot pepper oil *or*
        1 teaspoon cayenne
¼ cup chicken broth
    Dash of salt to taste (optional)
    Black pepper to taste
2 green scallions, minced
1 teaspoon sesame oil

Cut the bean curd into ½-inch cubes, and drain in a colander.

Marinate the pork in a mixture of the white wine and 1 teaspoon cornstarch for a few minutes. Then fry in a hot wok containing the peanut oil. Cook for just a moment, and then add the bean curd cubes. Add the hot bean sauce or mein see mixed with red chili and garlic paste, ginger, garlic, soy sauce, peas, and hot pepper oil or cayenne. Stir-fry for about 1 minute.

Add the chicken broth and optional salt, and stir over high heat until mixture comes to a boil. Thicken the sauce with a mixture of 1 tablespoon water mixed with 1 tablespoon cornstarch. Garnish with the black pepper, scallions, and sesame oil. Serve hot.

SERVES 4 AS SIDE DISH.

■ HINT:

You can make your own pepper oil by heating 1 cup of peanut oil to about 350° Fahrenheit. Add 4 tablespoons crushed red pepper flakes, and remove from the heat. Let this cool and stand for 2 days, and you are ready to cook.

Hunan Steamed Spareribs with Hot Black Bean Sauce

You can make these marvelous ribs as hot as you wish simply by increasing the amount of the red chili and garlic paste. I hope you go to the trouble of finding real Chinese condiments, such as the red chili and garlic paste and the dow see (fermented black beans). It will make a great difference in your cooking. Chinese condiments keep well.

- 2 **pounds pork spareribs**
- 2 **tablespoons light soy sauce**
- 1 **tablespoon dow see*, rinsed**
- 2 **cloves garlic, crushed**
- 2 **tablespoons dry sherry**
- 1 **teaspoon fresh-grated ginger**
  Dash of hot pepper oil *or* **Tabasco** *or* **red chili and garlic paste**
- ½ **tablespoon cornstarch mixed with ½ tablespoon water**
  Pinch of brown sugar

Cut the pork spareribs into 1-inch pieces. Blanch in boiling water for one minute; then drain, and cool.

Mix all the remaining ingredients. Add to the ribs. Steam for 1 hour.

SERVES 6 TO 9.

■ HINT: How to Use the Chinese Wok

See page 9 for a discussion of what kind of wok you should purchase.

Cure the wok by washing it once with soap and water...and then never put soap in it again. Heat the wok on the burner until it is very hot; then add 2 tablespoons peanut oil to it. Swish the oil around, and allow it to cool. Remove and discard the oil, and heat the wok to smoking. Add oil, and continue this routine until you

*See footnote page 306.

have done it three times. Now wash the wok. It will then be ready to use. Never again wash with soap, even if things stick at first. Soak the wok in water, and then brush out the remaining food particles. Always hang your wok on its side to that it will not rust.

Cold Glass Noodle and Chicken Salad in Peanut Sauce

With a name like the above, it must be an unusual salad. It is, and it is also most delicious. This one you must try.

This Hunan dish can be made as hot as you wish simply by adding more pepper sauce. I prefer a pepper sauce found in Chinese markets or delicatessens. Ask for red chili and garlic paste.

> 1 **8-ounce package cellophane noodles***
> 2 **chicken bouillon cubes**
> 2 **tablespoons peanut butter**
> 4 **tablespoons hot water**
> 5 **tablespoons light soy sauce**
> **Red pepper oil (page 353)** *or* **Tabasco**
> *or* **Red Chili Paste with Garlic (page 23)**
> **to taste or cayenne**
> 1 **cucumber**
> 1 **tablespoon rice wine vinegar**
> ¼ **teaspoon sugar**
> 2 **teaspoons sesame oil**
> 1 **cup cooked chicken, cut into julienne sticks**
> ¼ **cup dry roasted peanuts, chopped**

Soak the cellophane noodles in water to cover for 1 hour, and then add the chicken bouillon cubes. Simmer for about 10 minutes, or until the noodles are tender but not mushy. Drain nearly all the broth, and cool the noodles in the refrigerator.

Mix the peanut butter with the hot water. Stir with a fork until it has the consistency of heavy cream; you may need a bit more water. Add the 3 tablespoons soy sauce and the red pepper sauce or Tabasco or cayenne. Drain the noodles, and toss with this dressing.

*Also called glass noodles, Sai Fun, or bean threads.

Cut the cucumber into small julienne pieces, and marinate in a sauce of 2 tablespoons soy sauce, the rice wine vinegar, sugar, and sesame oil. Arrange the cucumber sticks on top of the noodles. Garnish with the cooked chicken with some chopped peanuts.

SERVES 6.

Dishes from the Court of Peking

This large city of China has a distinguished food history. In this country we often see the name used in conjunction with mandarin cooking, and we confuse the two. *Mandarin* means high-class or of the ruling class, and it is used often with Peking cuisine because the ruling classes, the royalty, spent so much time in the city of Peking (now spelled Beijing). However, Canton, the region that most Americans associate with Chinese cuisine, also had a high level of formal dining. So the term *mandarin* means high-class, while *Beijing* refers to a particular city and certainly to a particular style and time in history.

Peking Duck

This is one of the great dishes to come from the Peking region. In the United States we often think of duck as an unusual or exotic fowl, but throughout China the duck is common. You have to take care of a chicken, but you can send a duck out of the house in the morning and it will come home fed in the evening. It really does take care of itself. So here is a dish in which the Peking chefs take an everyday item and elevate it to a treasure.

I should warn you before you begin that you will need a tire pump equipped with a basketball pumping needle, as well as an electric fan and a piece of old bed sheet. Now, if you are still with me we can begin.

> 1   4½- to 5-pound frozen duck*,
>   defrosted completely
>   Salt
>   Peel from ½ orange
> 2   green onions, chopped
> 2   cloves garlic, sliced
> 1   tablespoon peanut oil
> 2   teaspoons brown sugar
> 2   tablespoons mein see or soybean jam
>   or condiment
> ½   cup hoisin sauce
> 2   tablespoons dark soy sauce
> ½   cup chicken broth
> 6   tablespoons honey
>   Green onions and hoisin sauce for
>   garnish

Remove the giblets from inside the duck. Remove the excess fat that hangs about the tail. Rub 1 tablespoon salt into the skin, and let the duck dry for 1 hour.

Sauté or chow the orange peel, the 2 chopped green onions, and garlic in the peanut oil for a moment. Then add ½ teaspoon salt, the brown sugar, mein see or soybean jam or condiment, hoisin, and the soy sauce. Simmer for a moment, and add the chicken broth. Allow mixture to cool.

Wipe the duck dry with paper towels. Using poultry lacing needles, firmly lace up the neck first, and tie it closed with twine. Begin lacing up the rear end of the bird; leave enough of an opening to pour the sauce into the duck's cavity. After pouring the sauce into the cavity, finish the lacing, being sure that the sauce does not leak out from either end of the bird. This lacing and sewing and tying process is very important to the success of the dish because the bird must be airtight when finished.

Now the fun part. You want to separate the skin from the body, and if you have laced it properly, the duck will blow up like a balloon and stay that way through the cooking process. Attach

*Long Island variety is fine.

the basketball needle to a tire pump and insert the needle into the neck of the bird, just under the skin, and on the body side of the string used for the upper neck. Place a second piece of string around the neck, just above the point of the needle insertion, so that you can tie the neck tightly after pumping and removing the needle. Now, slowly pump up the duck until the skin separates, remove the needle, and quickly tie the neck with string.

In a large kettle bring 6 quarts water to a boil. Add the honey. Make a sling out of a bit of old bed sheet, and place the bird in the sling. Lower the bird into the kettle, using the sling, and roll it gently about in the honey water for a few moments. Be careful not to lose the duck from the sling.

Remove the duck from the honey water, and make a sling of a long, narrow piece of bed sheet with which to hang the duck for frying. Bring the wings around to the back of the bird, and slip the cloth under the wings. Hang the bird so that it swings freely from the sling, and aim a fan at it. Allow it to dry in this condition, in a cool place, for 3 to 4 hours.

At the end of the 3 to 4 hours, remove the bird from the sling, and place it on a greased oven rack. Roast it at 425° for 30 minutes. Then turn the oven to 350°, and continue roasting until you have roasted the bird for a *total time* of 18 minutes per pound, including the first ½ hour. In other words, a 4½-pound duck should be in the oven a total of 1 hour and 20 minutes. Place a pan of water under the duck so that the drippings will be caught in the water and not cause the oven to smoke.

When the duck is golden brown, remove it from oven, and allow it to cool for just a moment.

Drain the juice from the cavity of the duck, and serve it in a separate bowl. To serve, slice a bit of the skin from the duck, and place it on a Peking Pancake (below), garnished with a thin slice of green onion and a tiny bit of hoisin sauce.

The meat of the duck is eaten in the same way, but the skin is the highlight and is to be shared by all.

SERVES 6 TO 8 AT A CHINESE DINNER PARTY.

Peking Pancakes

This is a cheater's recipe. The pancakes, in the original form, are too much work to make. So simply purchase some wheat tortillas, and brush half of them with sesame oil on one side. Place the oiled tortilla, oil side down, on an unoiled tortilla. Place these pairs in a steamer, and steam until hot. Serve with Peking Duck (above).

Shrimp with Gin

Where did they get gin in Peking? China has always had several distilled grain products. Our gin will work well in many Chinese dishes and certainly in this one. It is one of my favorite shrimp dishes.

 1 tablespoon peanut oil
 2 teaspoons salt
 2 cloves garlic, sliced
 ½ pound large shrimp, in shells
 1 teaspoon fresh-grated ginger
 2 green onions, chopped
 1 tablespoon light soy sauce
 2 tablespoons gin

Have all ingredients ready. This dish must be done very quickly and over very high heat. Do not peel the shrimp.

Heat the wok or frying pan until very hot. Add the oil, salt, and garlic all at once. Throw in the shrimp, and chow it for a moment. Add the ginger and the green onions, still at high heat. Toss about for a moment until the shrimp changes color from a gray to a bright orange-pink.

When the shrimp are cooked to your taste, and this should take only a moment, throw the soy sauce and the gin into the pan all at once. It should make a sizzling sound. Put a lid on the pan immediately, and turn off the heat. Serve while still hot. Each guest may peel his own shrimp, but many of us eat the shell and all. This dish is that good.

SERVES 3 OR 4.

Drunk Chicken

One the day we were doing this show at our studios in Chicago, the president of the station, WTTW, William McCarter, came into the studios for a visit.

Since he had several distinguished visitors with him, I attempted to take a moment to speak with them. I suddenly realized that they must have been wondering about my cooking ability, as on the counter was a full bottle of whiskey, used for this dish, and a full bottle of gin which was to be used for Shrimp with Gin. I explained, of course, that I was making Chinese food!

1 whole 3-pound chicken, cleaned
4 cups chicken broth
3 slices fresh ginger, each the size and thickness of a quarter
1 tablespoon light soy sauce
2 green onions, chopped
2 cups whiskey
   Sesame oil

Place the chicken in a small cooking pan that will just hold all the ingredients; the chicken should be submerged, if possible, in the broth and whiskey. Add all the remaining ingredients except the sesame oil to the pot, and bring to a simmer. Simmer, covered, for 45 minutes. Then leave the lid on the pot, and turn off the heat. Leave the chicken in the hot bath of whiskey for another ½ hour.

Remove the chicken. Drain the sauce, and save it for a soup stock (some soup!). Rub the chicken with sesame oil and serve.

SERVES 4 OR 5.

Canton

Asparagus and Beef

I hope you have a good steel wok. It will help you a great deal in
the kitchen. Try this recipe with broccoli, too.

    2 pounds asparagus
    ½ pound beef steak, sliced thin across the grain
    2 tablespoons light soy sauce
    1 tablespoon dry sherry
    ¼ teaspoon fresh-grated ginger
       Peanut oil
    2 cloves garlic, crushed

SAUCE
    ½ cup Chinese Chicken Soup (page 365) or beef
       stock
    1 tablespoon light soy sauce
    1 tablespoon dow see*
       Pinch of sugar

Slice the asparagus into pieces about ½ inch thick. Marinate the
beef steak in the soy sauce, sherry, and ginger. Place 1 tablespoon peanut oil in the hot wok, and add the drained meat. Do
not turn, but allow to cook until it is lightly browned on one side.
Remove from the wok.

Place 1 tablespoon peanut oil in the hot wok, and add the
garlic. Add the asparagus, and toss or stir-fry, covered, over high
heat until barely done, about 6 minutes (should still be crunchy).
Return the beef back to the wok. Combine the sauce ingredients,

*See footnote on page 306.

and add to the wok. Stir until the sauces blend, and serve immediately.

SERVES 4 TO 6.

Chinese Bean Curd with Oyster Sauce

Bean curd, a cheeselike product made from the soybean, is one of the most versatile food products in the world. It will take on any flavor and respond to almost any cooking technique. This is one of my favorites.

- 1 fresh bean curd cake
- 3 Chinese mushrooms, soaked for 1 hour, and drained
- ½ yellow onion, peeled
- 2 tablespoons peanut oil
- 1 teaspoon brown sugar
- 2 tablespoons dry sherry
- 1 tablespoon light soy sauce
- 2 tablespoons oyster sauce

Cut the bean curd cake up into ½- by 1-inch pieces. Drain. Slice the mushrooms. Slice the onion.

Lightly brown the bean curd in the hot peanut oil in a wok or frying pan. Remove. Sauté the yellow onion in the same pan. Add the bean curd and mushrooms, and cook for a moment. Add the brown sugar, sherry, soy sauce, and oyster sauce. Simmer for 1 minute more.

Serve with rice.

SERVES 4.

Chinese Beef with Leeks and Pepper

One of those dishes that take so little time to prepare and the rewards of which taste like weeks of labor.

> 1   **pound beef flank steak, cut thin across the grain**
> 1   **tablespoon dry sherry**
> 2   **tablespoons light soy sauce**
> 1   **teaspoon fresh-grated ginger**
> 2   **tablespoons peanut oil**
> 3   **cups leeks*, cleaned and sliced (page 160)**
>   **Black pepper**

Marinate the meat in the sherry, soy sauce, and ginger for 15 minutes. Chow or stir-fry very quickly in hot pan, and add leeks at the last minute. Add ample black pepper.

SERVES 4.

Chinese Boiled Chicken with Onions—Chow Yow Gai

Read these instructions carefully. This dish is so simple that you will think the instructions are incorrect. When I did this on the Phil Donahue show, he kept asking me if he had understood properly. He had. The dish is that simple.

> 1   **3- to 3½-pound chicken, cleaned**
> 2   **bunches green onions**
> 1   **tablespoon light soy sauce**
> 1   **tablespoon sesame oil**
> 2   **teaspoons salt**
> ½   **cup peanut oil, heated to smoking point**

Fill a large kettle with water, and bring it to a boil. Place the chicken in the boiling water. When the water stops boiling, take out the chicken. Cover the pot, and when the water boils again, place the chicken back in the pot. Cover. Turn off the burner. Leave the bird in the pot and the pot on the burner. After 1 hour the chicken is done. Remove, and cool.

Debone the chicken, and tear the meat into small strips. Place them on a large platter. Clean the green onions, and split each onion down the middle. Then cut them up into ½-inch pieces, and place over the mound of chicken. Pour the soy sauce and

---

*If leeks are not available, use green onions.

sesame oil over the chicken. Pour the salt over the onions. When you are ready to serve, pour the hot peanut oil over the onions and chicken. Toss like a salad. Serve.

SERVES 4 TO 6.

Chinese Chicken Soup

The plain, bland Chinese soup stock that you find in most American-Chinese restaurants is a simple blend of 1 chicken to 5 gallons water. A good stock is made according to the following recipe. Remember that Chinese soup stock is rather light and terribly versatile. If you wish a heavier stock, proceed with the recipe, but omit the draining and rinsing process in the middle. Just cover the bones with water, and cook. That is what I generally do.

> **3   pounds chicken necks and backs**
> **3   slices fresh ginger**
> **1   dried turnip ball (optional) (see Glossary)**

Place the chicken in a large kettle, and cover with cold water. Bring to a light simmer. When a scum begins to form on the water, drain the kettle completely, and rinse the bones. Cover with fresh cold water, and add the ginger and turnip ball if desired. Bring to a light boil, and simmer for 2 hours. Drain, and skim the stock.

MAKES 3 QUARTS.

Chinese Fish Paste

Chines fish paste is a most versatile substance and most easily made. It's versatile in that you can mold it or form it into many different shapes, and since it is made with a bit of sherry, soy sauce, and ginger, it does not have a fishy flavor. For this reason children are very fond of this.

- **2 pounds whitefish**
- **2 tablespoons dry sherry**
- **2 tablespoons light soy sauce**
- **2 green onions, chopped**
  Bit of grated fresh ginger
  Salt and pepper to taste
- **1 tablespoon sesame oil**
- **1 egg**

Carefully bone the whitefish; remove all the bones. Place the small pieces of fish in an Osterizer or grinder, and grind to a smooth paste. If you use an Osterizer, you must mix this in very small batches; if you use a food processor, you can mix in a bit larger batch. Remove the fish paste to a bowl, and add the remaining ingredients. Mix this carefully, and you have a basic fish paste.

MAKES 1¾ POUNDS.

Chowed Chinese Vegetables

You can vary this dish to suit your supplies. Most vegetables work well, and there is no point at which you must stop adding variations.

When you cook vegetables Chinese style, always remember to put the vegetables that take the longest to cook in the pan first.

- **2 cloves garlic, sliced thin**
- **2 tablespoons peanut oil**
- **2 yellow onions, peeled and chopped**
- **8 stalks celery, chopped**
- **6 Chinese mushrooms, soaked for 1 hour, drained, and chopped**
- **1 10-ounce package sugar peas or frozen peas**
- **1 teaspoon brown sugar**
- **1 tablespoon sesame oil**
- **2 tablespoons light soy sauce**
- **1 tablespoon dry sherry**

In a hot frying pan or wok sauté the garlic in the peanut oil. Add the onions, and cook for a moment. Add the celery. Cook for a few minutes more and then add the Chinese mushrooms and either sugar or frozen peas. Cook on high heat until all is hot, about 5 minutes, stirring very often. Mix the brown sugar with the sesame oil, soy sauce, and sherry. Throw this into the pan, mix, and serve.

SERVES 8 AS VEGETABLE.

Clams in Dow See

In San Francisco the Chinese restaurants that specialize in fresh seafood serve this dish as regularly as noodles. It is superb.

This is a favorite clam dish of mine and terribly simple to prepare. The dow see, or fermented black beans, may be purchased in any Chinese grocery store or good specialty shop.

> 2 tablespoons peanut oil
> 2 cloves garlic, sliced
>   Tiny bit of grated fresh ginger
> 1 quart clams, in shells, rinsed and drained
> 1 tablespoon dow see
> 2 tablespoons sherry

Gather all the ingredients, and be ready to go. Place the peanut oil in a hot wok on the stove or in a large heavy kettle. Add the garlic and ginger. Add the clams in the shell, and toss them in the oil. Cover, and allow to steam for a few minutes while you rinse the dow see. Then mash the dow see, and mix it with the sherry. Pour this sauce over the clams, and toss. Cover the clams, and continue cooking until all the clams are open, about 6 minutes. Be careful not to overcook. Serve the clams in the shell.

SERVES 3.

Cucumber Soup

Omit and substitute! That's how recipes should be written. Please don't ever get so hung up on published recipes that you forget that you can omit and substitute. You will like this dish.

2 **pork steaks, 1 pound total, deboned and
          coarsely chopped**
2 **thin-sliced cucumbers**

Proceed as in Peas and Egg Soup (page 372), using pork and cucumbers in place of eggs and peas.

SERVES 6.

Fish and Lettuce Soup

I know that this dish sounds strange, as we do little with cooked lettuce. In this dish neither the lettuce nor the fish is cooked for more than a moment, so the result is light and refreshing.

1 **tablespoon peanut oil**
2 **cloves garlic, chopped**
1 **quart Chinese Chicken Soup (page 365)**
2 **slices ginger**
½ **pound boneless thin-sliced whitefish fillet**
1 **head iceberg lettuce, chopped**
   Salt to taste
   Light soy sauce to taste
   Sesame oil to taste
3 **green onions, chopped**

Sauté the garlic in the peanut oil.

Bring the soup to a boil. Add the ginger and the garlic. Add the fish. Simmer for 5 minutes. Add the iceberg lettuce. Cook for 2 minutes. Add the salt, soy sauce, and sesame oil. Serve with the green onions on top.

SERVES 6 TO 8.

Fish Balls in Brown Gravy

Make the Fish Balls in Soup Stock (below). Drain the fish balls, and cover with a nice brown gravy (Bordelaise, page 262). A very nice addition to your meal.

SERVES 4 TO 6.

Fish Balls in Soup Stock

1   egg
3   green onions, chopped
1   pound Chinese Fish Paste (page 365)
6   cups Chinese Chicken Soup (page 365)

Add the egg and green onions to the fish paste. Mold into fish balls about 1 inch in diameter, and simmer very, very gently in the soup. This makes a delightful meal.

SERVES 6.

Fried Fish Toys for the Children

A great delight for children because most children are not upset by the flavor of fish but they are uncomfortable with the color and texture. Here is a perfect solution.

About ½ cup cornstarch
1   pound Chinese Fish Paste (page 365)
    Peanut oil

Add the cornstarch to a small amount of the fish paste until you get something that can be handled easily. The amount of cornstarch you may have to use depends on how moist the fish is. In any case, you want to prepare something that can be cut like cookie dough. Place the dough on a sheet of wax paper, and place another sheet on top. Roll the dough carefully into normal cookie dough thickness, and cut with your children's favorite cookie cutters. Fry these little creatures very slowly and very carefully in a bit of oil, and serve them with a flair. They make a delightful plate for children, and adults will get a kick out of them as well.

SERVES 8 CHILDREN OR 4 ADULTS WHO ARE IN A PARTY MOOD.

Fried Shrimp, Chinese Style

I love this dish. I first had it in San Francisco many years ago, and I've tried hard to duplicate it ever since.

- 1 pound large shrimp, in shells
- 1 tablespoon light soy sauce
- ½ tablespoon dry sherry
- ½ teaspoon grated fresh ginger
- 2 tablespoons peanut oil
- 2 cloves garlic, chopped
- 3 green onions, chopped
- 1 teaspoon salt
- 1 tablespoon sesame oil

Marinate the shrimp in the shells for 15 minutes in the soy sauce, sherry, and ginger. Drain. Stir-fry in a hot pan with the peanut oil and garlic until the color changes. Add the green onions. Add the salt and sesame oil. Toss until the onions barely wilt. Serve hot. Let each guest remove the shells at the table.

SERVES 6 AS PART OF CHINESE MEAL.

My Cousin David's Hot Szechwan Chicken

How do I tell you about my cousin David? He is a crazy ad exec in San Francisco, and he is a fine cook. Once a week friends call in and tell him that they are coming for dinner . . . and David tells them what they are to bring: "Bring two pounds of fish" or "Bring six skinned chicken breasts." They arrive, and he cooks dinner for everyone. This is always on Mondays. Do you know how this once-a-week restaurateur answers his phone on Monday? "This is Sum Dum Goi," he says.

> **4 chicken breasts**
> **2 tablespoons light soy sauce**
> **1 tablespoon dry sherry**
> **2 tablespoons cornstarch**
> **6 dried red peppers**
>
> SAUCE
> **2 tablespoons sherry**
> **2 tablespoons dark soy sauce**
> **2 teaspoons brown sugar**
> **1 tablespoon sesame oil**
> **1 teaspoon Worcestershire sauce**
> **1 tablespoon water**
> **1 tablespoon cornstarch**
> **3 tablespoons peanut oil**
>
> **Chopped green onions**
> **Chopped toasted peanuts**

Debone the chicken breasts, and cut into small pieces. Marinate them in the soy sauce, sherry, and cornstarch.

Remove the seeds from the red peppers. Cut them into small pieces.

Combine the sauce ingredients, and set aside.

Now place the peanut oil in a hot frying pan or wok, and add the red pepper pieces. Cook for 15 seconds. Add the chicken, marinade and all, and cook over high heat, stirring constantly for 10 minutes. Add the sauce mixture, and cook until it thickens. Top with chopped green onions and chopped toasted peanuts.

SERVES 4.

Peas and Egg Soup

This simple soup is served to persons who are ill and cannot digest more complex food. However, you will find that the flavor of this soup is so lovely that you will want to serve it at a formal dinner party, or better yet, to your family.

      1 **quart Chinese Chicken Soup (page 365)**
      1 **10-ounce package frozen peas**
         Chopped Chinese or fresh white mushrooms
      3 **eggs, whipped**
         Light soy sauce to taste
         Salt to taste
      1 **tablespoon sesame oil**
      3 **green onions, chopped**
         Pepper (optional)

To the soup add the peas and mushrooms. Bring to a boil. Remove from the heat and pour the eggs on top of the soup. Wait for a moment, and then stir. Season with soy sauce, salt, and the sesame oil. Serve with green onions on top. You might also enjoy pepper.

SERVES 6.

Pork Chow Yuk

You should make this dish for your children just so you can hear the funny name variations they will come up with. After all, *yuk* may mean "assorted vegetables" in Chinese, but in English it offers room for all kinds of fun. This is actually a very delicious dish.

2 or 3 pork steaks, cubed
4 tablespoons light soy sauce
3 tablespoons dry sherry
½ tablespoon grated fresh ginger
2 tablespoons peanut oil
2 cloves garlic, sliced
2 yellow onions, peeled and chopped
6 stalks celery
4 Chinese mushrooms, soaked for 1 hour and
    drained
1 cup Chinese celery cabbage or napa, chopped
    (see Glossary)
2 cups bok choy, chopped
2 cups bean sprouts
½ cup Chinese Chicken Soup (page 365)
1 tablespoon cornstarch
  Pinch of sugar
½ tablespoon sesame oil

Cut up the pork steaks into ½- by 1-inch pieces. Marinate them in a mixture of 3 tablespoons soy sauce, 2 tablespoons sherry, and ginger for 15 minutes. Sauté or chow the pork in a little peanut oil in a hot wok, stirring for no more than 5 minutes, or until cooked. Remove pork.

Add a little more oil and the garlic to the wok. Then chow the onions, celery, mushrooms, Chinese cabbage or napa, bok choy, and finally, bean sprouts in this order so that nothing is over-cooked when all are done. Mix the chicken soup, cornstarch, 1 tablespoon light soy sauce, 1 tablespoon sherry, sugar, and sesame oil. Add to the wok along with the pork and vegetables, and stir-fry until thickened—just a moment. Serve this right away because it will continue to cook in the wok.

Remember: Serve Chinese vegetables the minute they are done so that they are never overcooked. "Better a person should wait for a meal than the meal wait for the person."

SERVES 6 TO 8 AS PART OF A CHINESE MEAL.

Sesame Chicken, Chinese Style

This is probably not a proper Chinese way to produce this sesame chicken, but it is easy and delicious. So try it.

    10 chicken thighs
     3 tablespoons light soy sauce
     2 tablespoons dry sherry
    ½ teaspoon grated fresh ginger
     3 tablespoons cornstarch
     4 tablespoons raw sesame seeds
        Peanut oil for deep frying

Cut the chicken thighs in half across the bone. Marinate them in the soy sauce, sherry, ginger, and enough cornstarch to make a thick sauce for 1 hour. Add the sesame seeds. Deep-fry pieces in peanut oil at 375° until lightly browned.

SERVES 5 OR 6.

Shrimp in Oyster Sauce

My wife and I used to order this dish in a basement restaurant in New York's Chinatown. The menu was written on the wall with chalk, in Chinese. We did well just watching what was going on and ordering accordingly. One waiter spoke English, and he helped us more than once. I love to go into places like that. Calvin Trillin says that he will not order unless he is sure of what is coming. I like to order and see what happens.

Be careful that you do not overcook this dish. The solution to this problem is very simple. Have everything cut and ready to go before you ever turn on your wok. Oyster sauce and dow see may be purchased in any Chinese market or good gourmet shop.

1 **pound large shrimp, peeled**
2½ **tablespoons light soy sauce**
2½ **tablespoons dry sherry**
1 **teaspoon grated fresh ginger**
¼ **pound coarse-ground pork**
Peanut oil
A few sticks fresh ginger, matchstick size
2 **cloves garlic, sliced**
2 **green onions, chopped**
2 **tablespoons oyster sauce**
½ **tablespoon dow see, rinsed, drained, and mashed**
1 **egg**
Pinch of brown sugar (optional)

Marinate the shrimp in 2 tablespoons soy sauce, 2 tablespoons sherry, and a bit of grated ginger, for 15 minutes. In another bowl, marinate for the same time the pork in ½ tablespoon soy sauce, ½ tablespoon sherry, and again a bit of grated ginger.

Chow the pork in a bit of peanut oil in a wok or heavy frying pan. Cook it just for only a few moments, or until it changes color. Remove it, and rinse the wok. Heat the wok again, and add 2 tablespoons peanut oil. When the oil is hot, add the ginger sticks and the garlic. When they have cooked for a moment, add the *drained* marinated shrimp, and toss them in the hot oil. Cook for just a moment, and then add the green onions and cooked pork. Add the oyster sauce and dow see. Toss again, and add the egg to thicken the dish. You may wish to add a pinch of brown sugar to cut some of the saltiness.

SERVES 4 TO 6.

Smoky Beef Strips

Actually I must confess that this dish is more Korean than Chinese. I developed it after tasting such a treasure at a street fair in Tacoma. We have many Koreans living near us in the Northwest because of Fort Lewis and McChord Air Force Base. They have brought a delicious influence with them.

1½ pounds beef chuck roast, sliced thin across the
       grain
¼ cup light soy sauce
1 teaspoon grated fresh ginger
½ tablespoon brown sugar
1 teaspoon liquid smoke
1 tablespoon catsup or chili sauce
   Dash of Tabasco
2 tablespoons dry sherry
1 teaspoon sesame oil
1 tablespoon hoisin sauce*
2 cloves garlic, crushed
1 green onion, chopped

Marinate the beef strips in the remaining ingredients for 30 minutes. Broil quickly on one side, just until lightly browned.

SERVES 4 TO 6.

Squid, Chinese Style

I used to eat this dish when I was thirteen years old and living in
Seattle. I would save my allowance and then take the bus to
Seattle's Chinatown and eat at the old Tai Tung, now a tourist
restaurant. In the 1950s it served the best Chinese food one could
imagine, and often as a young boy I would be the only Caucasian
in the dining room. This was a favorite dish of mine.

*Available in Oriental markets and many supermarkets.

   1   **pound squid, cleaned (page 420)**
   ½   **peeled yellow onion**
   3   **stalks celery**
       A few water chestnuts
       Peanut oil
   2   **cloves garlic**
   4   **green onions, chopped**
   ¼   **teaspoon grated fresh ginger**
   1   **tablespoon light soy sauce**
   1   **tablespoon light dry sherry**
   ¼   **cup Chinese Chicken Soup (page 365)**
   ½   **tablespoon cornstarch**
       Pinch of sugar
   1   **tablespoon sesame oil**
   ½   **teaspoon Tabasco**

Clean the squid, and cut into small circles (page 420).

Chop up the onion, celery, and water chestnuts, and place a wok or a frying pan on the burner to heat. When the wok is hot, add a little peanut oil, and chop in the garlic. Immediately add the onion, celery, water chestnuts, and the green onions. Chow or sauté until the vegetables are barely cooked. In the meantime, marinate the squid circles in the grated ginger, soy sauce, and sherry.

Add the squid and vegetables, and toss for just a moment. Because you want all these ingredients to come to their points of fulfillment at the same time, do not overcook anything. To thicken the dish, simply mix together the soup, cornstarch, sugar, and sesame oil, pour into the hot wok, and toss the whole for just a moment. Serve immediately, for this must not be over cooked. It is a classic.

If you wish to serve it northern style, simply throw in a shot of a good Tabasco. Be careful; you do not want to make the dish so hot that you cannot taste the delicate flavor of the lovely squid.

SERVES 6.

Steamed Lingcod in Black Beans

To prepare this most unusual and delicious dish, you must find the Chinese food product called dow see (fermented black beans). It can be found in any Chinese community in most cities or in fancy specialty shops.

> 1½ pounds lingcod fillets
> 2 tablespoons light soy sauce
> 2 tablespoons dry sherry
>   Bit of fresh ginger
> 2 cloves garlic, crushed
> 2 scallions, chopped
>   Pinch of brown sugar
> 1 tablespoon dow see, rinsed, drained, and
>   mashed

Marinate the lingcod fillets in the light soy sauce, sherry, and ginger, for 15 minutes. Add the garlic, scallions, brown sugar, and dow see. Mix this carefully with the fish, and place the fish and marinade in a baking dish that will fit into a steamer (page 301). Cover, and steam for 20 minutes. The fish should steam quickly, so be careful not to overcook it.

SERVES 4 TO 6.

Stuffed Fish Noodles

Prepare won tons in recipe for Toasted Fish-Filled Noodles (below), but do not steam. Simmer in Chinese Chicken Soup (page 365) until tender. I like to add a few mustard greens to the soup stock.

Toasted Fish-Filled Noodles

My dear friend Mary Young, of San Francisco, is a fine cook and a beloved friend. She was born in Peking but came to San Francisco when she was a tiny girl. Her insight into creative and frugal Chinese cooking has always been a great joy. It was she who taught me about the meaning of the Chinese table and the necessity of always being ready for guests. Thus, the following recipe. She will make these noodles and freeze them, and when people appear at her door, it is only a moment before she can pop these under the broiler and offer a great treat to her guests.

Won ton noodles*
Chinese Fish Paste (page 365)
Chopped green onions
Sesame oil

Using won ton noodles, place 1 teaspoon fish paste on half of each noodle. Wet two adjoining edges of the square noodle and fold the two remaining edges over onto the wet edges. You now have a sealed triangle-shaped stuffed noodle. When sealing, be sure to work out the air in the noodle gently, or it will expand when heated. Place in a steamer (page 301), and steam for 15 minutes. Cool. When the noodles are ready to serve, brush them with a bit of sesame oil, and place them under a hot broiler until toasty brown and somewhat puffy. You may wish to turn them and broil them on both sides. This is a delicious hors d'oeuvre. If you wish to freeze it, do so prior to browning. Wrap well.

*Available at supermarkets.

France

Bouillabaisse

This basic French fisherman's stew is a classic from the old peasant world. Mama would prepare the stock while Papa was out on the fishing boat, and at the end of the day what Papa did not sell was thrown into the pot. Please understand that this is not a complex thing to make and that the stock may be made a day or so ahead of time, so that all you need do is heat up the stock as your guests wait anxiously.

This is one of the greatest fish dishes that I know. It is easy to make, but you must have everything as fresh as possible.

   ½ cup olive oil
    3 yellow onions, peeled and chopped
    4 or 5 leeks, cleaned and chopped
    5 or 6 ripe tomatoes, chopped
    1 head or full bulb of garlic, chopped (No, you
             don't have to peel it, and yes, I mean the
             whole thing.)
2½ quarts water
    3 pounds fish heads and bones
    1 head (bunch) parsley, chopped
    2 bay leaves
    1 teaspoon whole thyme
    1 teaspoon whole fennel seed
       Saffron*
    2 chunks (about 2 tablespoons) dried orange peel
       Salt and pepper to taste
       Shot of Tabasco (optional)

*If you use good saffron, a pinch will do; if you use Mexican saffron, you will need several pinches. This is an expensive herb, and you may wish to omit it. The dish will be delicious without it, but you will need to increase the pepper and coriander.

380

Whole coriander seed (optional)
Few tablespoons tomato paste†
5 **pounds clams, whitefish, squid, crab, or mussels**
Chopped parsley for garnish
6 **to 8 toasted slices French Bread (page 267)**

In a long stockpot, sauté in the olive oil the yellow onions, leeks, tomatoes, and garlic for about 10 minutes, or until tender. Add the water, fish heads and bones, parsley head, bay leaves, thyme, fennel, saffron, orange peel, salt, pepper, Tabasco if desired, coriander if desired, and tomato paste. Simmer for about 35 to 40 minutes. Strain.

When you are ready to serve dinner, bring the stock to a boil. Add the fish or shellfish. Simmer for a few minutes so that all is barely cooked, and serve with chopped parsley and toasted French bread in the bowl.

All you need to make this a complete meal is a large salad and your own French bread. Either a red or a white wine is fine.

SERVES 6 TO 8.

French Fish Bisque

This lovely bisque is terribly simple, provided you have some leftover stock from your Bouillabaisse (above). Strain the stock carefully, and heat. Add a bit of rich cream just before serving. Garnish with a bit of parsley. You may wish more Tabasco. I love this served along with a bit of Rouille Sauce (below) spread on toast squares.

---

†This varies according to the ripeness of the tomatoes. I like to add a few tablespoons for color and flavor.

Rouille Sauce

4 **dried red peppers, each 2 inches long**
¼ **cup water**
2 **large cloves garlic, cleaned**
½ **cup mashed potato**
2 **tablespoons olive oil**
½ **cup stock from bouillabaisse or clam juice**

Remove the seeds from the peppers and soak in the water for ½ hour. Drain, discard the water, and mash the peppers in a mortar and pestle along with the garlic. Work until smooth. Blend in the mashed potato and the oil. Gradually beat in the stock or clam juice until the rouille has the consistency of heavy cream. Strain and serve with toast squares, or use on the fish from the bouillabaisse. This is hot, but delicious.

MAKES 1 CUP.

Beef in Burgundy

Cooking with wine is common throughout Europe. I often tell my cooking students that one should never add water to a dish—stock, perhaps, and often wine, but never water. Wine has a cleansing ability, and a little dry sherry will greatly clean a sauce or gravy that tastes too much of oil or fat.

Beef in Burgundy is a classic dish from France.

6 **slices bacon**
3 **pounds good stewing beef**
Olive oil or peanut oil (optional)
3 **or 4 cups burgundy or dry red wine**
2 **cups Basic Brown Soup Stock (page 47)**
2 **tablespoons tomato paste**
3 **cloves garlic, crushed**
½ **teaspoon thyme**
1 **bay leaf**
Salt to taste
1 **pound mushrooms, browned in butter**
2 **or 3 yellow onions, peeled, chopped, and browned in butter**
Roux of ½ cup flour browned in ½ cup butter

Cut the bacon into little strips, and blanch them with boiling water. Fry gently, being careful not to burn them or to darken the fat.

Remove the bacon from the pan, and in the fat, brown the beef. You may wish to add a little olive or peanut oil to the pan. (Note that the meat is not floured before being browned.) Brown the meat carefully and rapidly so that it is a lovely deep brown on all sides. Place in a large 4-quart casserole.

Add the wine and soup stock. Add the tomato paste, garlic, thyme, a bay leaf, and a little salt. Careful with the salt—taste first.

Deglaze your frying pan by putting it back on the heat for a moment after you have removed the beef. When the pan is slightly hot, add a stiff shot of red wine, and move it around with a wooden spoon. Add this beautiful dark liquid to the casserole.

Bake the casserole in a 350° oven for 2 or 3 hours. (You may also cook this in a heavy kettle on the top of the stove.) When the beef is tender, add the mushrooms and yellow onions. Let all cook together for 20 minutes, and then thicken the whole with the roux.

Serve this dish with much too much wine for your guests, along with some cooked green vegetables and a huge salad. You will be famous in about a half hour.

SERVES 8.

■ HINT: On Browning Meat for a Stew

Please do not flour the meat when you brown it for a stew or cassoulet. Browning floured meat means that you have browned flour, and the point here is to brown and color the natural sugars in the meat. So do not flour. Heat the pan, and add a bit of oil. Sear or brown the meat very quickly, and then add to the stewpot. The color and flavor will be much improved.

Cassoulet

A classic dish from France that uses all sorts of meats and takes some time to prepare. However, each of my cooking students who have made this dish has reported great success. It is worth the effort, I promise. Yes, this is the ancestor of that terrible American dish called pork and beans with frankfurters.

Read this one through twice before you begin. It's not complicated, but you could get lost!

1 **frying chicken, cut up**
1 **or 2 pounds pork spareribs, cut into bite-size pieces**
2 **pounds white beans, soaked overnight**
   Fresh water or Chicken Soup Stock (page 53)
2 **yellow onions, peeled and each stuck with 2 cloves**
4 **carrots, quartered**
3 **cloves garlic, crushed**
1 **1-pound piece lamb breast**
1 **pound fatback or salt pork**
   Butter
   Peanut oil
3 **cups fine-chopped yellow onions**
1 **teaspoon crushed garlic**
1 **cup tomato purée**
   Salt and pepper to taste
1 **Polish sausage, cut up**

Brown the fryer pieces in the oven along with the pork spareribs at 350° until barely cooked through, about ½ hour.

Drain the beans, and place in a large kettle with a metal lid that can be placed in the oven, or use a very large casserole. Cover the beans with fresh water or soup stock, and add the yellow onions, stuck with cloves, the carrots, and 3 cloves garlic. Tie the lamb breast and fatback or salt pork into a little bundle (Simply use string and tie it up!). Place it in the pot with the beans and vegetables. Cook gently for about 1 hour, or until the beans are about half-cooked.

In the meantime, in another frying pan, melt a little butter. Add a little peanut oil, and sauté the fine-chopped onions and the 1 teaspoon garlic for about 4 minutes. Add the tomato purée and a little salt and pepper to the pan. Set aside.

When the beans are half-done, remove the lamb and fatback, and cut them into bite-size pieces. Add to the frying pan mixture. Mix, and cook for a moment.

To the pot of beans and vegetables, add the cut-up cooked

chicken, the cut-up spareribs, and the cut-up Polish sausage. Simmer for another 30 minutes.

Now we are ready!

Remove everything from the big pot if you are going to bake in it, or get a large casserole. Place a layer of the beans and vegetables in the bottom of the casserole, add a layer of the tomato sauce, and top with another layer of beans. Continue this until all ingredients are in the casserole. Cover the top with a piece of buttered wax paper, and place the lid on the casserole. Bake in a 350° oven for about 1½ hours, adding a little stock or water if needed.

Serve on large plates with a green salad on the side.

SERVES 12.

Clams Bordelaise

When I was a child, my mother used to take me to the beach and we would gather clams. I always thought that clam gathering was what poor people had to do. Can you imagine? Now I don't have time to gather clams, and I long for the days during which we could afford the time to gather our own. The Pacific Northwest is loaded with clams, and I am as happy as one.

Be sure to check the variations of this dish that appear at the end of the recipe. My older brother thinks that anyone who steams clams without garlic should be shipped out of the country.

> 6 shallots (optional), chopped, or 8 green onions
>   or 1 yellow onion, chopped
> ¼ cup olive oil
> 3 or 4 quarts clams, in shells, drained
> ¼ cup parsley
>   Pepper to taste
> 1 teaspoon whole thyme
> 1 cup dry white wine

In a large kettle with a tight-fitting lid, sauté a few shallots or green onions, or yellow onion, in a little olive oil. Add the clams, parsley, a few twists from your pepper mill, and a couple of pinches of whole thyme. Add the wine, and cover the pot. Place on high heat until the clams open, about 10 minutes. Serve with the sauce poured over the clams.

Variations: You may add 3 cloves of chopped garlic—wonderful! Or remove the clams from the pot, and thicken the sauce with a little roux, a paste made from melted butter and flour; pour the thickened sauce over the clams.

I like to serve these as a first course at a nice meal. They really will go with almost any menu.

SERVES 4 TO 6.

Ratatouille

The color of the eggplant must be one of God's favorites. And the name in French, *aubergine*, is simply wonderful. How can people say that they don't eat eggplant when God loves the color and the French love the name? I don't understand.

This is actually a very rich eggplant relish. It can be used as a vegetable dish or as an omelet filling, quiche flavoring, crepe filling, and on and on.

> 1 eggplant
> 2 tablespoons salt
> Olive oil
> 4 cups cut-up zucchini
> 2 yellow onions, chopped into coarse pieces
> 1 green pepper, cut up
> 3 or 4 tomatoes, chopped into coarse pieces
> Salt and pepper to taste
> 1 teaspoon basil
> ½ teaspoon coriander

Cut the eggplant into ½- by ½-inch squares, and toss with the 2 tablespoons salt. Place in a colander, and drain for ½ hour. In ¼ cup olive oil sauté the zucchini for 5 minutes. Add the yellow onions and green pepper. Cook for 15 minutes. In another pan sauté the eggplant for 15 minutes in a little olive oil; remove from pan. Sauté the tomatoes for a few minutes. Place all the vegetables in a large saucepan. Add salt, pepper, basil, and coriander. Cook for 45 minutes on top of stove. Be careful that the vegetables do not become too mushy.

Serve as a side dish with almost any meat.

SERVES 8 TO 10.

■ HINT:

When preparing vegetables for soup or stew or even red pasta sauce, be sure to sauté or brown them in a frying pan first. This will brown the natural sugar in the vegetables and give your soup, stew, or sauce additional color and flavor.

Glace de Viande

When you buy beef bouillon cubes, you are buying salt, and little else. Better you should make your own. This recipe for meat extract is simple to prepare, but you must begin with our good beef stock.

3 quarts Basic Brown Soup Stock (page 47)
     Cornstarch

Gently boil down the brown stock until there are about 2 cups. This will require changing pans once. The results should be dark and thick, like molasses. Cool, and place in the refrigerator. Cut into little blocks, cover with cornstarch, refrigerate, and use for flavoring and coloring soups and gravies.

MAKES 2 CUPS.

Hot Brie and Almonds

A good Brie can serve as an appetizer or as a dessert. In this case I could eat it at both ends of the meal.

> **Small wheel of Brie cheese**
> **Toasted almonds**
> **Flat rye crackers**

Place the Brie in a small oven dish. Cover the top with toasted almonds. Heat the Brie and almonds in a 350° oven until the cheese begins to melt, about 8 minutes. Then serve with flat rye crackers for dessert or for an appetizer.

Coeur à la Crème

It is always fun to find simple recipes for dishes that are supposed to be very complicated. Hearts of Cream, here offered in a simple version, are to be molded in little porcelain hearts from France. A small Chinese teacup will work just fine.

> **8 ounces cream cheese**
> **½ pint sour cream**
> **2 tablespoons lemon juice**
> **2 tablespoons sugar**

Blend together all the ingredients. Stir until creamy, and then place in any kind of mold you wish. Refrigerate.
   Serve with fresh berries or other fresh fruit!

SERVES 6.

Greece

The cuisine of Greece is ancient and delightful. Buy a bottle of retsina, a pound of Greek olives, some feta cheese, and you have one of the oldest takeout lunches in the world. That was the menu at the great Greek outdoor theater.

In the very early days of Greek civilization, at the time of Homer, the host, a male, did all the cooking for his guests. They were men of rank in the community, and they came to the dinner expecting to help.

Eventually the servants who helped with the cooking were given places of great responsibility, and their places as cooks were so honored and respected that the word went out that "when the cook makes a mistake, it is the flute player that receives the blows."

We are indebted to Greece for the frying pan, the bain-marie (double boiler), béchamel sauce (white sauce), and the following recipes.

Greek Menu Planning

This section offers entire feasts. You might also check the index under Greece for more help in planning a Greek dinner party. Remember that the Greeks have always loved good food, so start cooking.

Saganaki—Fried Cheese

Chris, one of the owners of the Parthenon Greek Restaurant in Chicago, brought this dish of flaming cheese to the Windy City. I have not seen it in other places, and it is very delicious. It is also dramatic and fun. During the dinner hour at the Parthenon you can watch waiters light five and six of these plates of cheese at a time.

> Kasseri cheese, ⅓ inch thick (⅓ pound)
> Egg
> 1 tablespoon milk
> Flour
> Olive oil for pan frying
> Brandy
> Lemon juice

Cut a slice of kasseri cheese about ⅓ inch thick. Mix the egg with the milk. Dip the cheese into the egg mixture. Then dip it into flour. Fry in a bit of oil in a heavy frying pan on medium heat until golden brown. Then turn. Flame with brandy if you wish, but be careful. Add a squirt of lemon juice when the flame dies down.

Serve with crackers or crusty French bread.

Plaki—Baked Fish

Olive oil, garlic, and oregano are three great treasures in Greece. When they are blended with vegetables and herbs and baked over fish fillets, they result in a flavor that smells the way the Greek islands must smell.

- 3 yellow onions, chopped
- 3 cloves garlic, crushed
- 3 tablespoons olive oil
- 2 cups canned tomatoes, crushed
- ½ cup chopped parsley
- 1 teaspoon oregano
- ½ cup red wine
- 2 pounds whitefish fillets
  Salt and pepper to taste
- 1 whole lemon, sliced thin

Sauté the onions and garlic in olive oil for 5 minutes. Add the tomatoes, parsley, and oregano, and simmer for 10 more minutes. Finally, add the red wine and simmer for 5 more minutes.

Grease a large casserole or baking dish with a bit of olive oil. Place the whitefish in the bottom of the pan, and add salt and pepper. Cover the fish with lemon slices.

Top the fish with the cooked sauce, and cover. Bake at 375° for 45 minutes.

SERVES 8.

Deep-Fried Squid

Squid may look funny to you, but the flavor and texture of these creatures are just wonderful. This recipe is a favorite of the Greeks, and the Italians as well.

- Squid
- Peanut oil for deep frying
- Flour

Clean each squid by pulling the head out from the tubular body. The insides should come right along with the head. Reach inside the tubular body, and remove the plasticlike backbone; discard.

If you wish to use the heads as well, cut off the body innards and remove the eyes. This can be done with a small paring knife and takes very little time. You will also want to remove the tiny beak found in the midst of the tentacles. Wash the body tubes, and cut the body into circles about ½ inch wide. Drain.

Heat a frying pan of about 1½ inches of oil to 375°. Dip the squid rings into flour, and fry them in the oil for only a minute, or until lightly browned.

Serve with Skorthalia (below).

Skorthalia—Garlic Sauce

Talk about a bright garlic flavor! This sauce is great as a dipping sauce for Deep-Fried Squid (above), but it also works well as a spread for snacks at your dinner party. Everyone will come to the table smelling like an old Greek fisherman. Wonderful!

- 1 **head garlic**
- 10 **slices white bread**
- 1 **cup olive oil**
- ½ **cup white vinegar**
- 2 **tablespoons lemon juice**
- 3 **tablespoons water**

Peel and crush the garlic—not just a clove, but the entire head. Remove the crusts from the white bread, and place the crustless bread in a mixing bowl. Add the garlic along with the olive oil and white vinegar. Let this soften for 1 hour.

Beat with an electric mixer until all is smooth. Then add the lemon juice, and slowly add the water while the mixer is running so that you will have a thick and fluffy sauce.

MAKES ABOUT 2½ CUPS.

Melitzanosalata—Eggplant Dip

I enjoy eggplant in any form possible. I love to see it sitting in the produce displays, and I love to see it in my kitchen. This dish is just a great first course for a Greek dinner party.

>   Olive oil
> 1   eggplant
> 1   tablespoon white vinegar
> 2   tablespoons lemon juice
> 1   tablespoon fine-chopped parsley
> 2   cloves garlic, crushed
> 1   cup yogurt
> 1   3-ounce package cream cheese
> 1   tablespoon bread crumbs
>   Salt and pepper to taste

Brush a baking pan with 1 tablespoon olive oil. Slice the eggplant in half, the long way, and place it, cut side down, on the oiled baking pan. Bake at 375° for 45 minutes, or until soft.

Cut the eggplant, including the skin, into small pieces, and place in a blender. Add 3 tablespoons olive oil, the vinegar, lemon juice, parsley, and garlic. Blend until smooth.

Add the yogurt, cream cheese, and bread crumbs. Blend again, and add salt and pepper. Refrigerate overnight.

Use as dip with bread, crackers, fingers, etc.

MAKES 2 CUPS.

Stuffed Squid

The squid is so cooperative. Its body forms a tube that can be stuffed with marvelous fillings. You don't have to be Greek to enjoy this one.

> 12 4- to 5-inch-long squid (1½ pounds)
> 1 cup chopped yellow onion
>   Olive oil
> ½ cup chopped parsley
> 1 tablespoon dried dill weed
> ½ cup long-grain rice, parboiled for 7 minutes,
>   then drained
> 2 tablespoons tomato paste
>   White wine
>   Salt and pepper to taste
> 4 tablespoons lemon juice
> ⅛ teaspoon paprika
>   Parsley for garnish

Clean the squid. Remove the heads from the bodies, and clean the body tubes. Cut the tentacles from the heads, and chop fairly fine. Set aside.

In a sauté pan, sauté the yellow onion in ¼ cup olive oil until golden. Add the chopped squid tentacles, chopped parsley, and dill weed. Sauté for a moment or two more, and then add the drained parboiled rice. Also add the tomato paste, ½ cup white wine, and salt and pepper. Simmer for a few minutes, and set aside to cool

Using a regular small kitchen spoon, loosely stuff each of the squid with the filling. Remember that the rice will expand some more, so do not pack the squid too tightly. Secure the open end with a toothpick, and place in an oiled baking dish.

Mix ¼ cup white wine with the lemon juice. Add 2 tablespoons olive oil and the paprika. Lightly salt and pepper the squid, and pour the dressing over the fish. Cover, and bake at 325° for about 45 minutes, or until tender.

Garnish with parsley. Serve with a great green salad and some heavy dry wine.

SERVES 4 TO 6.

Broccoli-Spinach Pie

The paper-thin dough from Greece, called phyllo or fillo, is actually pulled, not rolled. It takes great skill to do this, and I always seem to wind up with holes. Prepared phyllo is readily available, so you have no excuse for not preparing this unusual but very typical Greek dish.

Phyllo dough can be purchased in most delicatessens. It can be purchased fresh or frozen. Try to find the fresh type, even if you have to go to a Middle Eastern delicatessen. It is much easier to use.

> ½ **pound broccoli cooked or frozen, 10-ounce package**
> ½ **pound whole leaf spinach fresh or frozen, 10-ounce package**
> 1 **yellow onion, peeled and chopped fine**
> 2 **green onions, chopped fine**
> 2 **tablespoons olive oil**
> 8 **ounces feta cheese**
> 2 **eggs, beaten**
> 2 **tablespoons fresh chives, chopped**
> 2 **tablespoons fresh dill, chopped, *or* 1 tablespoon dried dill weed**
> ½ **cup parsley, chopped**
>   **Fresh-ground black pepper**
> 12 **phyllo leaves**
> ½ **cup melted butter**

Preheat the oven to 350°.

Defrost broccoli and spinach. If fresh spinach is used, wash thoroughly, cut into coarse pieces, and set aside. Fresh broccoli must be cooked first.

Sauté the yellow and green onions in the oil until golden brown. Add the broccoli and spinach, and cook for 5 minutes.

Stir in the cheese, eggs, chives, dill, parsley, and black pepper. Remove from the heat to cool a bit.

Fold the phyllo leaves in half, and cut to make 24 sheets to fit an oblong baking dish (12 by 7 by 2 inches). Using a pastry brush, butter the baking dish, and begin layering the first 12 phyllo leaves, brushing each as it is added.

Drain excess liquid from broccoli-spinach mixture, and spread it over the phyllo. Cover with remaining 12 sheets, repeating the buttering process.

Cut the pie into 10 (or more) pieces, using a sharp, pointed knife. Bake uncovered, for 1 hour, or until golden brown.

SERVES 6 TO 8 AS A MAIN COURSE.

SERVES 12 AS HORS D'OEUVRE.

Tzatziki—Greek Cucumber and Yogurt Salad

Just read this recipe and you will understand why this dish is a must at a Greek dinner.

    1 pint yogurt
    1 unpeeled cucumber, chopped fine
    1 clove garlic, crushed
    ½ cup olive oil
       Juice of ½ lemon
    1 teaspoon salt
       Parsley

To the yogurt add the cucumber, garlic, olive oil, lemon juice, and salt. Blend well with fork. Top with parsley. Refrigerate.

Serve with Melba toast as first course or as a side dish during dinner.

SERVES 4 TO 6.

Pastitso

This is Greek lasagne, but I hesitate to use the Italian term. The Greeks were making this dish before the Italians began with their noodle dishes. And the sauce used in this dish, a basic white sauce, is also Greek, though it is known in our culture only by its French name, béchamel. The Greeks had it first!

- 2 pounds hamburger
- 2 tablespoons olive oil
- 1 large yellow onion, peeled and chopped
- ½ cup chopped parsley
- 1 clove garlic, crushed
- ½ teaspoon cinnamon
- 1 8-ounce can tomato sauce
- ½ cup white wine
- 1 pound lasagne noodles
- ¼ pound butter, melted
- 3 eggs, beaten
  Fresh-grated Parmesan cheese
- 4 cups Béchamel Sauce for Pastitso (page 398)

Sauté the hamburger along with the yellow onion in the oil. When the onions are clear, add the parsley, garlic, cinnamon, tomato sauce, and white wine. Let this cook together gently for 30 minutes.

Meanwhile, boil the lasagne noodles until not quite tender. Drain, and soak in cold water.

When the sauce is done, drain the cold noodles, and place in a large bowl. Add the butter, 3 eggs, and a handful of Parmesan cheese. Toss the noodles, and place half the mixture in a buttered baking dish. Add the meat sauce. Place the rest of the noodles on top, and cover with the béchamel sauce for pastitso. Top with more grated cheese. Bake at 350° for about 1 hour, or until the top is bubbly.

SERVES 6 TO 8.

Béchamel Sauce for Pastitso

        4 cups milk
        ½ cup butter
        6 tablespoons flour
           Salt and pepper to taste
           Pinch or two of cinnamon

Heat the milk. Melt the butter, and stir in the flour. Stir the flour
and butter into the hot milk, and continue stirring, until thick.
Add the salt, pepper, and cinnamon.

MAKES 4 CUPS.

Tiropetákia

These little pillows filled with cheese and spinach are heaven!
The name refers to the shape, a triangle, or "three feet"—*tirope-
tákia*.

        ½ 10-ounce package frozen chopped spinach,
             defrosted
        ¼ pound feta cheese, chopped
        ½ pound small-curd cottage cheese, drained
        1 egg
        1 teaspoon grated lemon peel
           Nutmeg
           Salt and pepper to taste
           Melted butter
           Phyllo dough

Drain the spinach. Mix with the cheeses. Add the egg, some
lemon peel, a little nutmeg, salt, and pepper.
    Place a sheet of phyllo dough on a cutting board, and brush
with melted butter. With a sharp knife cut the sheet into 5 pieces,
each about 3 inches wide. Place 1 tablespoon filling at the bottom
of each piece, and roll up so as to form a triangle. Move one side
to the other until the whole is rolled up.
    Bake on a greased cookie sheet at 400° for 15 to 20 minutes,
or until lightly browned.

MAKES 30 TO 35.

Egg Lemon Soup

The combined flavor of egg yolk and lemon, *avgholemono*, is basic in Greek cuisine. Sauces, soups, and baked dishes often bear this mark. I consider this soup one of the classic soups of the world. The only Greek soup that I like better is an egg lemon soup with lamb tripe.

   2 **cups milk**
   2 **tablespoons cornstarch**
   6 **egg yolks, beaten**
  ½ **cup rice**
   2 **quarts Chicken Soup Stock (page 53)**
  ½ **stick (⅛ pound) butter**
      Chopped parsley
   1 **cup lemon juice**
      Grated lemon peel (optional)
      Salt and pepper to taste

To the milk, add the cornstarch, and then mix in the egg yolks. Add the rice to the soup stock, and cook until the rice is puffy and tender, about 25 minutes. Remove the soup from the heat, and add the egg and milk mixture, stirring carefully. Continue to cook for a moment until all thickens. Remove from the heat again, and add the butter, the chopped parsley, and lemon juice. You may wish to add some grated lemon peel as well. Add salt and pepper, and serve.

SERVES 10 TO 12.

Israeli and Jewish

The Nosher

The *nosher* is someone who simply loves to snack. Most of us are noshers.

Since Jews are found in many countries and come from many national backgrounds, one is hard pressed to say, "This dish is typical of Jewish cooking." However, some dishes are common among the Jews who came from Eastern Europe, and the dishes Americans call Jewish generally came from that area. Southern Europe and the Middle East have also given us great treasures.

This section will offer you enough dishes for entire Jewish menus. Please also check the index for additional suggestions. *L'chayim*!

Gefilte Fish

Mrs. Morris Kleiner, of Tacoma, a most gracious woman that I have known since my college days, gave me a lesson in making gefilte fish. Mine is almost as good as hers!

    3 **pounds fish***
    1 **large or 2 small yellow onions, peeled**
    3 **eggs**
    ¼ **to ¾ cup matzo meal**
    1 **cup cold water**
    1 **teaspoon sugar**
      Salt and pepper to taste
      Fish Stock for Gefilte Fish (below)

Put the fish and onion through a meat grinder, or have the fish-monger grind the fish for you. Place the mixture in a bowl, add the other ingredients, and mix thoroughly. Do not use all the matzo meal at once because you may not need much in order to make a firm and workable fish paste. Season generously with salt and pepper. Form into balls, and cook in the fish stock. Let come to a boil; then cook slowly for 1 hour with a lid on the kettle.

Serve the fish cold in some of the broth. Traditionally horse-radish is served on the side.

MAKES 20.

Fish Stock for Gefilte Fish

      Fish skin, bones, and heads
    2 **carrots, cut up**
    2 **small yellow onions, peeled and chopped**
    4 **stalks celery, chopped**
      Salt to taste

Cover all ingredients with water, and simmer until the vegetables are soft. Strain, and use the liquid for cooking the gefilte fish balls.

Matzo Ball Soup

This dish is heaven! When I was in graduate school, I became absolutely addicted to the matzo ball soup served at the Stage

---

*Use a mixture of different types such as red salmon, white salmon, cod, or any others you prefer.

Delicatessen in Manhattan. I wish it were still the same. This one is just as good, and it is not hard to make. I found it years ago on the Manischewitz matzo meal box.

SOUP STOCK
- 3 **pounds chicken backs and necks, rinsed with fat pulled off the backs and reserved**
- 3 **carrots, chopped**
- 1 **large yellow onion, peeled and chopped**
- 4 **stalks celery, chopped**
- 2 **quarts water**
- 6 **peppercorns**
- 1 **teaspoon salt or more to taste**

MATZO BALLS
   Reserved chicken fat
- 2 **eggs, slightly beaten**
- ½ **cup matzo meal**
- 1 **teaspoon salt**
- 2 **tablespoons soup stock**
   Chopped parsley for garnish

Cover, and simmer all the ingredients of the soup stock for 2 hours. Drain the stock, and remove the fat; or chill and remove the fat the next day.

Place the chicken fat in a small frying pan. Heat gently over medium heat until the fat is rendered from the solid part and the remains are small and lightly browned. Do not burn the fat. (Some people attempt to make matzo balls with oil or margarine, but the flavor is simply not the same.)

Cool the fat, and mix 2 tablespoons of the clear fat with the eggs. Mix together the matzo meal and salt, and add to the eggs. When all is well blended, add the soup stock. Cover the mixing bowl, and refrigerate for at least 20 minutes. Using a 2- or 3-quart pot, bring salted water to a brisk boil. Roll the cold mixture into 12 balls, and place on wax paper. When all the balls are complete, drop them into the slightly boiling water, cover, and cook for 30 to 40 minutes. Have the soup at room temperature, and place the drained matzo balls in the soup pot. When you are ready to serve, heat the soup at a simmer for about 5 minutes.

To serve, place two balls in each bowl of soup. Garnish with a bit of chopped parsley.

SERVES 6.

Carrot Ring

This dish is terribly rich, but it simply makes a buffet party. It was given me by one of the great dinner party planners, the woman to whom I dedicated my first cookbook years ago, Pearl Baskin. She and her husband, Lester, changed my life when I was a college student . . . and they did it around the table. Their friendship through the years has continued to be celebrated around the table, with a good Château Latour, of course.

       2 cups shortening
       1 cup brown sugar
       2 eggs, beaten
       2 tablespoons lemon juice
       6 cups grated carrots
    2½ cups flour
       2 teaspoons baking powder
       1 teaspoon salt
      ½ cup Wheaties

Cream the shortening, and add the sugar, then the eggs, and then the lemon juice. Stir in the carrots. Mix the flour, baking powder, and salt together, and stir into the carrot mixture.

Grease a 3- to 4-quart ring mold, and line it with the Wheaties. Pour in the carrot mixture, and bake the mold in a pan of hot water, coming up to one-third the height of the ring mold, in a 350° oven for 1 hour.

Invert onto a plate to serve.

SERVES 8 TO 10 AT DINNER.

Cheesecake, New York Style

As served at the Chaplain's Pantry for ten years. My wife was brought up in Brooklyn, so she knew real cheesecake. After a long search she came up with this recipe, and she has never given it out. So, this is a first. You will enjoy the richness of this dessert and the clarity of flavor.

>   1 cup graham cracker crumbs
> ¾ cup sugar
> ¼ cup plus 2 tablespoons melted butter
> 1½ cups sour cream
>   2 eggs
>   2 teaspoons vanilla
>   1 pound cream cheese, broken into small pieces

Blend the cracker crumbs, ¼ cup sugar, and ¼ cup melted butter, and line the bottom of an 8- or 9-inch ungreased spring-form pan.

Blend the sour cream, ½ cup sugar, eggs, and vanilla in a food blender for 1 minute. Add the cream cheese. Blend until smooth.

Pour 2 tablespoons melted butter through the top of the machine. Pour into the spring-form pan.

Bake in the lower third of a 325° oven for 45 minutes.

When baking is finished, remove from oven, and turn oven on to broil. Broil the cheesecake just until the top begins to show attractive spots of brown.

Refrigerate for 4 hours, preferably overnight, before cutting and serving.

This is not a low-calorie version. Cut into small pieces—it is very rich.

SERVES 8 TO 12, DEPENDING ON THE SIZE OF THE SLICE.

Cucumber Salad

This salad has a flavor very close to what Jewish New Yorkers call a "new pickle." It will become a family favorite, I promise!

>   4 cucumbers
>   1 yellow onion, peeled and sliced thin
> ¾ cup sugar
> ½ cup water
>   1 cup white vinegar
> ½ tablespoon dried dill

Peel and cut the cucumbers into thin slices. Mix with the yellow onion. Bring to a boil the sugar, water, white vinegar, and dill. Pour over the cucumber and onion, and chill.

SERVES 4 TO 6.

Sesame Chicken

We know that sesame seeds and sesame oil were used in cooking prior to biblical times. This dish is not only from Israel but probably from early times.

> 1 **cup flour**
> 1 **cup sesame seeds**
> 2 **tablespoons good paprika**
>   **Salt to taste**
> 2 **pounds chicken thighs**
> 2 **eggs, whipped**
> ½ **cup chicken broth**

Blend together in a large bowl the flour and sesame seeds, along with the paprika and a little salt. Coat the chicken thighs in this mixture, and dip them first in a mixture of the eggs and chicken broth, and then back into the flour again. You may brown these lightly in a frying pan and finish in the oven, or you may simply bake them at 350° for about 30 minutes.

SERVES 6.

Herring and Sour Cream

A favorite appetizer of every Jewish grandma.

> **Pickled herring**
> **Sliced yellow onions**
> **Sour cream**

Buy some good, firm pickled herring from your fishman, and drain it. Mix it with yellow onions and sour cream.

Serve on a bed of lettuce with brown rye crackers.

Blintzes—Jewish Egg Pancakes

The egg pancake, or egg crepe, is raised to new heights in the Jewish blintz. This is a stuffed pancake that is so rich you can hardly eat it . . . and so delicious you cannot stop eating.

        2 eggs
        ¾ cup milk
        1 ounce butter, melted and cooled
           Salt to taste
        ¼ cup flour
           Butter or peanut oil for frying

FILLING
        1 pound large-curd cottage cheese, drained for at
              least 2 hours
        1 egg
           A few raisins
        ¼ cup sour cream
           Grated peel from 1 lemon
           Sugar to taste
           Salt to taste
           Melted butter
           Sour cream and jam for topping

In your blender, place the eggs, milk, butter, salt, and flour. Blend for a moment; then allow to cool in the refrigerator for a couple of hours.

Make the pancakes as you would a crepe. But do not turn them. They should be thin and not at all browned. Fry them in very little butter or oil in a medium-heat pan until the top is dry in appearance, but the bottom is not brown. Keep them separated with wax paper until all are cooked.

Prepare a filling by putting the drained cottage cheese through a ricer. Add the egg, raisins, sour cream, lemon peel, sugar, and salt. Blend well with a fork, and fill the blintzes with a little of the mixture. Then fold them up like little envelopes. Place on an oiled cookie sheet, and brush the tops with melted butter. When you are ready to serve, place the blintzes under a broiler until the tops begin to brown. Serve with more sour cream on top along with your favorite jam.

MAKES 10.

Italy

Edible Italian History

I am firmly convinced that the Chinese are the oldest and the most influential cooks in the world. And the Italians are the second. No, it has not been the French or even the Greeks, but the Italians.

The first cookbook that we know of in the Western world was compiled by Apicius during the first century in Rome, and the recipes give us an exciting insight into what was going on at the Roman table. These fellows were wealthy, to be sure, and the descriptions of the sausages, spicy meat loaves, vegetable dishes, and meats cooked with figs and sweet sauces cause one to wonder just how much time was spent at table. Of course, people of wealth also had a full complement of slaves to do the kitchen work. Slaves were taught to be fine chefs, but they endangered their lives if they made a mistake or served an ill-prepared dish. Rather than being reprimanded, they were often hauled into the dining room and flogged in the presence of the guests.

The list of ingredients available to the cooks at that time is made even more clear when we consider the finds of the ruins of Pompeii. The volcanic eruption of A.D. 79 preserved for us breads, wine, oil, figs, lentils, barley, even taverns and bars. Those were good days if you were a part of the aristocracy. Even if not, your diet was rather sophisticated by the then current standards of the rest of the Mediterranean. However, missing from the list are several food items that are now common in Italy: the tomato, corn for polenta, and several forms of beans. All these dishes came from the New World and became popular in Italy during the past 300 to 400 years. The cuisines of northern Italy, for instance, still do very little with tomato sauce.

This whole section can be used to create full Italian meals. Please remember that a formal meal begins with an antipasto plate, followed by a soup, the pasta course, then the main course. The salad is usually served with the main course or at the end of the meal. Yes, at the end. Consult the index under "Italy" for more suggestions.

Tuna Sauce

This is actually a tuna mayonnaise. Because it is very versatile and rich, you can keep a small jar of this in the refrigerator and be ready for a party at any time.

    1 7-ounce can tuna, drained
    8 or to taste flat anchovies
    ¼ cup lemon juice
    ¾ cup olive oil, at room temperature
    1 tablespoon capers, chopped

Place the tuna, anchovies, and lemon juice in a blender. Blend for a few moments, and then slowly add the olive oil. Stir in the capers.

Serve over meats and salads. Traditionally this sauce is served over thin slices of veal, but it is just great with chicken.

MAKES 1½ CUPS.

Eggs Tonnata—Eggs in Tuna Sauce

Wedge hard-boiled eggs, and serve them in a shallow pool of Tuna Sauce (above). Garnish with lettuce for a full salad or antipasto.

Spaghetti Frittata

This antipasto dish shows that there are endless possibilities when you are set loose in an Italian kitchen. This dish is very close to that served at a fine antipasto house in San Francisco called Little City Antipasto.

⅛ pound thin spaghetti, cooked, drained, rinsed, and cooled
1 egg, beaten
2 tablespoons fresh-grated Parmesan or Romano cheese
Salt and pepper to taste
Pinch each of oregano and basil
Olive oil for frying

Blend all the ingredients together, and brown on one side in a small frying pan in a bit of olive oil.

Top with more cheese, and place under broiler until crusty and brown on top.

SERVES 2 OR 3 AS AN ANTIPASTO.

Pork Piccata

This dish is traditionally made with veal, but with pork it is much cheaper and very enjoyable.

1 pound pork butt, sliced very thin
¼ teaspoon pepper
1 cup flour
Olive oil
1 clove garlic, crushed
Juice of ½ lemon
½ cup white wine
1 tablespoon capers, chopped
3 tablespoons parsley, chopped

Pound the pork very thin between two sheets of wax paper or plastic wrap. Mix the pepper with the flour, and dredge each slice of pork. In a large frying pan heat a bit of olive oil, and add the garlic. Lightly brown the pork slices on both sides, very quickly (you may have to do this in two or three stages, removing the meat as it is browned). When all the meat is browned, remove it from the pan, and add the lemon juice, white wine, and capers. Reduce the sauce for just a moment, and replace the meat in the pan. Add the parsley, and shake the pan a bit so that the sauce is thickened by the flour on the meat. Remove, and serve hot.

SERVES 4 TO 6.

■ HINT: To Pound a Piece of Meat or Fish Thin and Flat

Purchase a 2- by 2-foot piece of 8-millimeter vinyl at a lumberyard or hardware store. Ask to be sure that the material can be used on food. Wash and then fold the sheet in half, and place the thin-sliced meat in between. Pound with a wooden meat mallet or a piece of two-by-four wood. The meat will spread very thin and will not tear because of the protection of the plastic. This works well for fish and meat.

Peas and Pasta

This very simple and satisfying dish is from my wife's Aunt Suzy in Brooklyn. It is very common Italian family food.

    2 cloves garlic, chopped
    3 tablespoons olive oil
    3 stalks celery, chopped
    2 ripe tomatoes, chopped
    1 10-ounce package frozen peas
    ½ pound pasta, cooked and drained

Sauté the garlic in the olive oil until barely browned. Add the celery and the tomatoes, and cook for 5 minutes. Add the frozen peas, and cook for 10 minutes more. Serve over hot pasta.

SERVES 4 OR 5.

Italian Sausage

I rarely trust a butcher to grind up pork for a sausage for me. I usually buy a pork butt roast and grind it myself, thus assuring me of a fresh grind and much less fat.

> 2 pounds coarse-ground lean pork
> 1 tablespoon coarse-ground fennel*
> 2 bay leaves, crushed
> 1 tablespoon dried parsley
> 3 cloves garlic, crushed
> ⅛ teaspoon hot dried red pepper flakes (optional)
> 2 teaspoons salt or to taste
> ½ teaspoon fresh-ground black pepper
> 4 tablespoons water

Mix together all the ingredients, and let rest in refrigerator for 1 hour. Then mix again.

Stuff into casings, or use as is.

MAKES 2 POUNDS OF SAUSAGE.

Beef Stew with Marsala

The dried mushrooms and the Marsala wine in this dish create a flavor combination that is so rich you will be able to eat only a bit of this dish. But then that is the point of the frugal kitchen. We eat too much meat, and if we begin to use meats as flavorings for our table rather than as the main course, we will all be much better off.

---

*Buy whole fennel seed, and pound it up in a mortar and pestle or a small electric coffee grinder.

3   pounds lean stewing beef
2   tablespoons olive oil
2   yellow onions, peeled and chopped
3   cloves garlic, chopped
½   cup dry white wine
1   cup Marsala wine
2   ounces dried mushrooms, soaked in 1½ cups
        warm water for 1 hour (see note on Dried
        European mushrooms, page 231) *or* ½ pound
        mushrooms, sliced, and ½ cup beef broth
½   teaspoon dried rosemary
½   teaspoon dried oregano
½   teaspoon dried basil
     Salt and pepper to taste

Brown the meat in the oil very quickly over high heat. Remove from the pan, and sauté the yellow onions and the garlic together until the onions brown a bit. You may have to add oil.

Add the remaining ingredients to a stewpot (use only ½ cup of the broth from the dried mushrooms, and reserve the rest of the juice in case the stew gets too dry). Simmer for 1½ hours, or until all is tender.

Serve with rice or polenta (cornmeal mush that is cooked until it is very thick; it is served in Italy much like mashed potatoes).

SERVES 8 OR 9.

Pork Chops with Fennel

The fennel, garlic, and pork will cause you to think of good Italian sausage, but you will be eating a chop with little fat. This is very simple yet elegant enough for a fine dinner party.

1   pork chop or thick pork steak
½   clove garlic, crushed
     Salt and pepper to taste
¼   teaspoon whole fennel seed
1   teaspoon olive oil
     Red wine

Rub the chop with the garlic, salt, and pepper, and press the fennel seeds into the meat. Push hard on the meat with another plate so that the seeds stay in place.

Brown on both sides in the oil. Use medium heat, and do not overcook.

Add a bit of red wine*, cover the pan, and simmer for a few minutes, or until the meat is tender.

Serve with Italian green beans and perhaps some rice or pasta. Green salad and a white wine complete the meal.

SERVES 1.

Pork Roast Stuffed with Sausage and Spinach

When I was in high school, I was hired as a clerk at a delicatessen in the Pike Place Farmers Market, a Seattle institution and one of the great markets of the world. Now in the midst of a grand restoration, the market is drawing some fine restaurants. I found this dish, or one very close to it, in a tiny but sophisticated eatery called Place Pigalle. The cooks are very creative. This dish will take some doing, but you will love it.

     3 pound pork shoulder roast, deboned
     ½ pound Italian Sausage (page 413)
     1 bunch spinach, *or* 1 package frozen leaf spinach
        Salt and pepper to taste
     2 eggs, hard-boiled and sliced
     ½ pound ricotta cheese *or* ½ pound small-curd
           cottage cheese, well drained
     1 medium yellow onion, peeled and chopped
        Olive oil for frying

Lay the pork roast out flat, fat side down, and decide whether you can fill it and roll it like a jelly roll or whether you must cut some of the meat from the center so that you have room for a stuffing. (Use the meat removed to make the sausage.)

*½ cup for 4 chops.

Wash, chop, and quickly fry the spinach in olive oil. Drain. (If you use frozen spinach, defrost, drain, and squeeze it dry.)

Salt and pepper the meat. Place the sausage, spinach, eggs, cheese, and onion in the center of the roast. You may not need all the fillings, depending on how the meat is cut; just use what you can, and save the rest for another dish. Roll up the roast, and tie it like a jelly roll. Place it on a baking rack, and bake at 350° for about 1 hour and 15 minutes, or until golden on the outside.

Slice thin across the roll, and serve.

A salad and wine along with some buttered noodles make a fine meal.

SERVES 6 TO 8.

Cold Roast Veal with Tuna Sauce

Roast the veal, and chill. Slice it very thin. Place a little puddle of Tuna Sauce (416) in the middle of each plate. Place a few slices of the veal in the sauce. Serve vegetables and/or salad on the side.

Sausage and Spinach Meatballs

There is no reason why we should not add a few items to a good meatball. I began cooking these meatballs simply because I had made too much filling for a pasta dish. The boys loved the meatballs better than the pasta dish.

  2   pounds Italian Sausage (page 413)
  1   large yellow onion, peeled and chopped
  1   package frozen spinach, defrosted, drained, and
        squeezed dry
     Salt and pepper to taste
½   pound ricotta cheese
  2   eggs
⅛   teaspoon nutmeg
  1   cup dry white wine
  2   tablespoons olive oil

Mix together all the ingredients, except the white wine and oil. Form into meatballs, and brown in oil on both sides. Add the white wine, cover the pan, and allow to simmer for 20 minutes. You may need to add more wine so that the pan does not dry out.

Serve with vegetables, pasta or rice, a large green salad, and good heavy red wine.

SERVES 6 TO 8.

■ HINT:

To make your meatballs moist if they have a tendency to dry out, try putting a small ice cube in the midst of each meatball before you brown it. Then proceed as you usually do, and be ready to accept compliments from your guests on the moist meatballs. Do not tell about the ice cube.

Lamp Chops with Rosemary

I really prefer this dish with fresh herbs. But if you cannot obtain fresh ones, dried herbs still give you a great dish.

1   **tablespoon fresh rosemary** *or* ½ **tablespoon
       dried rosemary**
½   **tablespoon fresh sage or marjoram** *or* ¼
       tablespoon dried sage or marjoram
6   **lamb chops or lamb steaks**
2   **cloves garlic, crushed**
2   **tablespoons olive oil**
1   **tablespoon lemon juice
       Salt and pepper to taste**

Crush up the rosemary and sage or marjoram, and place in a bowl
along with the lamb. Add the garlic and oil, and allow to marinate for 3 hours or longer if you wish.

Place the meat on a broiling rack, and broil, under high heat,
for about 5 minutes a side or to your taste. Splash with the lemon
juice, add salt and pepper, and serve hot.

Serve with broiled tomatoes, polenta, and a green salad. Either a red or a white wine is fine.

SERVES 6.

■ HINT: How to Clean Squid

Squid is probably the most maligned fish from the sea.
You remember the great stories from Jules Verne's clas-
sics about gigantic squid that swim under the sea. What
a horrible fright to put upon the squid lovers of the
world. While it is true that squid grow to great length,
the kind that you and I buy in a fish market, either
frozen or fresh, are little rascals, being about 5 or 6
inches long total. They are easy to clean. You simply cut
the head off each and remove the filling from the tube,
or body. Don't forget the plasticlike backbone of the
squid. You will find it within the tube of the fish while
digging around. Rinse the tubes, and you are ready to
begin. I also save the tentacles, though not the head, for
other dishes.

Squid in Tomato Sauce

Do not overcook this dish. Squid becomes tough when over-cooked, and like most seafoods, it should be simply threatened with heat and then celebrated with joy. This dish is a classic for pasta or simply eaten as is.

TOMATO SAUCE
- 3 cloves garlic, chopped
- ¼ cup olive oil
- ½ yellow onion, peeled and chopped
- 3 stalks celery, chopped
- ¼ green pepper, chopped
- 2 carrots, chopped fine
- ½ cup parsley, chopped
- 2 14-ounce cans tomato sauce
- ½ cup red wine
- ½ cup Basic Brown Soup Stock (page 47)
  Salt and pepper to taste
- 1 teaspoon oregano
- ½ teaspoon rosemary
- 2 1-inch pieces lemon peel
  Pinch of sugar
- 3 pounds squid, cleaned and cut into ¼-inch circles
- ½ cup fresh-grated Parmesan or Romano cheese

Sauté the garlic in the olive oil. Add the yellow onion, celery, green pepper, carrots, and parsley. When all the vegetables are tender, add the tomato sauce. Add the wine and the soup stock. Bring to a simmer, and add salt, pepper, oregano, rosemary, and lemon peel. Add the sugar, and simmer the whole gently for about 1 hour.

When you're ready for dinner, add the squid to the preheated tomato sauce. Simmer for just a few moments. When the squid is tender, add the Parmesan or Romano cheese. Serve over hot pasta.

SERVES 5 TO 6.

Squid Salad

I first tasted this dish at the North Beach Italian Restaurant in San Francisco. I know this may seem a bit weird to you, but it is actually a classic bit of Italian antipasto.

> 1 pound squid
> 1 cup chopped celery
> 1 yellow onion, peeled and sliced
> ⅓ cup olive oil
> ¼ cup white wine vinegar
> 1 teaspoon crushed oregano
> ½ cup parsley, chopped
> Fresh-ground pepper to taste
> Lemon wedges

Clean the squid by pulling off the head and rinsing out the body tube that remains. Remove the cuttlebone. Cut the squid into little circles. You may also use the head if you remove the eyes with a small paring knife, and remove the beak in between the legs by just pinching it out. Wash the squid pieces, and drop them into boiling water. Squid will be done when the edges curl or when the water resumes boiling. Drain immediately. Place in a salad bowl with the celery, yellow onion, olive oil, wine vinegar, oregano, parsley and pepper. Toss, and chill for about 2 hours before serving. Serve with lemon wedges.

SERVES 4 TO 6.

Mussels in a Light Italian Sauce

Mussels are available in many fish markets or available on beaches. If you can't find mussels, use clams. They are just as good, if not better. They are certainly larger. On the West Coast, mussels are free to be had on the beaches. In New York City you can buy them by the bushel basket, and I believe this is true of most fish markets across the country. They are lovely eating.

    3 to 4 pounds mussels
    2 tomatoes, chopped
    ½ stick (⅛ pound) butter
    3 tablespoons olive oil
    4 or 5 green onions, chopped
    2 cloves garlic, chopped
       Pinch of oregano
       Pinch of rosemary
       Tiny handful fresh-chopped parsley
       Salt and pepper to taste
    ½ cup dry white wine

To clean the mussels, scrub each in fresh water. Remove all barnacles, and use a pair of pliers to pull off the little beard that was used by the mussel to attach itself to the rock. Do not use mussels that are already opened unless they will close when you tap them with the back of a table knife.

In a 6-quart kettle, sauté the tomatoes in butter and olive oil. Add the green onions, garlic, oregano, rosemary, and parsley. Sauté for a few minutes until soft. Now add a bit of salt and pepper and finally a good white wine. When all is simmering severely, throw in the mussels.

Cover the pot, and simmer until the mussels are open and tender. Be careful; this takes only a few moments.

The joy of this dish stems from the fact that after you have eaten the mussels, you will have a sauce remaining in the bottom of your bowl that simply cries out for fresh pasta. Cook spaghettini or other favorite pasta, and use the sauce over the top.

SERVES 4.

Lebanon (also Armenia)

As a very young child I became acquainted with the unusual and creative foods of Lebanon. A marvelous Lebanese fellow married my Norwegian mother's sister, thus giving rise to a series of whole new possibilities in the preparation of food. While I have no Lebanese blood in me, I really believe that in terms of food history we all were from the Middle East at some time in our past. Wine, bread, cheese—all came from the desert, and in my culinary mind, I retreat to the desert often.

My uncle Vic's mother, a tender and tough woman from the old country, fed me many of these dishes. Her name was Selma. She and her husband, Joseph Abdo, came to this country in 1913. I can remember how important a meal was to her, and not just because we were to eat to grow up strong. She wanted us to enjoy, and taste, and delight in these dishes from the Old World. And believe me, I did, and I do.

Mezza refers to an appetizer, or first course, though it is very possible to make an entire meal out of it.

Lebanese Menu Planning

I am sure that after you have read through these recipes, menus will make sense very quickly. In the desert one does not eat as we do, with a main course and perhaps a soup or salad. Many dishes are served, and the more important the occasion or the guest, the more complex the menu becomes. I have been to my uncle's home when nearly everything in this entire section was served at once and from one buffet! Consult the index for more dishes from the cuisine of Lebanon.

Hommus

This is a staple in the Middle East, and a delicious one at that!

> 2 16-ounce cans garbanzo beans
> ½ cup tahini*
>   Juice from 1 lemon
> 2 cloves garlic, crushed
> 2 tablespoons olive oil
>   Chopped parsley

Drain the juice from 1 can garbanzo beans. Place the drained beans in a food blender or processor, and then add the second can of beans, water and all. Add the tahini, lemon juice, and garlic, and blend until very smooth. Pour onto a large plate, and pour olive oil over the top. Garnish with parsley.

Serve with sliced vegetables for a dip, along with Middle

*Sesame paste. Available in Middle Eastern groceries or delicatessens.

Eastern bread cut into wedges. Sliced cucumber, olives, radishes
—all are traditional.

SERVES 8 TO 10 AS FIRST COURSE (MEZZA).

Bread with Zaartar

Zaartar, a blend of herbs, is very popular with those in the Middle
East. It is made up of thyme, sesame seeds or chick-peas, and
sumac bark. You can buy this mixture in any Middle Eastern
grocery or delicatessen. You can use it for many dishes.

>   2 **loaves Middle Eastern or Arab or pocket bread**
>   4 **tablespoons olive oil**
>   2 **tablespoons sesame seeds**
>   2 **tablespoons zaartar**
>   ⅛ **teaspoon salt**

Cut each loaf of bread into 8 wedges. Separate the wedges so that
each loaf offers 16 wedges.

Mix the remaining ingredients together to form a paste. Brush
the coarse side of each of the wedges with a bit of the paste.
Place on a cookie sheet, and broil until lightly browned on top.
Watch these carefully.

MAKES 32 PIECES.

Rolled Grape Leaves

It is necessary to recognize the fact that many great dishes came
out of desperate times. When you have to eat the grape leaves off
the vine, you must be in trouble. From that difficult spot came a
dish that is now a basic in the diet of the Middle East. Everyone
has his or her variations of the fillings, but I think you will like
this one.

> 1 16-ounce jar grape leaves in brine*
> ¾ cup long-grain rice
> 1 pound lean lamb, chopped into coarse pieces
> 1 teaspoon salt
> ¼ teaspoon pepper
> ¾ teaspoon ground cinnamon
> ¾ teaspoon ground allspice
>   Juice of 1 lemon
> 3 cloves garlic, crushed
> 1 teaspoon dried or fresh mint leaves

Remove the grape leaves from the jar, and drain. Wash the rice, and soak for a few minutes in water; drain well. Mix together the rice, lamb, salt, pepper, cinnamon, and allspice. Blend well.

Place a leaf on a flat surface, and set ¾ tablespoon of the lamb and rice filling in the center. Roll into a little bundle with the ends tucked in, as you would wrap a package of meat. Continue until all the filling has been used.

Place a few of the larger unused leaves on the bottom of a 3-quart kettle. Layer the rolled grape leaves, seam sides down, very close together; they should be snug. Place another layer of plain leaves on top, and continue to layer. When all are in the pot, add water almost to cover. Cover the pot, and simmer over medium heat for ½ hour.

Blend the lemon juice, garlic, and mint leaves. Add water to this mixture to make up 1 cup liquid. Pour on top of rolled leaves in pot, and replace the lid. Simmer for an additional ½ hour.

Serve with yogurt for dipping. Can be eaten hot or cold, but I prefer them cold.

MAKES 35.

Lamb with Beans or Okra

No, this dish will not taste strongly of lamb. It is spicy but not heavy, and it has everything in one pot. How much fun it is for all to eat from one pot!

*Available at Middle Eastern groceries or delicatessens.

2 **pounds lamb shoulder steaks, boned**
1 **large yellow onion, peeled and chopped**
3 **tablespoons olive oil**
2 **cloves garlic, crushed**
1 **15-ounce can tomatoes**
½ **teaspoon cinnamon**
½ **teaspoon allspice**
Salt and pepper to taste
2 **10-ounce packages frozen green beans or okra,
defrosted**

Trim the lamb of bone and fat, and cut the meat into ½-inch pieces. Brown the lamb and onion in the olive oil and garlic. Place tomatoes, juice and all, in a food blender, and blend for a few seconds. Pour over the lamb and onions. Add the cinnamon, allspice, salt, and pepper, and simmer for ½ hour. Finally, add the green beans or okra, and simmer for ½ hour or until tender.

Serve over Lebanese Rice Pilaf (below).

SERVES 6 TO 8.

Lebanese Rice Pilaf

¼ **cup Chinese egg noodles or spaghetti, broken
into ½-inch pieces**
3 **tablespoons olive oil**
2 **cups Texas or Chinese long-grain rice**
4 **cups cold water**
Salt to taste

In a small frying pan, sauté the noodle pieces in the olive oil until they are a golden brown. Careful, these will burn!

Wash the rice, drain it, and place it in a small pan with a tight-fitting lid. Add the water and the toasted noodles and oil. Add salt. Bring to a boil without the lid, and then move to another burner, which you have already turned on to low. Cover the pot, and cook for 20 minutes.

SERVES 6 TO 8.

Eggplant with Lamb and Pine Nuts

These rounds of eggplant covered with a flavorful sauce not only look fantastic but taste of the summer nights on the desert.

- 1 **pound ground lean lamb**
- 1 **medium yellow onion, peeled and chopped**
- 2 **cloves garlic, crushed**
- 4 **tablespoons olive oil**
  Salt and pepper to taste
- ½ **cup tomato sauce, canned**
- ¼ **cup red wine**
- ½ **teaspoon cinnamon**
- ½ **teaspoon allspice**
- 3 **tablespoons pine nuts**
- 1 **eggplant**

Brown the lamb along with the onion in the garlic and oil. Add the salt, pepper, tomato sauce, red wine, cinnamon, allspice, and pine nuts. Cook for about 15 minutes while the sauce reduces a bit.

Cut the eggplant into ½-inch-thick slices. Lightly brown them in a frying pan with just a touch of olive oil. Turn, and brown the other sides. Do not overcook.

Place the slices of eggplant on a baking sheet, and spread some of the filling on each. When you are ready to serve dinner, place the tray in a 375° oven, and bake for 15 to 20 minutes, or until all is hot and the eggplant tender.

SERVES 6 TO 8 AS A VEGETABLE.

Lebanese Poultry Stuffing

I know that in your house anyone who suggested that you change the recipe for the turkey stuffing would be shot. Give this one a try, perhaps not on a holiday, and see what the family says. It is one of the great memories of my childhood, a childhood filled with Middle Eastern dishes as a result of the presence of my Lebanese uncle.

¼ cup orzo (rice-shaped pasta) *or* Chinese egg
noodles or spaghetti, broken into ½-inch
pieces
3 tablespoons olive oil
1 small yellow onion, peeled and chopped
½ pound lean lamb, ground
2 cups long-grain rice
4 cups water
Salt and pepper to taste
½ teaspoon cinnamon
½ teaspoon allspice
½ cup pine nuts (optional)

Sauté the orzo in the olive oil just until they begin to turn a light golden brown. Add the onion to the pan, and sauté until clear. Remove from the heat.

Sauté the lamb, and pour off the fat.

Place the onions and orzo, along with the rice, in a saucepan with a tight-fitting lid. Add the water, and bring to a boil with the lid off. Move to another burner, which is on low, and cover the pot. Cook for 20 minutes. Remove the lid, and allow the rice to cool a bit.

In a large bowl mix the rice with the lamb, salt, pepper, cinnamon, and allspice. Add the pine nuts; while these are optional, they add a great deal to this dish.

MAKES ENOUGH STUFFING FOR 1 SMALL 8- TO 10-POUND TURKEY OR 2 3- TO 4-POUND CHICKENS.

Lebanese Zucchini

The Lebanese do not use our thick-skinned dark green zucchini. They grow one that is much more delicate, but it is hard to find. I have eliminated the lamb that would normally be present in this dish so that you can prepare this for a vegetable and starch dish. Your family will love it.

> 4 medium zucchini
> 1 cup long-grain rice
> 1 yellow onion, peeled, chopped, and browned
>   Salt and pepper to taste
> 1 tablespoon lemon juice
> ½ teaspoon allspice
> ½ teaspoon cinnamon
> 1 teaspoon dried dill
> 2 cups tomato sauce, canned

Cut the zucchini in half, the long way, and scoop out the seeds. Cook the rice, but keep it firm and nice. Mix the rice with the yellow onion, salt, pepper, lemon juice, allspice, cinnamon, and dill. Use to stuff the zucchini shells. Lay them, face up, in a baking dish, and add tomato sauce to the bottom of the pan. Do not cover the squash with the sauce. Cover, and bake in a 350° oven until tender but firm, about 1 hour. Serve with a little of the sauce on top.

SERVES 8.

Cucumbers and Yogurt

In Lebanon this dish is called *leben*, the same word that Germans use for "life." It is so called because yogurt is actually alive with a bacterium that at once flavors the milk and preserves it. The flavor which results from the yogurt, mint, garlic, and cucumber is very refreshing.

   3 cucumbers, peeled
   2 cups yogurt
      About 12 fresh mint leaves
   2 cloves garlic
      Salt to taste

Cut the cucumbers into thin slices, and set aside in refrigerator. Mix the yogurt with a paste that you pounded in a teacup or a mortar and pestle from the mint leaves and garlic. Add to the drained cucumbers along with a little salt. Refrigerate before serving.

SERVES 6 TO 8.

Lentil Salad
(Armenia)

This is such an unusual salad. Lentils have a slightly peppery flavor, and when they are coupled with the rest of these ingredients, you have a very heavy but delightful dish.

   1½ cups lentils
   ½ teaspoon salt
   ½ cup chopped parsley
   6 green onions, chopped
   8 tablespoons olive oil
      Juice of 2 lemons
   2 cloves garlic, crushed
      Black pepper to taste
   ¼ teaspoon ground coriander
   ¼ teaspoon ground cumin

Soak the lentils in ample water to cover for a few hours. Then bring them to a boil, and simmer until tender, but not mushy, about 30 minutes. Drain and cool them. Place the lentils in a salad bowl, and add the salt, parsley, and green onions.

   Mix the olive oil, lemon juice, garlic, black pepper, coriander, and cumin. Toss with the lentils, and chill.

SERVES 6.

Poland

The cuisine of Poland, which is certainly misunderstood in this country, is a combination of many cultures. Poland has had many rulers from foreign lands, and each brought with him an addition to the already creative Polish cuisine. In the early days flamboyant dishes were prepared for the royalty just as they were prepared in the rest of Europe, and the Polish chef had a grand tradition and a wealth of fresh foodstuffs to fall back upon. Sour cream and buttermilk, cabbages and pickles, dill and fresh herbs —all remain in the basic Polish diet.

Polish Menu Planning

We can add to the rather heavy diet of Poland with a few green salads and some additional vegetables. Boiled Red Cabbage (page 229) would be traditional in Poland, as would be Cucumber Salad (page 405). So there is no limit to your planning of a Polish meal. Remember, these dishes were eaten by royalty and by the peasants alike. So get out the sour cream and get started.

Pierogi—Stuffed Dough Pockets

This is a classic Polish dish. The dough is easy, and the fillings are endless.

> 1 cup flour
> 1 egg
> ¼ teaspoon salt
> About 4 tablespoons cold water
> Filling (below)
> Melted butter
> Bread crumbs for topping

Mix the flour, egg, and salt with enough water to make a medium-soft dough. Knead well; then roll out until thin. Cut into squares to make 40 pierogi or into 40 circles about 3¼ inches in diameter.

Place 1 teaspoon of filling in the center of each square or circle, and fold the dough in half to make a triangle or half-circle. Pinch the edges well to keep the dumpling from falling apart.

To cook, drop into salted water, and cook, covered, until all the pierogi float to the top, about 10 minutes. Cook, still covered, for 5 minutes longer. Drain, and place on heated platter. Drizzle melted butter over the dumplings, and sprinkle with a few bread crumbs.

MAKES 40.

Fillings

CHEESE
½ pound cottage cheese, drained well
1 egg yolk
1 teaspoon butter, melted
  Pinch of salt

Mix all ingredients thoroughly.

SAUERKRAUT AND MUSHROOM
1½ tablespoons cooked dried mushrooms*, soaked
      for 1 hour
2 cups sauerkraut, drained
  Salt and pepper to taste
  Pinch of sugar
  Browned butter†
  Bread crumbs

---

*These mushrooms are necessary to good Polish cooking and they can be found in fancy food shops. You do not need expensive dried imported Italian mushrooms, and you will find domestic varieties as well as good varieties from South America, mainly Chile. Ask for domestic or South American dried boletus.
†To prepare, simply melt butter in a saucepan, and gently heat until it browns.

Drain the mushrooms, reserving the liquid for a later soup stock. Chop the mushrooms, and sauté in a bit of the butter along with the sauerkraut, pepper, and sugar. You do not want to brown the sauerkraut but only to cook it a bit with the mushrooms; much of the moisture of the sauerkraut will evaporate. Top with bread crumbs and more browned butter.

POTATO

- 1 large potato, cooked and mashed
- ¼ yellow onion, peeled, chopped, and browned
- 1 tablespoon melted butter
  Salt and pepper to taste
- 2 tablespoons cottage cheese, drained

Mix together all ingredients.

Pot Roast with Dill Pickles

This is a very rich dish. You may use chuck roast, but I prefer a bottom round roast since there is much less fat in the bottom roast, and this dish is rich enough!

- 3 pounds bottom or top round roast
- 2 tablespoons peanut oil
- 1 large yellow onion, peeled and chopped
- 3 or 4 dried mushrooms (optional)*
- 6 peppercorns
- 1 bay leaf
- ¼ cup beef stock or bouillon
- 3 dill pickles, chopped
- 1 cup sour cream

Brown the roast well in the oil (be sure that pan is hot before you put in the oil or the meat). Place the meat in a covered casserole, and add all the remaining ingredients except the sour cream. Simmer for about 2 hours, or until the meat is very tender. Add the sour cream, and simmer for ½ hour more. Slice, and serve with the rich sauce on the top.

SERVES 6 TO 8.

*See footnote on facing page.

Bigos—Traditional Hunters' Stew

This marvelous dish is one of the oldest found in Polish cuisine. In earlier times a week was spent in the preparation of this dish, but our adaptation is very good indeed, and unless you want to have the hunters hunting you, you had best produce this in just a few hours.

Cut into a very large dice 4 to 6 pounds of cooked meats, using any or all of the following:

> 4 to 6 pounds roast beef or pot roast, roast lamb, roast pork, venison or rabbit, chicken or duck, ham, Polish sausage, or roast veal*
> 2 yellow onions, peeled and chopped
> ¼ pound salt pork, diced and browned
> 2 tablespoons flour
> 3 quarts sauerkraut
> 1½ ounces cooked dried mushrooms†, with water, or 2 cups fresh mushrooms, sautéed
> Salt and pepper to taste
> 1 tablespoon brown sugar
> 1 cup dry red wine

Cut the meat into very large dice.

Cook the onions in the fat from the salt pork until limp. Add the flour, and blend well. Stir in the sauerkraut and mushrooms, along with the juice from the dried mushrooms. Add all the diced meats, including the salt pork, and the salt, pepper, and sugar. Simmer, covered, for 1 hour. Add the wine, boil up once, and remove from the heat. Keep the pot covered until you are ready to serve.

Traditionally so much time was spent in preparing this dish that one is not expected to eat it on the first day. It keeps for several days in your refrigerator, and it is much better heated up.

SERVES 10 TO 12.

---

*If you just do not have all these meats sitting around already cooked, simmer each *individually* in a covered casserole along with a bit of onion, carrots, celery, and a few peppercorns. Add just a tiny bit of water or broth to the pot so that the meat does not stick during cooking. Simmer until not quite tender.
†See note on dried mushrooms on page 434. Cook the mushrooms in a bit of water until soft enough to cut into thin strips. Save the water.

Kielbasa—Polish Sausage

Kielbasa means "sausage" in Polish, and it refers to many kinds. However, in this country *kielbasa* refers to a sausage that was made famous in Krakow. In this case we are using bulk sausage, and it works well in many fine Polish dishes.

    1½ pounds pork, ground coarse
    ½   teaspoon ground allspice
    1   teaspoon plus ½ teaspoon fresh-ground black
          pepper
    6   cloves garlic, crushed
    1   teaspoon salt
    1   teaspoon liquid smoke
    ⅓   cup water

Mix together all the ingredients except the water. Then add the water slowly, and continue to mix so that you form an even texture.

Seal in plastic bags in form of sausage. Use bags that can be sealed and then placed in boiling water. Boil in water for 45 minutes. (Sausage can be frozen at this point.) Remove from the pouch, and brown in the frying pan. Seasoning can be varied to suit individual taste.

MAKES 1½ POUNDS.

Index

About the Author

JEFF SMITH is an ordained minister and former chaplain at the University of Puget Sound in Tacoma. He became more involved with cooking after he taught a course called Food as Sacrament and Celebration. A popular lecturer in the Northwest on food and wine history, he has appeared on numerous television and radio shows, as well as filming his own TV series. He lives in Tacoma, Washington, with his wife and two sons.